The Creative Curriculum® for Preschool, Sixth Edition

Volume 6: Objectives for Development & Learning: Birth Through Third Grade

Diane Burts, EdD
Kai-leé Berke, MHD
Cate Heroman, MEd
Heather Baker, MLS
Toni Bickart, MSW
Patton Tabors, EdD
Steve Sanders, EdD

TeachingStrategies® · Bethesda, MD

Teaching Strategies, LLC
Bethesda, Maryland

www.TeachingStrategies.com

Library of Congress Control Number: 2016934452

978-1-60617-703-7

Printed and bound in China

2025 2024 2023 2022 2021
14 13 12 11 10 9 8 7 6

Acknowledgments

We would like to acknowledge many people for their essential role in developing this tool. We appreciate the thorough research work of Jennifer Mosley who oversaw extensive field testing. Dr. Richard Lambert of the University of North Carolina deserves recognition for his evaluation and research work, as does Dr. Renee Casbergue for drafting language and literacy items.

We would also like to thank our content reviewers who reviewed the items as they expanded through third grade: Dr. Jennie M. Bennett, University of Houston Central Campus; Jenna Bilmes, MEd, author and early childhood consultant; Kristy Feden, Early Childhood Program Administrator; Dr. Francis (Skip) Fennell, McDaniel College; Kim Hughes, Conscious Connections founder and principal consultant; Dr. Lea McGee, Ohio State University; Carol Mohn, Instructional Resource Teacher, Wake County Public Schools; Julia Rucci, MAT, literacy specialist, Wake County Public Schools; Dr. Dorothy Strickland, Rutgers University; Jean Ubbelohde, special educator and early childhood educator; Dr. GG Weisenfeld, EdD, Director of the Executive Office on Early Learning Honolulu. We also thank Colleen DuPre, DeAnna Ranheim, Steve Sather, and Jeff Sawyer from The Raleigh School for their participation in the content pilot of the expanded items.

The *Objectives for Development & Learning: Birth Through Kindergarten*, and the *Objectives for Development & Learning: Birth Through Third Grade* underwent extensive piloting and field testing at many schools across the country. We would like to thank all those who participated for their invaluable contribution.

We thank Dr. Dina Castro, Dr. Linda Espinosa, Antonia Lopez, Dr. Lisa Lopez, and the late Dr. Patton Tabors of our Latino Advisory Council and Dawn Terrill for their assistance in developing our dual-language learning component. We deeply appreciate the contributions of Dr. Espinosa and Dr. Lopez to the Spanish literacy and language objectives.

The creation of the *Objectives for Development & Learning: Birth Through Third Grade* was an ambitious undertaking that would not have been possible without a unified effort. We recognize the entire staff of Teaching Strategies, who used their relentless energy to make this product the best for our users.

Contents

Foreword

At Teaching Strategies, we've always been committed to finding the best and most effective ways to support the critically important work of early childhood educators. Over the years, that has meant engaging with educators to support best practices, bringing innovation to all of our resources, and rethinking what it means to offer solutions that are truly supportive of positive outcomes for all children. That's why it gives me such great pleasure to introduce you to our newly-expanded *The Creative Curriculum® for Preschool, Volume 6: Objectives for Development & Learning: Birth through Third Grade.* This groundbreaking resource takes our more than 35 years of commitment to programs serving children from birth and expands that commitment across the whole of the early childhood years.

The 38 objectives that are outlined in this resource are at the heart of everything we do at Teaching Strategies. They represent our goals for young children, and they are critical to every decision we make in the classroom. Keeping the objectives central to all that we do is what helps us ensure that children are fully supported in building the knowledge, skills, and abilities that they need to succeed.

Consider an example: one of our goals for young children is that they are able to persist with an appropriately challenging task. So we have to:

- start by building some professional knowledge about that goal, giving teachers information on how to support children's development of persistence and why it is so important both in the short term and for future success in school and in life;
- provide curriculum experiences that explicitly support the development of persistence and that are easily individualized to meet the needs of each child in the classroom;
- have an assessment tool that shows what the progression of development of the ability to persist looks like over the early childhood years and makes it easy for the teacher to decide where a child's abilities lie along that progression; and
- build relationships with families and provide resources that help them support their specific child's development of persistence at home.

The objectives for development and learning cover all areas:

- Social–Emotional
- Physical
- Language
- Cognitive
- Literacy
- Mathematics
- Science and Technology
- Social Studies
- The Arts

A tenth area for English Language Acquisition allows us to measure the expressive and receptive language learning of English-language or dual-language learners.

These objectives are based on an extensive review of the most current research and professional literature in the field of early childhood education. They include predictors of school success and are aligned with the Common Core State Standards, state early learning guidelines, and the *Head Start Child Development and Early Learning Framework*. Each objective shows the seamless progression of learning and development in every area that's critical to children's success from birth through third grade, outlining research-based, widely-held expectations for a child's age, class, or grade.

To me, what's especially significant about expanding these research-proven objectives to include first through third grade educators is that for the first time, we're beginning to set our expectations for success in elementary school at birth. As educators, we've all faced the fact that often times policymakers, curriculum developers, and school leaders begin with the standards for the oldest of students and work backwards—all the way to kindergarten, and then preschool. Sometimes, this can lead to a push down of expectations—and unfortunately, an inappropriate push down of teaching practices. But at Teaching Strategies, we prefer to think of child development and learning in the natural order—it begins in infancy and grows. The first three years of life lay the foundation for all future learning and development—so we can't gloss over those foundational skills and expect success in preK, kindergarten, and beyond. That's why our expanded progressions highlight the critical importance of those foundational skills, and how they build upon each other to support children's development and learning through the early elementary grades.

By bringing our objectives for development and learning to early elementary school classrooms and shifting the focus from building skills in just math and literacy to developing the whole child, we're changing the way that teachers support each child's development. We're giving the teachers of our youngest learners the tools to see how their role in supporting children's development and learning is essential to all of their future development and learning. We're giving our kindergarten, first-, second-, and third-grade teachers the opportunity to look back along that progression to see how each child's development and learning has been scaffolded over time. And we're placing as much importance on social–emotional skill development as we are on mathematics and literacy development, knowing that these skills are equally essential for future success, in school and in life.

The complete picture of the early childhood years that is outlined by these objectives for development and learning supports teachers to better understand what their students know and can do. Teachers can meet children where they individually are along the progression and clearly see a path for supporting their development and learning moving forward. It is my hope that these objectives will become an essential source of support for your teaching practice, and that they help you to see the powerful role that you play in building a strong foundation for every child's learning and development, birth through third grade.

Kai-leé Berke

Kai-leé Berke
Author, *The Creative Curriculum*®

Introduction

As a teacher, you make decisions every day that help lay a solid foundation for children's learning, now and in the future. In order to make good decisions, you need a deep knowledge and understanding of three aspects of early childhood education:

1. child development
2. content knowledge
3. instructional strategies

The effective teacher knows and understands **child development**—who children are and how they learn. She uses this information to guide her planning and decision-making. She understands children as individuals—their interests, abilities, backgrounds, needs, language, and family background—so that she can individualize in ways to help each child succeed. She knows and understands general areas of development—social–emotional, physical, language, and cognitive.

Effective teachers also know **content**—the subject matter appropriate for the early childhood years. They are familiar with the knowledge, skills, and understanding of concepts that are important for children to acquire. They know the learning progressions that children typically follow as they develop the foundation for competence in literacy and mathematics and begin to explore science and technology, social studies, and the arts.

Effective teachers also have a broad range of **caring and teaching strategies** that interweave their knowledge of child development and their content knowledge in ways that support children's development and make learning meaningful and engaging for each child. *Volume 6: Objectives for Development & Learning: Birth Through Third Grade* is like a compass that will point you in the right direction as you plan each day. Using it in conjunction with the wide variety of *Daily Resources* that are part of the curriculum will help you make decisions about what to teach, the materials and resources you select, and how you will interact and scaffold children's learning. Use this volume as a reference for information about child development, content knowledge, and appropriate instructional strategies.

Objectives for Development & Learning:
Birth Through Third Grade

Social–Emotional

1. Regulates own emotions and behaviors
    a. Manages feelings
    b. Follows limits and expectations
    c. Takes care of own needs appropriately
2. Establishes and sustains positive relationships
    a. Forms relationships with adults
    b. Responds to emotional cues
    c. Interacts with peers
    d. Makes friends
3. Participates cooperatively and constructively in group situations
    a. Balances needs and rights of self and others
    b. Solves social problems

Physical

4. Demonstrates traveling skills
5. Demonstrates balancing skills
6. Demonstrates gross-motor manipulative skills
7. Demonstrates fine-motor strength and coordination
    a. Uses fingers and hands
    b. Uses writing and drawing tools

Language

8. Listens to and understands increasingly complex language
    a. Comprehends language
    b. Follows directions
9. Uses language to express thoughts and needs
    a. Uses an expanding expressive vocabulary
    b. Speaks clearly
    c. Uses conventional grammar
    d. Tells about another time or place
10. Uses appropriate conversational and other communication skills
    a. Engages in conversations
    b. Uses social rules of language

Cognitive

11. Demonstrates positive approaches to learning
    a. Attends and engages
    b. Persists
    c. Solves problems
    d. Shows curiosity and motivation
    e. Shows flexibility and inventiveness in thinking
12. Remembers and connects experiences
    a. Recognizes and recalls
    b. Makes connections
13. Uses classification skills
14. Uses symbols and images to represent something not present
    a. Thinks symbolically
    b. Engages in sociodramatic play

Literacy

15. Demonstrates phonological awareness, phonics skills, and word recognition
    a. Notices and discriminates rhyme
    b. Notices and discriminates alliteration
    c. Notices and discriminates discrete units of sound
    d. Applies phonics concepts and knowledge of word structure to decode text
16. Demonstrates knowledge of the alphabet
    a. Identifies and names letters
    b. Identifies letter–sound correspondences
17. Demonstrates knowledge of print and its uses
    a. Uses and appreciates books and other texts
    b. Uses print concepts
18. Comprehends and responds to books and other texts
    a. Interacts during reading experiences, book conversations, and text reflections
    b. Uses emergent reading skills
    c. Retells stories and recounts details from informational texts
    d. Uses context clues to read and comprehend texts
    e. Reads fluently
19. Demonstrates writing skills
    a. Writes name
    b. Writes to convey ideas and information
    c. Writes using conventions

Mathematics

20. Uses number concepts and operations
    a. Counts
    b. Quantifies
    c. Connects numerals with their quantities
    d. Understands and uses place value and base ten
    e. Applies properties of mathematical operations and relationships
    f. Applies number combinations and mental number strategies in mathematical operations
21. Explores and describes spatial relationships and shapes
    a. Understands spatial relationships
    b. Understands shapes
22. Compares and measures
    a. Measures objects
    b. Measures time and money
    c. Represents and analyzes data
23. Demonstrates knowledge of patterns

Science and Technology

24. Uses scientific inquiry skills
25. Demonstrates knowledge of the characteristics of living things
26. Demonstrates knowledge of the physical properties of objects and materials
27. Demonstrates knowledge of Earth's environment
28. Uses tools and other technology to perform tasks

Social Studies

29. Demonstrates knowledge about self
30. Shows basic understanding of people and how they live
31. Explores change related to familiar people or places
32. Demonstrates simple geographic knowledge

The Arts

33. Explores the visual arts
34. Explores musical concepts and expression
35. Explores dance and movement concepts
36. Explores drama through actions and language

English Language Acquisition

37. Demonstrates progress in listening to and understanding English
38. Demonstrates progress in speaking English

Objectives for Development and Learning

Child development and learning is complex. It would be overwhelming to try to identify every skill and behavior children demonstrate in these early years. *Volume 6, Objectives for Development & Learning* includes the knowledge, skills, and abilities that are most predictive of school success. It also includes objectives that help you focus on competencies valued in state early learning standards and standards of professional organizations. The objectives will guide your program planning and decision making.

Thirty-six of the **objectives** are organized into nine **areas of development and learning.** The first four areas describe major areas of child growth and development:

- Social–Emotional
- Physical
- Language
- Cognitive

The following five areas focus on content learning that are often described as outcomes in early learning standards:

- Literacy
- Mathematics
- Science and Technology
- Social Studies
- The Arts

A tenth area, English Language Acquisition, helps you to follow a child's progress in acquiring both receptive and expressive language in English.

Many of the objectives include **dimensions** that are more specific descriptions of aspects of the objective. For example, dimensions of Objective 1, "Regulates own emotions and behaviors," include managing feelings, following limits and expectations, and taking care of own needs appropriately.

A complete list of the objectives can be found on pages x–xii.

Volume 6, Objectives for Development & Learning is based on an extensive review of the most current research and professional literature in the field of early childhood education. The following is a brief description of each part of this resource:

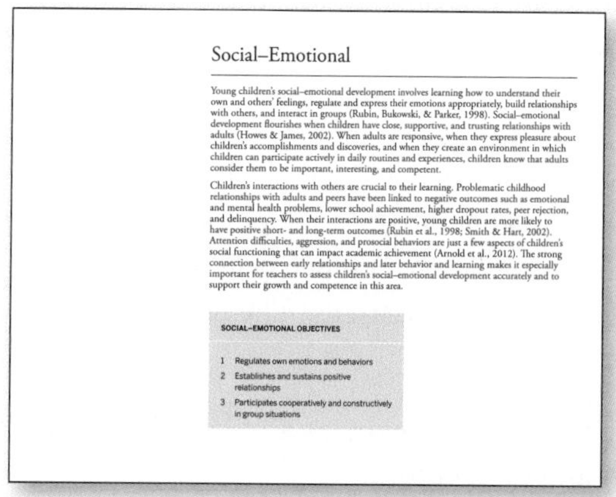

Social–Emotional

Young children's social–emotional development involves learning how to understand their own and others' feelings, regulate and express their emotions appropriately, build relationships with others, and interact in groups (Rubin, Bukowski, & Parker, 1998). Social–emotional development flourishes when children have close, supportive, and trusting relationships with adults (Howes & James, 2002). When adults are responsive, when they express pleasure about children's accomplishments and discoveries, and when they create an environment in which children can participate actively in daily routines and experiences, children know that adults consider them to be important, interesting, and competent.

Children's interactions with others are crucial to their learning. Problematic childhood relationships with adults and peers have been linked to negative outcomes such as emotional and mental health problems, lower school achievement, higher dropout rates, peer rejection, and delinquency. When their interactions are positive, young children are more likely to have positive short- and long-term outcomes (Rubin et al., 1998; Smith & Hart, 2002). Attention difficulties, aggression, and prosocial behaviors are just a few aspects of children's social functioning that can impact academic achievement (Arnold et al., 2012). The strong connection between early relationships and later behavior and learning makes it especially important for teachers to assess children's social–emotional development accurately and to support their growth and competence in this area.

SOCIAL–EMOTIONAL OBJECTIVES

1 Regulates own emotions and behaviors
2 Establishes and sustains positive relationships
3 Participates cooperatively and constructively in group situations

Objective 1

Regulates own emotions and behaviors

1

In order to manage emotions and regulate his behavior, a child must learn to control impulses, tolerate frustration, cope with strong emotions, follow limits and expectations, and delay gratification. A crying infant calms when rocked by a loving adult. A 2-year-old sits in a quiet place hugging a stuffed bear after his mother leaves for work. A preschooler acts out a birthday party, thanking her guests for coming. A 5-year-old tells you when others are not following the rules. A second grader takes a deep breath when a peer grabs the pencil she was going to use.

To be able to regulate their emotions and behaviors, children must: 1) develop a basic understanding that actions have positive and negative consequences, 2) know what behaviors are acceptable, 3) be aware that they are capable of controlling their behavior, and 4) know that they have the power to manage their emotions (Bilmes, 2004). Children learn how to manage their emotions and regulate behavior in an environment that is warm and nurturing, and where the adults are trustworthy and responsive to each child's needs. Discussing the reasons for limits and the consequences of behavior helps children know why limits and rules are necessary. Teachers usually provide reasons for moral rules that apply in every setting, such as not hitting or taking another child's toy. They usually do not explain the social reasons for rules such as putting blocks back on the shelf neatly (Charlesworth, 2007; Smetana, 1984).

Children who regulate their emotions positively do better in school (Blair & Razza, 2007; Bronson, 2000) and have an easier time getting along with peers (Copple & Bredekamp, 2009; Ponitz, McClelland, Jewkes, Conner, Farris, & Morrison, 2008). Noncompliant, problematic behavior in preschool tends to continue in later school years (Campbell, 1995; Charlesworth, 2007; Campbell, Pierce, March, Ewing, & Szumowski, 1994). Self-regulation is ranked as the most important characteristic necessary for school readiness by kindergarten teachers, who also indicate that over half of their children lack effective self-regulatory skills (Rimm-Kaufman, Pianta, & Cox, 2000). Children who have warm, supportive, secure relationships with their teachers exhibit fewer behavioral problems than children who do not have positive relationships (Bronson, 2006; Howes & Ritchie, 1998), so teachers' role in helping children follow limits and expectations is important to children's future school success.

The **overview of each area of development and learning** explains the research about why the area is important. The objectives included in the area are listed in a shaded box.

The **research foundation page** summarizes the important research findings related to the objective. It provides a broad picture of development and learning from birth through kindergarten, and it explains what is being measured and why. Cultural and linguistic considerations, as well as considerations for children with disabilities, are included in this foundation.

Progressions of development and learning include indicators and examples based on standard developmental and learning expectations for various age-groups and for classes or grades.

Objective 1 Regulates own emotions and behaviors

a. Manages feelings

Levels →

Indicators (in bold) →

Examples (bulleted) →

Expectations for ages or classes/grades →

Not Yet	1	2	3	4	5	6	7	8	9	10	11	12	13
		Uses adult support to calm self • Calms self when touched gently, patted, massaged, rocked, or hears a soothing voice • Turns away from source of overstimulation and cries but is soothed by being picked up		**Comforts self by seeking out special object or person** • Gets teddy bear from cubby when upset • Sits next to favorite adult when sad		**Is able to look at a situation differently or delay gratification** • When the Block area is full, looks to see what other areas are available • Scowls and says, "I didn't get to paint this morning." Pauses and adds, "I have an idea. I can paint after snack."		**Controls strong emotions in an appropriate manner most of the time** • Asserts, "I'm mad. You're not sharing the blocks!" • Says, "I'm so excited! We're going to the zoo today!" while jumping up and down		**Manages strong emotions using known strategies** • When feeling overwhelmed, talks with teacher about a plan for completing an assignment • Finds a quiet place in the classroom to read after a disagreement with a friend • Talks to a friend about being reprimanded by the teacher		**Demonstrates patience with personal limitations; controls feelings based on how they will affect others** • When practicing cursive writing, says, "I need to go slowly when I write the letter Q so I won't get frustrated." • Smiles and says, "thank you" for a gift, and then later tells an adult, "I already read that book, and I didn't like it."	

The **levels** (numbers above each box) are used to label each point along the progression of development and learning. The "in-between" boxes allow for more steps in the progression, so teachers have a way to show that children's skills are emerging in this area but not yet solid. These in-between levels also enable the teacher to show whether a child needs adult support (verbal, physical, or visual) to accomplish the indicator.

Colors are used to indicate the age or class/grade ranges for these expectations. Red, orange, and yellow code each year of life for the first 3 years. Green, blue, and purple code classes/grades for the next 3 years, and pink, silver, and brown code first through third grades.

Birth to 1 year

1 to 2 years

2 to 3 years

Preschool 3 class

PreK 4 class

Kindergarten

First Grade

Second Grade

Third Grade

Notice that some colored bands of a progression are longer or shorter than others. Some bands begin in the "Not Yet" column. While there is a typical progression for each objective, it is not rigid; development and learning are uneven, overlapping, and interrelated. Sometimes a skill does not begin to develop until a child is 2 years old, and another skill may not emerge until age 3 or 4. The colored bands might show you at a glance that it is typical, for example, for children to enter the pre-K year with a particular skill emerging at level 5 and for the children to progress to level 8 by the end of the year if they are given appropriate support and experiences.

Finally, the **strategies page** offers ways to promote development and learning in relation to the objective.

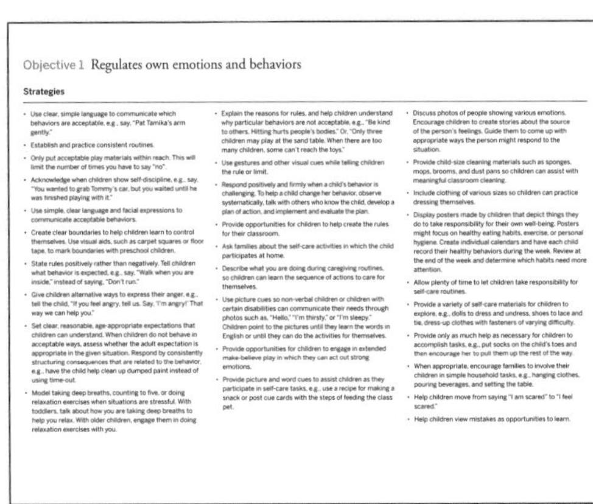

Objective 1 Regulates own emotions and behaviors

Strategies

- Use clear, simple language to communicate which behaviors are acceptable, e.g., say, "Pat Tamika's arm gently."
- Establish and practice consistent routines.
- Only put acceptable play materials within reach. This will limit the number of times you have to say "no".
- Acknowledge when children show self-discipline, e.g., say, "You wanted to grab Tommy's car, but you waited until he was finished playing with it."
- Use simple, clear language and facial expressions to communicate acceptable behaviors.
- Create clear boundaries to help children learn to control themselves. Use visual aids, such as carpet squares or floor tape, to mark boundaries with preschool children.
- State rules positively rather than negatively. Tell children what behavior is expected, e.g., say, "Walk when you are inside," instead of saying, "Don't run."
- Give children alternative ways to express their anger, e.g., tell the child, "If you feel angry, tell us. Say, 'I'm angry!' That way we can help you."
- Set clear, reasonable, age-appropriate expectations that children can understand. When children do not behave in acceptable ways, assess whether the adult expectation is appropriate in the given situation. Respond by consistently structuring consequences that are related to the behavior, e.g., have the child help clean up dumped paint instead of using time-out.
- Model taking deep breaths, counting to five, or doing relaxation exercises when situations are stressful. With toddlers, talk about how you are taking deep breaths to help you relax. With older children, engage them in doing relaxation exercises with you.
- Explain the reasons for rules, and help children understand why particular behaviors are not acceptable, e.g., "Be kind to others. Hitting hurts people's bodies." Or, "Only three children may play at the sand table. When there are too many children, some can't reach the toys."
- Use gestures and other visual cues while telling children the rule or limit.
- Respond positively and firmly when a child's behavior is challenging. To help a child change her behavior, observe systematically, talk with others who know the child, develop a plan of action, and implement and evaluate the plan.
- Provide opportunities for children to help create the rules for their classroom.
- Ask families about the self-care activities in which the child participates at home.
- Describe what you are doing during caregiving routines, so children can learn the sequence of actions to care for themselves.
- Use picture cues so non-verbal children or children with certain disabilities can communicate their needs through photos such as, "Hello," "I'm thirsty," or "I'm sleepy." Children point to the pictures until they learn the words in English or until they can do the activities for themselves.
- Provide opportunities for children to engage in extended make-believe play in which they can act out strong emotions.
- Provide picture and word cues to assist children as they participate in self-care tasks, e.g., use a recipe for making a snack or post cue cards with the steps of feeding the class pet.
- Discuss photos of people showing various emotions. Encourage children to create stories about the source of the person's feelings. Guide them to come up with appropriate ways the person might respond to the situation.
- Provide child-size cleaning materials such as sponges, mops, brooms, and dust pans so children can assist with meaningful classroom cleaning.
- Include clothing of various sizes so children can practice dressing themselves.
- Display posters made by children that depict things they do to take responsibility for their own well-being. Posters might focus on healthy eating habits, exercise, or personal hygiene. Create individual calendars and have each child record their healthy behaviors during the week. Review at the end of the week and determine which habits need more attention.
- Allow plenty of time to let children take responsibility for self-care routines.
- Provide a variety of self-care materials for children to explore, e.g., dolls to dress and undress, shoes to lace and tie, dress-up clothes with fasteners of varying difficulty.
- Provide only as much help as necessary for children to accomplish tasks, e.g., put socks on the child's toes and then encourage her to pull them up the rest of the way.
- When appropriate, encourage families to involve their children in simple household tasks, e.g., hanging clothes, pouring beverages, and setting the table.
- Help children move from saying "I am scared" to "I feel scared."
- Help children view mistakes as opportunities to learn.

Scaffolding Children's Learning

Teacher–child interactions play an important role in guiding children's learning. It is through these interactions that you *scaffold* children's learning. Just as a carpenter uses a scaffold as he works on part of a building that is out of reach, you provide the children with support as they work on developing skills that are just beyond their reach. As children acquire the skills, you offer less and less support until the children can accomplish the task independently.

For example, consider Objective 14b, "Engages in sociodramatic play." You notice that a child is at level 4, "Acts out familiar or imaginary scenarios; may use props to stand for something else." You look ahead to level 6, "Interacts with two or more children during pretend play, assigning and/or assuming roles and discussing actions; sustains play scenario for up to 10 minutes." To scaffold a child's learning, you consider the instructional strategies you will use to support children on their path to the next level. In this example, you might use one of the instructional strategies provided in the section following the progression:

> *Extend children's pretend play by interacting with them. Imitate what they are doing, comment and ask questions, or take a role, using a play voice and gestures.*

Keep the objectives for development and learning in mind as you consider how to support children's learning, and use a wide range of instructional strategies.

Planning for Children's Learning

You make many decisions each day as you observe children and respond in appropriate ways. Often your observations lead you to ask questions as you think about each child and consider how best to provide support. *Objectives for Development & Learning: Birth Through Third Grade* is an important resource to help you see where a child is in relation to each objective. Because the objectives show all areas of development and learning, they give you a comprehensive picture of the whole child's development and learning.

Planning for children is an art. There are no formulas or quick solutions. It would be wonderful to say that if you do this one activity, the child will progress to the next level. It takes time, practice, and reflection to determine what support a child or group of children needs.

However, you can plan for the specific needs of individual children. Think about what you know about your group of children, the expected outcomes included in this volume, and in your state early learning standards. Use this information to shape what you do each day. Think about the progressions to guide how and when you need to make adaptations to an activity or make it simpler or more complex.

Intentional Teaching Cards™ are a resource you can use to help you plan for individuals and groups of children. These are carefully selected activities that are linked to the progressions included in this volume. While *Objectives for Development & Learning* describes the path that children follow as they develop specific skills and behaviors, the *Intentional Teaching Cards*™ provide the teaching sequence for you to follow.

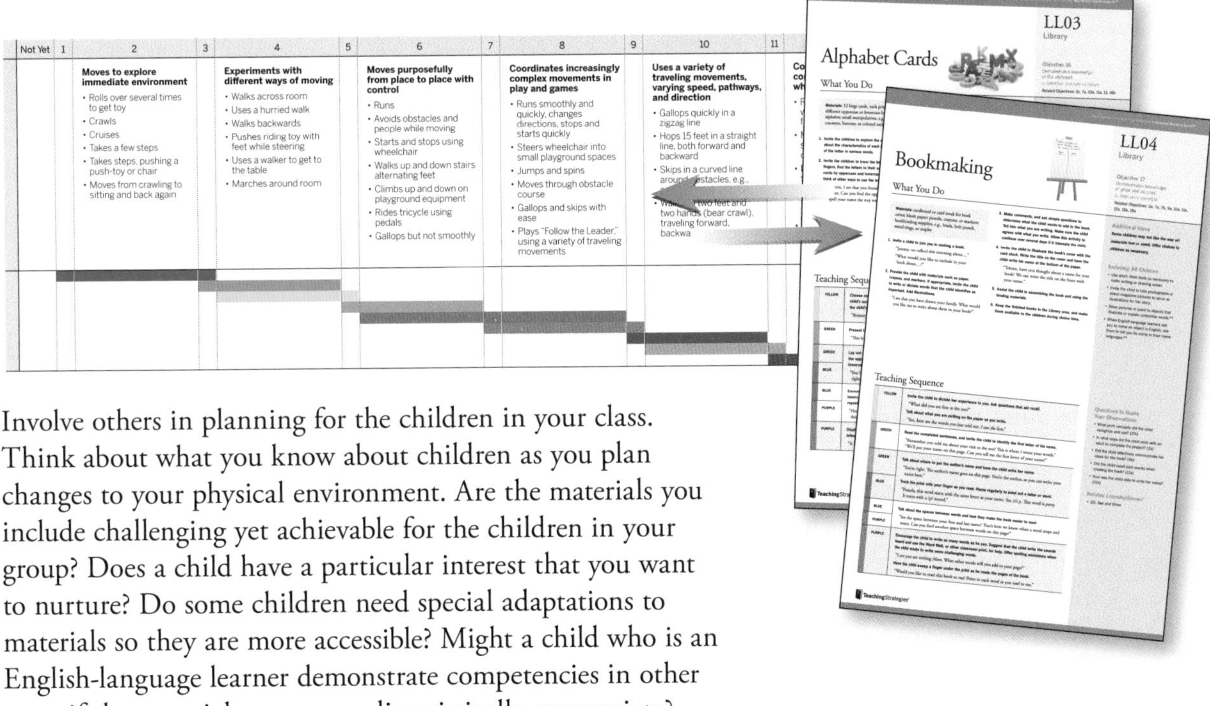

Involve others in planning for the children in your class. Think about what you know about children as you plan changes to your physical environment. Are the materials you include challenging yet achievable for the children in your group? Does a child have a particular interest that you want to nurture? Do some children need special adaptations to materials so they are more accessible? Might a child who is an English-language learner demonstrate competencies in other areas if the materials were more linguistically appropriate?

Working With Children With Disabilities

To ensure that all children, including those with disabilities, are making progress, teachers recognize the many possible emergent skills that precede the development of these widely expected skills of children in the early years. A wide range of progressive skills and behaviors for objectives are included in this volume. They serve as a guide to seeing how all children are progressing in the nine areas of development and learning, while acknowledging that children show what they know in different ways. The progressions of development and learning emphasize to teachers that all children have skills and behaviors upon which to build.

The Creative Curriculum® objectives for development and learning help you plan for children who may be struggling in some areas by understanding the individual skills and specific needs of each child. You can then identify support strategies such as simplifying instructions or a change in materials used, to make it easier for children to participate and make progress through daily experiences.

Because *Volume 6, Objectives for Development & Learning* provides a picture of development through kindergarten, children with disabilities or those who struggle to learn, are able to demonstrate progress. Keep the child with disabilities in mind as you read this volume and consider the intent of the objectives for individual children. Observe how each child progresses toward meeting the objective while using individualized modifications, assistive devices, or adult supports as necessary. For example, a child with a physical impairment might use a walker or a wheelchair to move around the classroom. The intent of Objective 4, "Demonstrates traveling skills" is that the child is able to move or propel herself to get where she wants to go. Any means that a child uses, such as adaptive equipment, scooting on her bottom, or crawling, meets the intent of the objective.

Volume 6, Objectives for Development & Learning: Birth Through Third Grade can be used to support tiered models of supportive instruction and individualize intervention by identifying a child's strengths in relation to those of classmates. You can design learning experiences for skill building and practice for natural groupings of children that create opportunities to learn new skills. For some children, *Objectives for Development & Learning* can help identify areas of need so that collaborative teams of educators, other professionals, and family members can design more explicit interventions to assist with skill attainment and expansion.

You can use *Objectives for Development & Learning* to guide the development of Individualized Education Program (IEP) goals for each child. IEPs look closely at the child's skill level and the instructional plans and interventions that will take place in a given period of time. The progressions can be used to identify more advanced skills and behaviors that a child is most likely to develop next. In addition, the "in-between levels" in the progressions can be used to indicate the support a child requires as he or she makes progress. IEP goals can then indicate the appropriate supports and opportunities needed to achieve the IEP goals. IEP goals are often similar to the objectives, as they reflect interrelated and progressive skills that help a child to participate and progress in the general curriculum.

Working With English-Language or Dual-Language Learners

In areas other than language and literacy, the objectives presented in this book will help you gather information, no matter which language children prefer to use as they demonstrate what they know and can do. However, the indicators, dimensions, and examples for the language and literacy objectives (8–10 and 15–19) show the progression of English-language development (e.g., Is the child able to understand directions given in English? Does the child associate English sounds with the letters of the alphabet?).

Dual-language learners are children who are learning two or more languages at the same time, and they are continuing to develop their first language(s). If you are in a program that uses a dual-language approach and Spanish is one of the languages, also refer to *El Currículo Creativo para educación preescolar, Volumen 6: Objetivos para el desarrollo y el aprendizaje.*

Objectives 37 and 38 are the English language acquisition objectives. They are to be used with English- and dual-language learners in preschool 3, pre-K 4, and kindergarten classrooms. Use the "Home Language Survey" on the next page to identify those children. In order to determine whether or not to use the English language acquisition objectives, you will need to gather information about what language the child and his or her family members use at home, and what language the child uses while he or she is in the classroom talking with the teachers and other children. While the English language acquisition objectives are not used with younger children, survey information is helpful while planning and individualizing learning experiences.

Answer the survey questions about the child and the family members who care for the child. Respond, using a scale ranging from "only English" to "only home language." Try to gather as much information as possible to help you answer the questions. If you are unable to answer a question because you do not know the answer or because the child is not yet speaking, circle "N/A" for "not applicable."

Add the numbers you have circled and put the sum in the space provided. Then divide this value by the number of questions you were able to answer, not counting any questions for which you circled "N/A." The value you obtain will help you make a determination about whether or not to use the English Language Acquisition objectives. If the value is 2 or greater, use Objective 37, "Demonstrates progress in listening to and understanding English," and Objective 38, "Demonstrates progress in speaking English," to guide your planning and instruction.

Home Language Survey*

☐ Check here if the child's parents or legal guardians decline to provide information for this survey.

A. What language do family members use when speaking to the child in the home?

	1	2	3	4	5
	only English	mostly English but sometimes home language	both equally	mostly home language but some English	only home language (not English)

(write in home language: ____________)

B. What language does the child use when speaking to family members in the home?

N/A	1	2	3	4	5
Not applicable	only English	mostly English but sometimes home language	both equally	mostly home language but some English	only home language (not English)

C. What language does the child use when speaking to other children in the classroom?

N/A	1	2	3	4	5
Not applicable	only English	mostly English but sometimes home language	both equally	mostly home language but some English	only home language (not English)

D. What language does the child use when speaking to the teachers?

N/A	1	2	3	4	5
Not applicable	only English	mostly English but sometimes home language	both equally	mostly home language but some English	only home language (not English)

Sum of circled numbers		Number of questions answered		
________	/	________	=	______

If this value is 2 or greater and the child is in a preschool 3, pre-K 4, or kindergarten class, use Objectives 37 and 38.

***These research reports helped guide our thinking in the development of the "Home Language Survey":**

Aikens, N. L., Caspe, M. S., Sprachman, S., López, M. L., & Atkins-Burnett, S. M. (June 2008). *Paper Symposium: Development of a language routing protocol for determining bilingual Spanish–English speaking children's language of assessment.* Biennial Head Start Research Conference. Washington, DC.

Puma, M., Bell, S., Cook, R., Heid, C., López, M. L., et al. (2005). *Head Start impact study: First year findings.* Washington, DC: U.S. Department of Health and Human Services, Administration for Children and Families.

Gutiérrez-Clellen, V. F., & Kreiter, J. (2003). Understanding child bilingual acquisition using parent and teacher reports. *Applied Psycholinguistics, 24*(2), 267–88.

Widely Held Expectations

Objectives and Dimensions	Ranges (color-coded)								
SOCIAL–EMOTIONAL									
1. Regulates own emotions and behaviors									
a. Manages feelings	■	■	■	■	■	■	■	■	■
b. Follows limits and expectations	■	■	■	■	■	■	■	■	■
c. Takes care of own needs appropriately	■	■	■	■	■	■	■	■	■
2. Establishes and sustains positive relationships									
a. Forms relationships with adults	■	■	■	■	■	■	■	■	■
b. Responds to emotional cues	■	■	■	■	■	■	■	■	■
c. Interacts with peers	■	■	■	■	■	■	■	■	■
d. Makes friends		■	■	■	■	■	■	■	■
3. Participates cooperatively and constructively in group situations									
a. Balances needs and rights of self and others	■	■	■	■	■	■	■	■	■
b. Solves social problems	■	■	■	■	■	■	■	■	■
PHYSICAL									
4. Demonstrates traveling skills	■	■	■	■	■	■	■	■	■
5. Demonstrates balancing skills	■	■	■	■	■	■	■	■	■
6. Demonstrates gross-motor manipulative skills	■	■	■	■	■	■	■	■	■
7. Demonstrates fine-motor strength and coordination									
a. Uses fingers and hands	■	■	■	■	■	■	■	■	■
b. Uses writing and drawing tools		■	■	■	■	■	■	■	■
LANGUAGE									
8. Listens to and understands increasingly complex language									
a. Comprehends language	■	■	■	■	■	■	■	■	■
b. Follows directions	■	■	■	■	■	■	■		
9. Uses language to express thoughts and needs									
a. Uses an expanding expressive vocabulary	■	■	■	■	■	■	■	■	■
b. Speaks clearly	■	■	■	■	■	■	■	■	■
c. Uses conventional grammar	■	■	■	■	■	■	■	■	■
d. Tells about another time or place		■	■	■	■	■	■	■	■
10. Uses appropriate conversational and other communication skills									
a. Engages in conversations	■	■	■	■	■	■	■	■	■
b. Uses social rules of language	■	■	■	■	■	■	■	■	■

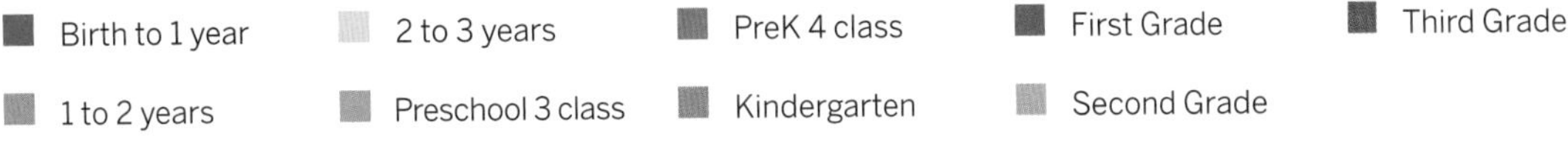

Objectives and Dimensions	Ranges (color-coded)
COGNITIVE	
11. Demonstrates positive approaches to learning	
a. Attends and engages	
b. Persists	
c. Solves problems	
d. Shows curiosity and motivation	
e. Shows flexibility and inventiveness in thinking	
12. Remembers and connects experiences	
a. Recognizes and recalls	
b. Makes connections	
13. Uses classification skills	
14. Uses symbols and images to represent something not present	
a. Thinks symbolically	
b. Engages in sociodramatic play	
LITERACY	
15. Demonstrates phonological awareness, phonics skills, and word recognition	
a. Notices and discriminates rhyme	
b. Notices and discriminates alliteration	
c. Notices and discriminates discrete units of sound	
d. Applies phonics concepts and knowledge of word structure to decode text	
16. Demonstrates knowledge of the alphabet	
a. Identifies and names letters	
b. Identifies letter–sound correspondences	
17. Demonstrates knowledge of print and its uses	
a. Uses and appreciates books and other texts	
b. Uses print concepts	
18. Comprehends and responds to books and other texts	
a. Interacts during reading experiences, book conversations, and text reflections	
b. Uses emergent reading skills	
c. Retells stories and recounts details from informational texts	
d. Uses context clues to read and comprehend texts	
e. Reads fluently	
19. Demonstrates writing skills	
a. Writes name	
b. Writes to convey ideas and information	
c. Writes using conventions	

Objectives and Dimensions	Ranges (color-coded)
MATHEMATICS	
20. Uses number concepts and operations	
a. Counts	
b. Quantifies	
c. Connects numerals with their quantities	
d. Understands and uses place value and base ten	
e. Applies properties of mathematical operations and relationships	
f. Applies number combinations and mental number strategies in mathematical operations	
21. Explores and describes spatial relationships and shapes	
a. Understands spatial relationships	
b. Understands shapes	
22. Compares and measures	
a. Measures objects	
b. Measures time and money	
c. Represents and analyzes data	
23. Demonstrates knowledge of patterns	
SCIENCE AND TECHNOLOGY	
24. Uses scientific inquiry skills	No evidence yet Emerging Meets program expectations
25. Demonstrates knowledge of the characteristics of living things	
26. Demonstrates knowledge of the physical properties of objects and materials	
27. Demonstrates knowledge of Earth's environment	
28. Uses tools and other technology to perform tasks	
SOCIAL STUDIES	
29. Demonstrates knowledge about self	No evidence yet Emerging Meets program expectations
30. Shows basic understanding of people and how they live	
31. Explores change related to familiar people or places	
32. Demonstrates simple geographic knowledge	
THE ARTS	
33. Explores the visual arts	No evidence yet Emerging Meets program expectations
34. Explores musical concepts and expression	
35. Explores dance and movement concepts	
36. Explores drama through actions and language	
ENGLISH LANGUAGE ACQUISITION	
37. Demonstrates progress in listening to and understanding English	Progressions included, but not age-level designations
38. Demonstrates progress in speaking English	

Key Parts of the System

Here are definitions of important terms used in *Volume 6: Objectives for Development & Learning:*

area of development and learning
the broadest domains of development and learning, e.g., "Social–Emotional"

objective
a statement of expectations of knowledge, skills, and abilities, e.g., "Regulates own emotions and behaviors"

dimensions
a specific aspect or subskill of an objective, e.g., "Manages feelings," "Follows limits and expectations"

indicators
descriptions of knowledge, skills, or behaviors that children demonstrate along each developmental progression. These statements are in **bold** above bulleted examples, e.g., "Accepts redirection from an adult"

examples
different ways that children show what they know and can do, e.g., "Moves to the sand table at the suggestion of an adult when too many children are at the art table"

colored bands
colored lines (red, orange, yellow, green, blue, purple, pink, silver, and brown) that show the age or the class/grade ranges for widely held developmental and learning expectations

progressions of development and learning
paths, or trajectories, that children typically follow when acquiring a skill or behavior

levels
the rating scale that describes specific points along the progression for each objective

teaching strategies
what teachers can do to support and scaffold children's learning as it relates to a particular objective

Areas of Development and Learning

Social–Emotional

Young children's social–emotional development involves learning how to understand their own and others' feelings, regulate and express their emotions appropriately, build relationships with others, and interact in groups (Rubin, Bukowski, & Parker, 1998). Social–emotional development flourishes when children have close, supportive, and trusting relationships with adults (Howes & James, 2002). When adults are responsive, when they express pleasure about children's accomplishments and discoveries, and when they create an environment in which children can participate actively in daily routines and experiences, children know that adults consider them to be important, interesting, and competent.

Children's interactions with others are crucial to their learning. Problematic childhood relationships with adults and peers have been linked to negative outcomes such as emotional and mental health problems, lower school achievement, higher dropout rates, peer rejection, and delinquency. When their interactions are positive, young children are more likely to have positive short- and long-term outcomes (Rubin et al., 1998; Smith & Hart, 2002). Attention difficulties, aggression, and prosocial behaviors are just a few aspects of children's social functioning that can impact academic achievement (Arnold et al., 2012). The strong connection between early relationships and later behavior and learning makes it especially important for teachers to assess children's social–emotional development accurately and to support their growth and competence in this area.

SOCIAL–EMOTIONAL OBJECTIVES

1 Regulates own emotions and behaviors

2 Establishes and sustains positive relationships

3 Participates cooperatively and constructively in group situations

Regulates own emotions and behaviors

1

In order to manage emotions and regulate his behavior, a child must learn to control impulses, tolerate frustration, cope with strong emotions, follow limits and expectations, and delay gratification. A crying infant calms when rocked by a loving adult. A 2-year-old sits in a quiet place hugging a stuffed bear after his mother leaves for work. A preschool child acts out a birthday party, thanking her guests for coming. A 5-year-old tells you when others are not following the rules. A second grader takes a deep breath when a peer grabs the pencil she was going to use.

To be able to regulate their emotions and behaviors, children must: 1) develop a basic understanding that actions have positive and negative consequences, 2) know what behaviors are acceptable, 3) be aware that they are capable of controlling their behavior, and 4) know that they have the power to manage their emotions (Bilmes, 2004). Children learn how to manage their emotions and regulate behavior in an environment that is warm and nurturing, and where the adults are trustworthy and responsive to each child's needs. Discussing the reasons for limits and the consequences of behavior helps children know why limits and rules are necessary. Teachers usually provide reasons for moral rules that apply in every setting, such as not hitting or taking another child's toy. They usually do not explain the social reasons for rules such as putting blocks back on the shelf neatly (Charlesworth, 2007; Smetana, 1984).

Children who regulate their emotions positively do better in school (Blair & Razza, 2007; Bronson, 2000) and have an easier time getting along with peers (Copple & Bredekamp, 2009; Ponitz, McClelland, Jewkes, Conner, Farris, & Morrison, 2008). Noncompliant, problematic behavior in preschool tends to continue in later school years (Campbell, 1995; Charlesworth, 2007; Campbell, Pierce, March, Ewing, & Szumowski, 1994). Self-regulation is ranked as the most important characteristic necessary for school readiness by kindergarten teachers, who also indicate that over half of their children lack effective self-regulatory skills (Rimm-Kaufman, Pianta, & Cox, 2000). Children who have warm, supportive, secure relationships with their teachers exhibit fewer behavioral problems than children who do not have positive relationships (Bronson, 2006; Howes & Ritchie, 1998), so teachers' role in helping children follow limits and expectations is important to children's future school success.

Objective 1 Regulates own emotions and behaviors

Various factors, such as a disability, life experiences, and family practices, influence the way children express their feelings and emotions. Some children are taught to avoid expressions of emotion, while others are encouraged to express their feelings openly (Trawick-Smith, 2006). Difficulty in learning to manage emotions may be an early warning sign of a disability or future psychological problems (Diamond, 2002; National Scientific Council on the Developing Child, 2004). Infants who have trouble remaining calm may need special help to develop self-regulatory skills (Cook, Klein, & Tessier, 2004). Children who cannot control their emotions at age 4 are likely not to be able to follow the teacher's directions at age 6 (Bodrova & Leong, 2005).

Differences in family beliefs and expectations affect the way children respond to classroom limits. The ways people express opinions, discuss ideas and feelings, and take turns in conversations differ from one culture to another and often from one family to another. Children from some cultural backgrounds look others straight in the eye during conversations while other children are taught to avoid eye contact (McAfee & Leong, 2007). There are also differences in the strategies families use when children do not follow the established limits (Trawick-Smith, 2006). Frequent communication between teachers and families is therefore necessary to guide children's behavior and to work toward shared goals.

Children's ability to meet their own needs appropriately is valued and typically expected by some cultures (Pierce & Schreibman, 1994). When children take care of themselves in these cultures, they build their confidence, and this influences their emotions and behaviors. Children who feel competent, or who have belief in their abilities, are better able to face life's challenges (Curry & Johnson, 1991). Children develop confidence by participating successfully in everyday activities. When children can communicate their needs, move from place to place, use tools, and participate in classroom routines, they have more opportunities to build self-confidence.

Children with physical disabilities may be viewed by their nondisabled peers as being less able to perform certain tasks or to participate fully in everyday classroom activities (Diamond & Hestenes, 1996). It is therefore important for teachers to support children with disabilities appropriately in their efforts to do things for themselves and to give them, whenever possible, the same opportunities to participate in classroom activities as their typically developing peers. Teachers may need to provide children with disabilities as well as English-language learners with pictorial examples depicting various sequences of a routine or activity. The pictures support children's abilities to complete tasks by themselves (Macrina, Hoover, & Becker, 2009; Pierce & Schreibman, 1994).

When students enter grade school, they are expected to follow directions, solve problems, and possess social skills that allow them to successfully interact with others (Lane, Givner, & Pierson, 2004; O'Shaughnessy, Lane, Gresham, & Beebe-Frankenberger, 2002). Students in middle childhood strengthen the coping strategies they used as preschool children (including "problem-solving, support-seeking, distancing, internalizing and externalizing, distraction, reframing/redefining, and denial") (Denham, 2007) so that they are able to navigate the social and academic demands of elementary school. They gradually develop a repertoire of strategies that work for them, such as reading a book, listening to music, or getting a drink of water (Thompson, Winer, & Goodvin, 2011).

Objective 1 Regulates own emotions and behaviors

a. Manages feelings

Not Yet	1	2	3	4	5	6	7	8	9	10	11	12	13
		Uses adult support to calm self • Calms self when touched gently, patted, massaged, rocked, or hears a soothing voice • Turns away from source of overstimulation and cries but is soothed by being picked up		**Comforts self by seeking out special object or person** • Gets teddy bear from cubby when upset • Sits next to favorite adult when sad		**Is able to look at a situation differently or delay gratification** • When the Block area is full, looks to see what other areas are available • Scowls and says, "I didn't get to paint this morning." Pauses and adds, "I have an idea. I can paint after snack."		**Controls strong emotions in an appropriate manner most of the time** • Asserts, "I'm mad. You're not sharing the blocks!" • Says, "I'm so excited! We're going to the zoo today!" while jumping up and down		**Manages strong emotions using known strategies** • When feeling overwhelmed, talks with teacher about a plan for completing an assignment • Finds a quiet place in the classroom to read after a disagreement with a friend • Talks to a friend about being reprimanded by the teacher		**Demonstrates patience with personal limitations; controls feelings based on how they will affect others** • When practicing cursive writing, says, "I need to go slowly when I write the letter *Q* so I won't get frustrated." • Smiles and says, "thank you" for a gift, and then later tells an adult, "I already read that book, and I didn't like it."	

Objective 1 Regulates own emotions and behaviors

b. Follows limits and expectations

Not Yet	1	2	3	4	5	6	7	8	9	10	11	12	13
		Responds to changes in an adult's tone of voice and expression • Looks when adult speaks in a soothing voice • Appears anxious if voices are loud or unfamiliar • Touches the puddle of water when adult smiles encouragingly		**Accepts redirection from adults** • Moves to the sand table at suggestion of adult when there are too many at the art table • Initially refuses to go inside but complies when the teacher restates the request		**Manages classroom rules, routines, and transitions with occasional reminders** • Indicates that only four persons may play at the water table • Cleans up when music is played • Goes to rest area when lights are dimmed		**Applies basic rules in new but similar situations** • Walks and uses a quiet voice in the library • Runs and shouts when on a field trip to the park • Listens attentively to a guest speaker		**Understands and explains reasons for rules** • Explains why running in the gym is safe but running in the hallway is not • When playing a block-balancing game, says, "You have to sit back when it's not your turn so the table doesn't get bumped."		**Demonstrates an understanding of the "big rule" concepts of safety, kindness, respect, and care for the objects and materials in the environment** • Asks to stand on a chair to reach a high shelf, and says it's safe because the chair is sturdy • Suggests organizing a book drive after hearing about a fire at a nearby elementary school's library	

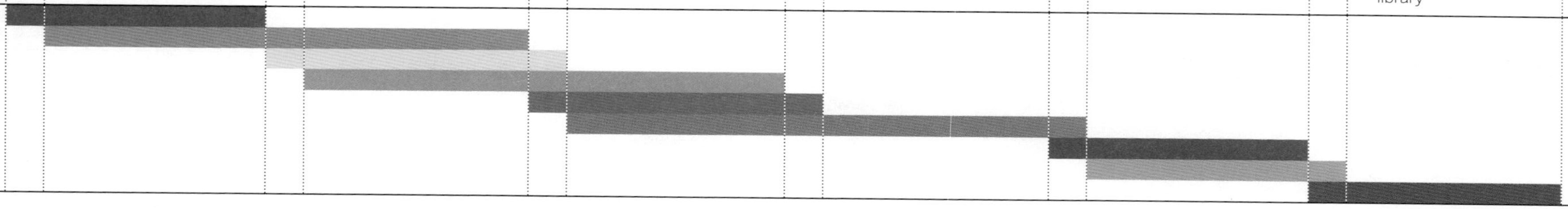

Objective 1 Regulates own emotions and behaviors

c. Takes care of own needs appropriately

Not Yet	1	2	3	4	5	6	7	8	9	10	11	12	13
		Indicates needs and wants; participates as adult attends to needs • Cries to show discomfort, hunger, or tiredness • Opens mouth when food is offered • Raises knees to chest when on back for diaper changing • Pulls off own socks • Raises arms while being lifted out of buggy		**Seeks to do things for self** • Asserts own needs by pointing, gesturing, or talking • Holds hands under faucet and waits for adult to turn on water • Tries to zip jacket but throws to ground in frustration • Attempts to clean up toys		**Demonstrates confidence in meeting own needs** • Washes hands and uses towel to dry • Stays involved in activity of choice • Uses materials, utensils, and brushes appropriately • Takes off coat and hangs it up • Puts away toys • Volunteers to feed the fish		**Takes responsibility for own well-being** • Completes chosen task • Waits turn to go down slide • Creates a "Do not touch" sign for construction • Tells why some foods are good for you • Takes care of personal belongings		**Practices skills to reach desired level of personal achievement** • Says, "I'm going to practice riding my bike every day so I can ride with my big brother." • Re-ties shoes when first attempt results in laces that are too loose • Writes poetry both at school and at home, claiming, "The more I write, the better I get."		**Accurately identifies own strengths and challenges (self-assessment, self-appraisal); develops and works toward personal goals** • After watching another child play basketball, says, "I'm not good at basketball. I'm better at soccer." • Completes self-assessment of math skills, checking off the ability to count by 2s, 5s, 10s, 20s, and 100s but not by 6s or 12s • Sets a goal for the amount of money to collect for the local animal shelter fundraiser and then solicits donations	

Objective 1 Regulates own emotions and behaviors

Strategies

- Use clear, simple language to communicate which behaviors are acceptable, e.g., say, "Pat Tamika's arm gently."
- Establish and practice consistent routines.
- Only put acceptable play materials within reach. This will limit the number of times you have to say "no".
- Acknowledge when children show self-discipline, e.g., say, "You wanted to grab Tommy's car, but you waited until he was finished playing with it."
- Use simple, clear language and facial expressions to communicate acceptable behaviors.
- Create clear boundaries to help children learn to control themselves. Use visual aids, such as carpet squares or floor tape, to mark boundaries with preschool children.
- State rules positively rather than negatively. Tell children what behavior is expected, e.g., say, "Walk when you are inside," instead of saying, "Don't run."
- Give children alternative ways to express their anger, e.g., tell the child, "If you feel angry, tell us. Say, 'I'm angry!' That way we can help you."
- Set clear, reasonable, age-appropriate expectations that children can understand. When children do not behave in acceptable ways, assess whether the adult expectation is appropriate in the given situation. Respond by consistently structuring consequences that are related to the behavior, e.g., have the child help clean up dumped paint instead of using time-out.
- Model taking deep breaths, counting to five, or doing relaxation exercises when situations are stressful. With toddlers, talk about how you are taking deep breaths to help you relax. With older children, engage them in doing relaxation exercises with you.
- Explain the reasons for rules, and help children understand why particular behaviors are not acceptable, e.g., "Be kind to others. Hitting hurts people's bodies." Or, "Only three children may play at the sand table. When there are too many children, some can't reach the toys."
- Use gestures and other visual cues while telling children the rule or limit.
- Respond positively and firmly when a child's behavior is challenging. To help a child change her behavior, observe systematically, talk with others who know the child, develop a plan of action, and implement and evaluate the plan.
- Provide opportunities for children to help create the rules for their classroom.
- Ask families about the self-care activities in which the child participates at home.
- Describe what you are doing during caregiving routines, so children can learn the sequence of actions to care for themselves.
- Use picture cues so non-verbal children or children with certain disabilities can communicate their needs through photos such as, "Hello," "I'm thirsty," or "I'm sleepy." Children point to the pictures until they learn the words in English or until they can do the activities for themselves.
- Provide opportunities for children to engage in extended make-believe play in which they can act out strong emotions.
- Provide picture and word cues to assist children as they participate in self-care tasks, e.g., use a recipe for making a snack or post cue cards with the steps of feeding the class pet.
- Discuss photos of people showing various emotions. Encourage children to create stories about the source of the person's feelings. Guide them to come up with appropriate ways the person might respond to the situation.
- Provide child-size cleaning materials such as sponges, mops, brooms, and dust pans so children can assist with meaningful classroom cleaning.
- Include clothing of various sizes so children can practice dressing themselves.
- Display posters made by children that depict things they do to take responsibility for their own well-being. Posters might focus on healthy eating habits, exercise, or personal hygiene. Create individual calendars and have each child record their healthy behaviors during the week. Review at the end of the week and determine which habits need more attention.
- Allow plenty of time to let children take responsibility for self-care routines.
- Provide a variety of self-care materials for children to explore, e.g., dolls to dress and undress, shoes to lace and tie, dress-up clothes with fasteners of varying difficulty.
- Provide only as much help as necessary for children to accomplish tasks, e.g., put socks on the child's toes and then encourage her to pull them up the rest of the way.
- When appropriate, encourage families to involve their children in simple household tasks, e.g., hanging clothes, pouring beverages, and setting the table.
- Help children move from saying "I am scared" to "I feel scared."
- Help children view mistakes as opportunities to learn.

Objective 1 Regulates own emotions and behaviors

Strategies, *continued*

- Foster a classroom climate of caring and cooperation. Set a tone that fosters kindness, helpfulness, tolerance, responsibility, and respect. Model a caring attitude as you respond to children with heartfelt compassion. Believe in your students and have high expectations for their learning.
- Be aware of your own emotional state. Show and tell students how to manage strong feelings and unexpected emotions. Take deep breaths, enjoy composure walks, or employ another calming strategy. Talk with children as you model these composure techniques so they understand the feelings that prompted your behavior, thus allowing them to use similar strategies when their strong emotions arise.
- Prepare children for unexpected change, e.g., if a special event is canceled. Be clear, concise, and direct about substitute plans in hopes of decreasing stress, e.g., tell the students that they will enjoy a cooperative learning activity instead. Understand that the unknown, unfamiliar, and unforeseen can promote distress and anxiety.
- Create a quiet space in your classroom for children to use when they need some time and space in order to deal proactively with strong feelings. This area will foster their ability to calm down and regain composure in order to maintain control when upset, angry, or frustrated.
- Offer ongoing opportunities for children to emotionally reflect on their day via journaling, visualization or imagery, self-reflective activities such as completing an exit ticket, sharing thoughts with a peer, and/or talking with the class as a whole.
- Listen empathetically to children when they share their concerns, worries, fears, and other emotional thoughts. Feeling heard can reduce stress and help children learn to internally work through strong feelings.

Establishes and sustains positive relationships

2

Being able to establish caring relationships and to enter successfully into ongoing social interactions are essential skills for school and for success in life. There are four dimensions to this objective: establishing and sustaining positive relationships with adults; making and keeping friends; relating to other children in groups; and interpreting the emotional cues of others and responding appropriately.

Relationships With Adults

The ability to establish caring relationships between a child and the important people in her life is called *attachment*. An infant squeals with laughter as a trusted adult plays with him. A toddler struggles to say good-bye to her mother at drop-off time. A 2-year-old runs into the room and hugs her teacher hello every morning. A preschool child works and plays with friends but knows when to ask an adult for help. A first grader engages a teacher in a conversation about their shared interest in horses.

Children's ability to form positive relationships with adults is important to their social development and academic success (Berk, 2006; Bronson, 2006; Howes, 2000; Howes et al., 2008; Palermo, Hanish, Martin, Fabes, & Reiser, 2007; Pianta, 1999). The model for all future relationships begins with the infant's early interactions with parents and other primary caregivers (Lamb, Bornstein, & Teti, 2002; Rubin, Bukowski, & Parker, 1998). Responding to infants' signals is critical to the development of a trusting, secure relationship with their primary caregivers (Petersen & Wittmer, 2008).

Various factors can interfere with a child's ability to form secure attachments with adults. Risk factors such as poverty, disabilities, or stress may influence the formation of secure attachments (Diamond, 2002; Ray, Bowman, & Brownell, 2006; Sigman & Ruskin, 1999; Trawick-Smith, 2006). Family socialization practices, such as encouraging dependence, may also affect how the child separates from the primary caregiver, how the child responds to other adults, and how other adults respond to the child (Chen, 1996; Harwood, Miller, & Irizarry, 1995; Trawick-Smith, 2006).

The classroom is an important setting for the development of positive relationships with adults outside the family (Pianta, 1999). Just as in the parent–child relationship, the quality of the teacher–child relationship can support or limit children's development and learning (Howes et al., 2008; Palermo et al., 2007; Schmidt, Burts, Durham, Charlesworth, & Hart, 2007). Teacher–child relationships may be close and affectionate, distant and formal, filled with conflict, or overly dependent (Coplan & Prakash, 2003; Howes & Matheson, 1992; Pianta, 1999). Overly dependent relationships and teacher–child relationships marked by lots of conflict can interfere with children's learning and academic achievement (Coplan & Prakash, 2003; Palermo et al., 2007; Ray et al., 2006). Teachers must build respectful and trusting relationships with children and their families. This is particularly true when the family's home culture and socioeconomic background differs from the teacher's (Ray et al., 2006).

Objective 2 Establishes and sustains positive relationships

Supportive relationships with teachers can help children overcome the challenges associated with living in high-risk circumstances and help children whose early relationships have not been positive (Pianta, 1999). Children who have secure attachment relationships with primary caregivers and teachers have an easier time interacting with peers, forming positive relationships, and being a part of the group.

Students' attachments to teachers continue to play a significant role in the primary grades. Students who have warm, close relationships with their teachers often have a more positive attitude toward school and higher scores on achievement tests, and they participate more in class (Hamre and Pianta, 2001). In middle childhood, students tend to have secure relationships with teachers who are "open to communication, responsive to the child's requests for help, and aware of the child's needs" (Bergin & Bergin, 2009).

Interpreting the Emotional Cues of Others and Responding Appropriately

Learning to recognize and respond to the emotional cues of other people involves learning a set of skills that adults model. When an infant smiles back at a smiling face and a toddler moves near a crying child, they are beginning to recognize and respond to the emotions of others. Two-year-olds respond to others with empathy and understanding when they offer a crying child a special toy and tell the teacher, "He's sad." Preschool and kindergarten children understand the reasons for people's emotions and begin to learn that other peoples' feelings about a situation may be different from their own. Middle childhood brings the ability to deduce others' emotional states via a multitude of indicators, such as body language, former experiences, and situations, and to offer increased empathy for one's peers.

Emotional understanding is critical to positive social relationships and peer acceptance (Denham, von Salisch, Olthof, Kochanoff, & Caverly, 2002; Eisenberg et al., 1997; Hubbard & Coie, 1994; Hyson, 2003). Social acceptance depends on a child's ability to understand, predict, and interpret the emotions of others (Mostow, Izard, Fine, & Trentacosta, 2002). Children who can accurately interpret emotional signals are more likely to respond appropriately to others and less likely to become angry or aggressive. Children who exhibit challenging behaviors may not recognize what others are feeling (Webster-Stratton & Herbert, 1994). But some children who bully others may "read" emotions correctly, but respond inappropriately. Adults must combat bullying behavior by being proactive and taking preventive actions.

Families introduce young children to cultural rules about ways of feeling and displaying emotions (Denham et al., 2002). Some children are taught to openly express their emotions, while others are encouraged to avoid outward expressions (Day, 2006; Trawick-Smith, 2006). Children who have suffered abuse or witnessed abuse often have difficulty managing their own emotions (Beland, 1996; Ontai & Thompson, 2002).

Some disabilities may affect children's sensitivity to emotions. For example, some children with Autism spectrum disorders have difficulty reading the emotions of others (Baron-Cohen, 1995). They may not recognize the meaning of basic emotional signals such as facial expressions, tone of voice, or words (Ayoub & Fischer, 2006). The more adults acknowledge children's emotional reactions and describe emotional signals, the better children become at interpreting them (Berk, 2006; Denham & Kochanoff, 2002).

There are links between students' emotional understanding and academic performance in primary school. Students who can accurately discern and respond to relevant emotional cues in the school environment tend to focus well on academic tasks (Trentacosta et al., 2006). This finding also extends to at-risk students living below the poverty line. In one study, competence in "detect[ing] and label[ing] emotion cues" assisted at-risk children in positive social interactions, whereas "a deficit in this ability contributed to behavioral and learning problems" (Izard et al., 2001).

Objective 2 Establishes and sustains positive relationships

Interacting With Peers and Making Friends

The ability to enter successfully into ongoing social interactions is an important social skill. This ability begins with an infant's early interactions with a primary caregiver and quickly grows into an interest in watching other children at play. A toddler who laughs with another child as they both finger paint with their own materials becomes a 2-year-old who takes turns dipping his fingers in a shared pot of paint. The preschool child who talks about friendships becomes a kindergarten child who establishes and maintains relationships over time. By third grade, he understands that friendships can continue even after a disagreement occurs.

Children's ability to build positive relationships with peers affects their social competence, school adjustment, academic success, and mental health in adulthood (Berk, 2006; Katz, Kramer, & Gottman, 1992; Ladd, Birch, & Buhs, 1999; Ladd, Buhs, & Seid, 2000; Peisner-Feinberg et al., 1999; Raver & Zigler, 1997; Shonkoff & Phillips, 2000; Wentzel & Asher, 1995). Some children's interactions put them at risk for developing negative relationships with peers. Once children develop negative reputations, they are likely to be rejected by their peers unless adults intervene (Black & Hazen, 1990; Kaiser & Rasminsky, 2003). Children who are not well liked often exhibit expressions of anger, hostility, or aggression (Cillessen & Bellmore, 2002; Denham et al., 1990; Hartup & Abecassis, 2002). Aggressive behaviors are not only physical. Aggression also may be verbal, e.g., name calling; nonverbal, e.g., mean faces; or relational, e.g., excluding children from an activity (Ostrov, Woods, Jansen, Casas, & Crick, 2004). Both the aggressor and the victim need adult intervention and support to develop positive peer relationships.

Children who are successful in their peer relationships use strategies such as making comments that are appropriate to the ongoing interaction. Children who are not well liked use behaviors such as calling attention to themselves or trying to control the interaction (Cillessen & Bellmore, 2002; Dodge, Schlundt, Schocken, & Delugach, 1983; Putallaz & Gottman, 1981). Many children need adult assistance to learn how to enter group play successfully. Children with disabilities may need help to enter the group or to initiate social contacts with potential social partners (Buysse, Goldman, & Skinner, 2003; Hart, McGee, & Hernandez, 1993; Kantor, Elgas, & Fernie, 1993; Pettit & Harrist, 1993; Robinson, Anderson, Porter, Hart, & Wouden-Miller, 2003).

Through interactions with peers over time, children begin to form friendships. These friendships can help children acquire positive social skills and develop more complex social competence (Katz, Kramer, & Gottman, 1992; Shonkoff & Phillips, 2000). Friend relationships are different from other relationships that children have with peers.

Friends are more likely to be the same sex, ethnicity, and have similar behaviors, both positive and negative. They spend more time with one another (Hartup & Abecassis, 2002). Most children with disabilities who are in programs with typically developing peers have at least one friend (Buysse, 1993).

Play is an important context for developing close relationships. Creative learning activities such as fantasy play, block play, and open-ended art activities provide opportunities for children to build positive relationships with peers (Wishard, Shivers, Howes, & Ritchie, 2003).

In middle and late childhood, peer groups begin to change significantly as special groups form, students socialize more outside of the school and home environments, and they communicate more via technology, e.g., cellular phones, Internet, and social networks (Gifford-Smith & Brownell, 2003). Students in this age range begin to feel more pressure to be accepted by their peer group and also come to realize that friendships can persist over time more than they did at younger ages (Zembar & Blume, 2009).

Objective 2 Establishes and sustains positive relationships

a. Forms relationships with adults

Not Yet	1	2	3	4	5	6	7	8	9	10	11
		Demonstrates a secure attachment to one or more adults • Appears uneasy when held by a stranger but smiles broadly when mom enters room • Calms when a familiar adult offers appropriate comfort • Responds to teacher during caregiving routines		**Uses trusted adult as a secure base from which to explore the world** • Moves away from a trusted adult to play with a new toy but returns before venturing into a new area • Looks to a trusted adult for encouragement when exploring a new material or physical space		**Manages separations without distress and engages with trusted adults** • Waves good-bye to mom and joins speech therapist in a board game • Accepts teacher's explanation of why she is leaving the room and continues playing		**Engages with trusted adults as resources and to share mutual interests** • Talks with teacher every day about their pets • Asks librarian to help find a book about surfing • Readily asks teacher for help when struggling with a number game		**Respectfully engages adult with a different viewpoint; considers adult's alternative ideas when engaged in discussion** • Listens to adult share a viewpoint about a presentation and offers another opinion • Participates in discussion about ideas presented in an opinion article about NASA	

Objective 2 Establishes and sustains positive relationships

b. Responds to emotional cues

Not Yet	1	2	3	4	5	6	7	8	9	10	11	12	13
		Reacts to others' emotional expressions • Cries when hears an adult use an angry tone of voice • Smiles and turns head to look at person laughing • Moves to adult while watching another child have a tantrum		**Demonstrates concern about the feelings of others** • Brings a crying child's blanket to him • Hugs a child who fell down • Gets an adult to assist a child who needs help		**Identifies basic emotional reactions of others and their causes accurately** • Says, "She's happy because her brother is here." "He's sad because his toy broke." • Matches a picture of a happy face with a child getting a present or a sad face with a picture of a child dropping the banana she was eating		**Recognizes that others' feelings about a situation might be different from his own** • Says, "I like riding fast on the trike, but Tim doesn't." • Shows Meir a picture of a dinosaur but doesn't show it to Lucy because he remembers that she's afraid of dinosaurs		**Recognizes that people can experience more than one emotion at the same time** • Talks about a book character who is excited and worried about going to a new school • Says, "When I broke my leg, I was really sad about it, but I was super excited to have everybody sign my cast!" • Says, "I think Brian is disappointed that he didn't get the role of the pirate in the play, but I think he's still happy about playing one of the shipmates."		**Uses situational context and past experiences when interpreting another's feelings; gauges reactions of others to determine response** • Remembers that a friend prefers to be left alone when upset and waits to be approached before talking to her • When a classmate is embarrassed about not knowing the answer to a homework question, says discreetly, "I figured out the answer. Do you want me to tell you?" • Notices someone alone on the playground and invites her to play	

Objective 2 Establishes and sustains positive relationships

c. Interacts with peers

Not Yet	1	2	3	4	5	6	7	8	9	10	11	12	13
		Plays near other children; uses similar materials or actions • Sits next to child playing an instrument • Imitates other children building with blocks • Looks at other child's painting and chooses the same color		**Uses successful strategies for entering groups** • Watches what other children are doing for a few minutes and then contributes an idea • Asks, "Can I run with you?"		**Initiates, joins in, and sustains positive interactions with a small group of two to three children** • Sees group pretending to ride a bus and says, "Let's go to the zoo on the bus." • Enters easily into ongoing group play and plays cooperatively		**Interacts cooperatively in groups of four or five children** • Takes turns being "it" during tag game on the playground • Invites multiple peers to join in play		**Works with a group toward a shared goal; participates in group games with rules** • As a member of a group, decides on a board game and compromises in order to make the game go smoothly • On the playground, collects "treasure" and builds a snow fort around it, with a small group of children taking turns as guards, builders, and treasure seekers		**Fluidly alternates between the roles of leader and follower in order to sustain play** • When preparing for a soccer game, says, "I'm going to be the goalie," but later changes positions when a teammate asks to be the goalie • Says, "You got to be the choreographer yesterday. I want a turn today."	

Objective 2 Establishes and sustains positive relationships

d. Makes friends

Not Yet	1	2	3	4	5	6	7	8	9	10	11	12	13
		Seeks a preferred playmate; shows pleasure when seeing a friend • Leaves Library area to greet another child upon his arrival • Seeks preferred child to sit next to at group time		**Plays with one or two preferred playmates** • Builds block tower with another child during choice time and then looks at books with same child later in the day • Joins same two friends for several days to play a running game outside		**Establishes a special friendship with one other child, but the friendship might only last a short while** • Talks about having friends and what friends do together • Seeks out particular friend for selected activities on a regular basis		**Maintains friendships for several months or more; forms friendships around similar play interests** • Finds her friend's favorite purple marker and gives it to her • Works through a conflict and remains friends after a disagreement • Chooses to play with a child who also likes to pretend he is a dragon		**Forms friendships based on personal qualities** • Says, "Teddy is my friend because he's really nice, and he's funny." • Explains that a good friend is someone who is helpful and kind		**Forms friendships based on mutual trust and assistance; understands that friendship can still exist when disagreements occur** • Says, "Tai and I are friends because he doesn't tease me when I get upset. He doesn't let other kids tease me, either." • Chooses to play alone after disagreeing with a friend, but seeks out that friend later in the day • Says, "My friend, Kami, and I are going to sit next to each other in music because she can help me count out my part, and I can help her read the notes."	

Objective 2 Establishes and sustains positive relationships

Strategies

- Label and talk about emotions and their causes, e.g., "Christina is angry because you took her truck," and "Willard is sad because he dropped his sandwich."
- Read books showing different emotions. Discuss why the people look and feel the way they do, e.g., say, "She's smiling because she is happy. She's happy because her mommy is home."
- Discuss and read books about friendships, e.g., how friends treat one another, the things they do for each other.
- Build positive relationships with each child by making purposeful observations every day, talking to each child respectfully, being sensitive to the child's feelings, and validating accomplishments and progress.
- Interact one-on-one with children daily, playing and talking with them.
- Display family pictures in the classroom to validate children's most important relationships.
- Respond promptly and consistently to children's needs.
- Smile frequently at children as you interact with them. This helps to establish positive relationships.
- Show appropriate affection, e.g., rub backs at nap time, hold children's hands as you walk around the playground, give hugs as children arrive in the morning.
- Talk to children at their eye level.
- Make each child feel special. Make time for him to share special interests with you, e.g., show you a favorite book or tell you about a recent experience. Tell children about your interests, e.g., things you like to do, what you liked to do as a child.
- Model respectful relationships with other adults in the program, e.g., tell children how other adults help. Say, "Mr. Jonas keeps our play yard clean and safe," or, "Thank you, Ms. Kelly, for getting the trikes out for us."
- Provide duplicates of favorite toys.
- Model cooperative behavior.
- Make accommodations for children with disabilities. You may need to pair a child with a disability with a peer partner, hold a prop for the child to use during group play, or give guidance and language for entering a peer group.
- Pay close attention to a child who is likely to act aggressively. Help the child control her emotions and behavior before another child gets hurt.
- Help children detect and interpret cues about how someone feels, e.g., say, "He looks angry. His forehead is wrinkled, his mouth turns down, and his fists are tight."
- Read stories to about various emotions. Discuss why the characters in the story look, feel, and act the way they do.
- Observe children as they try to enter group activities both indoors and outdoors. Help children who need assistance find play partners. Teach them positive strategies for entering and participating in group activities.
- Address all types of aggressive behavior. Assist the victim and the aggressor to develop prosocial behaviors such as helping, sharing, and including others in group activities and play. Call attention to positive changes in the child's behavior. Guide the other children toward responding to the child in new, more positive ways.
- Create spaces in the room for two children to work together.
- Help children learn how to enter a group by
  1) waiting, watching, and listening without speaking;
  2) imitating the actions of the children in the group; and
  3) saying something positive that relates to what the group is doing such as suggesting roles they could play.
- Explain that people have a variety of emotional responses to particular events (loss, injury, pain, birthday, going home, etc.), and they do not always react the same way.
- Explain that people express the same emotion in different ways, e.g., sometimes when people are sad they cry; sometimes they turn the corners of their mouths down like this and furrow their brows like this, but they do not cry.
- Engage children in informal conversations about your life and theirs. Listen attentively while they speak.
- Label your own feelings as you share experiences from your life and how you felt. Talk about things that made you happy, sad, or excited. Explain and model some of the ways you expressed your emotions.
- Provide opportunities for children to work together on group projects over time. Model how children can help each other and work through conflict situations.
- Encourage children to inform you of significant events, particularly those that threaten someone's emotional or physical safety. Recognize that "tattling" can offer an opportunity to teach the missing skills of self-advocacy, empowerment, and problem solving. Too often, children are confused by the message that "no tattling" sends, thus creating a culture of silence. Send the message that if an event is unsettling, teachers want children to advise them of this situation.

Objective 2 Establishes and sustains positive relationships

Strategies, *continued*

- Enthusiastically greet each child as she arrives each morning; ask open-ended, meaningful questions; and connect with a smile or a "high five" to promote positive, respectful relationships.
- Read literature that depicts main characters experiencing social–emotional struggles. Encourage children to recognize the social dilemma and/or the emotions found in the story, and lead a discussion about potential causes. Ask children to suggest possible coping strategies or situational solutions. Consider having the children role-play various social and emotional situations by identifying the problem, modeling the process of change, and proposing solutions in hopes of dealing with social–emotional challenges.
- Share photographs displaying various emotions and lead a discussion about recognizing others' feelings via situational clues and cues. Think about using behavioral rehearsal so children can practice and strengthen their social–emotional skills.

Participates cooperatively and constructively in group situations

3

Functioning as a member of a group requires an understanding of the feelings and rights of others and the ability to balance personal needs and desires with those of other people. When an infant babbles to the children at the lunch table, he is showing his interest in belonging to the group. When a 2-year-old waits for a turn on a bike, she is learning that other people's needs are important, too. When a preschool child works with others to paint a class mural, he is cooperating and sharing materials and ideas. And, an experienced kindergarten child knows how to negotiate a trade of toys so that he gets what he wants. Middle childhood generates an appreciation for reciprocity in sharing thoughts, feelings, and ideas so that social problem solving often results in a compromise. The foundational skills for being a productive member of social and learning groups are established during the early childhood years, and they are important for early school success (Ladd et al, 1999).

Being a productive member of a group involves complex interactions. Children must gradually learn to cooperate, negotiate, lead and follow, and express their feelings and ideas in socially acceptable ways. Positive group participation includes work-related skills like listening, following directions, behaving appropriately, staying on task, and organizing work materials. Poor work-related skills in kindergarten are related to behavioral difficulties and lower academic achievement in the primary grades (McClelland, Morrison, & Holmes, 2000).

Children who are socially competent interpret social situations and match their behavior accordingly. They comply with group expectations, and they work and play collaboratively. Social, cultural, and ethnic differences may create a mismatch between the kinds of behaviors expected at school, e.g., working independently to complete a task, and those expected at home, e.g., working together to complete a task (Ray, Bowman, & Brownell, 2006). Adult guidance helps children learn how to act and adapt to the different expectations they encounter in diverse group settings.

Younger children and children with poor peer relationships may use negative strategies, such as grabbing or hitting, to meet their needs (Berk, 2003; Downey & Walker, 1989; Yeates, Schultz, & Selman, 1991). Children with peer difficulties often assert their needs in ways that drive friends away (Erdly & Asher, 1999; Youngstrom et al., 2000). Some children come from homes where violence is the most frequently used problem-solving strategy. Children who experience difficulty processing social information often give up easily and resort to aggression (Kaiser & Rasminsky, 2003). Aggressive children are especially at risk for developing more serious problems throughout childhood and adolescence (Campbell, 1995; Parker & Asher, 1987), but intervention can help (Burton & Denham, 1998; Denham & Burton, 1996, 2003; Shure, 1997). Limited language skills can also be a barrier to social problem solving.

Objective 3 Participates cooperatively and constructively in group situations

Conflicts are important opportunities for children to learn the give-and-take necessary for mature, successful social interactions that require negotiation and compromise (Kimple, 1991). It is tempting for an adult to fix children's social problems, but children need opportunities to think about and implement their own solutions. Good social problem-solving skills enable children to speak up for themselves, build self-esteem, and develop competence in other areas (Dinwiddle, 1994; Gonzalez-Mena, 2002), and such skills deter aggressiveness (Richard & Dodge, 1982; Spivack & Shure, 1997). Children who think of multiple ways to solve a problem are better able to solve problems without resorting to aggression.

Children are more likely to use prosocial behaviors, such as cooperating or consoling and helping others, when their teachers use positive guidance strategies and a curriculum that emphasizes the values of a community (DeVries, Haney, & Zan, 1991; Schmidt, Burts, Durham, Charlesworth, & Hart, 2007).

In addition, adult guidance helps children develop a repertoire of effective problem-solving strategies. Children benefit from learning a process for solving social problems (see strategies at the end of this section) (Committee for Children, 2002; Gonzalez-Mena, 2002; Kaiser & Rasminsky, 2003; Levin, 2003; Slaby, Roedell, Arezzo, & Hendrix, 1995).

In the primary grades, empathy and perspective taking play an important role in balancing the needs and rights of self and others, as well as in solving social problems. Empathy has been correlated with more advanced conflict resolution skills in adolescents, so it is critical to promote understanding from an early age (de Wied et al., 2007; McDonald & Messinger, 2011). When students understand and can relate to others' emotions and motives, they are more likely to collaborate and work constructively in group situations. Primary school teachers rate cooperation and self-control as equally essential for success (Lane, Givner, & Pierson, 2004).

Objective 3 Participates cooperatively and constructively in group situations

a. Balances needs and rights of self and others

Not Yet	1	2	3	4	5	6	7	8	9	10	11	12	13
		Responds appropriately to others' expressions of wants • Gives another child a ball when asked • Makes room on the sofa for a child who wants to look at the book with him		**Takes turns** • Waits behind another child at the water fountain • Says, "It's your turn now; the timer is up."		**Initiates the sharing of materials in the classroom and outdoors** • Gives another child the gold marker to use but asks to use it again when the other child is done • Invites another child to pull the wagon with her		**Cooperates and shares ideas and materials in socially acceptable ways** • Moves to make space for someone else to work at the table • Pays attention to group discussions, values the ideas of others, and contributes own ideas in a respectful manner		**Completes cooperative projects with other children** • Says, "Let's split up the questions and take turns using the book to find the answers." • Disagrees with another child by saying, "I don't think that's the right answer. Let's see if we can figure it out." • Works with a partner to complete a project about Egypt by dividing the research and writing		**Accurately completes self-assessment of role in group work** • Says, "I didn't do as much work on this as Connor did. He worked really hard." • Completes a written self-assessment after a group science project	

Objective 3 Participates cooperatively and constructively in group situations

b. Solves social problems

Not Yet	1	2	3	4	5	6	7	8	9	10	11	12	13
		Expresses feelings during a conflict • Screams when another child touches his crackers • Gets quiet and looks down when another child pushes her		**Seeks adult help to resolve social problems** • Goes to adult crying when someone takes the princess dress she wanted to wear • Calls for the teacher when another child grabs the molding dough at the same time he does		**Suggests solutions to social problems** • Says, "You ride around the track one time, then I'll take a turn." • Says, "Let's make a sign to keep people from kicking our sand castle like we did in the Block area." • Asks teacher to make a waiting list to use the new toy		**Resolves social problems through basic negotiation and compromise** • Says, "If I let you use the ruler, will you let me use the hole-punch?" • Responds, "Hey, I know! You two can be the drivers to deliver the pizza."		**Seeks conflict resolutions based on interest in maintaining the relationship in the future** • Says, "I'll let you keep the best bracelet I made today in art since you gave me my favorite swing on the playground." • Says, "Maybe we should play a different game for now because I told Henry and Myra we wouldn't start playing tag until they are ready. I don't want them to be mad at me."		**Considers multiple viewpoints when solving conflicts** • Thinks about each person's feelings and wants when solving a problem • Asks friend to explain his viewpoint before sharing a solution	

Objective 3 Participates cooperatively and constructively in group situations

Strategies

- Explain conflicts to children when they take place, describing people's feelings and the reasons for those feelings.
- Carefully watch a situation that is becoming a conflict. Allow children the chance to work out difficulties for themselves if no one will be hurt, but be prepared to offer support if needed.
- Coach children to use assertive (not aggressive) language, e.g., say, "Zory, you tell him, 'It's my turn now'."
- Establish respectful and meaningful interactions between families and teachers. Share the objectives and expectations of your program.
- Communicate what you and other adults at school do to support children in group situations. Explain how family members can help their children develop work- and play-related skills, to assume responsibility, and to cooperate.
- Give children opportunities to help in the classroom, e.g., setting out the mats at nap time, looking for another child's missing shoe.
- Help children learn about cooperation by providing ample time, materials, and opportunities for children to engage in play and other cooperative activities with multiple children.
- Use positive strategies to guide children's behavior and to help them learn how to cooperate with others. Encourage cooperative interactions by suggesting turn-taking and sharing and by modeling cooperation.
- Use role-play, games, and books to help children practice conflict resolution when there is not an immediate problem. When a conflict does arise, help children think about the sequence of events that led to it. Guide children through the problem-solving process and help them experiment with possible solutions.
- Teach children the steps involved in resolving conflicts:
  1) Identify and model how to state the problem, e.g., say, "Juan wants the truck, but you're playing with it."
  2) Brainstorm solutions. Discuss possible solutions with the children involved. Accept all ideas as possibilities.
  3) Evaluate solutions. Use open-ended prompts to help children predict outcomes, e.g., say, "I wonder what would happen if...."
  4) Help children choose and try a solution.
  5) Help children evaluate the outcome. Discuss what worked and what did not. Encourage the children to try other solutions if necessary.
- Encourage children to watch for and record, through drawings or writings, the cooperative acts of others. Keep them in a special place, e.g., a "kindness jar." Before the day is over, read the children's notes aloud (Whitin, 2001).
- Coach children as needed about taking turns and sharing.
- Help children work in pairs (they work/play best when in pairs).
- Value social–emotional learning as much as you value the acquisition of cognitive skills. Weave social–emotional learning into your daily curriculum.
- Notice the positive, kind, helpful, and respectful actions and interactions of your students. Give specific feedback rather than a judgment, e.g., say, "You gave Sasha a pencil so she could finish her work" instead of "Good job." Detailed information helps students learn what they did specifically that was helpful so they can begin to internalize and then repeat these actions. Work diligently to notice all children, especially those who may struggle with social–emotional skills.
- Model that making mistakes can offer opportunities to learn something truly new.
- Regularly hold class meetings so that children can collaboratively discuss and determine behavioral norms and make decisions that impact the classroom climate. Encourage children to focus on the solution rather than the problem.
- Plan cooperative learning activities that encourage children to work together.
- Encourage children to play "stop and go" games during outside time (e.g., "Freeze Tag," "Simon Says," "Red Light/ Green Light") to strengthen their self-regulation skills and ability to control impulses.

Physical

Physical development includes children's gross-motor (large muscle) and fine-motor (small muscle) skills. Balance; coordination; and locomotion, or traveling, are part of gross-motor development. Motor development progresses predictably, from simple to complex, in a head-to-toe direction. An infant lifts his head, lifts his trunk, rolls, crawls, sits, stands, walks, and then becomes a toddler who runs. Children gain control of their bodies in a predictable sequence as well, from the center of their bodies and outward to their fingers and toes. A child first catches a ball by trapping it against her whole body, then by holding out her arms to catch it, and finally by catching it with her hands. Similarly, fine-motor skills progress from the child's grabbing an object with a whole hand, picking up a small item with thumb and index finger, and eventually controlling the fine hand muscles needed for writing. Children need many opportunities to practice their gross-motor skills, e.g., pulling, climbing, running, kicking, throwing, jumping, and their fine-motor skills, e.g., cutting, drawing, and writing.

As they develop physically, children master increasingly sophisticated tasks and are able to meet more of their own physical needs, such as feeding and dressing themselves. Motor and other aspects of physical development are influenced by gender, heredity, nutrition, health, environment, economic level, experience, culture, and disabilities (McKenzie, et al., 1997; Spaulding, Gottlieb, & Jensen, 2008; Trawick-Smith, 2006).

Physical development affects other areas of development. Brain research points to the importance of early, positive movement experiences to brain development (Gabbard, 1998; Robert, 1999). Physical development is linked to children's emotional development and their school performance (Pica, 2006; Rule & Stewart, 2002; Sanders, 2002; Son & Meisels, 2006). The ability to be physically active influences social well-being and mental health. Regular physical activity helps children build and maintain healthy bones, muscles, and joints. It helps them to control weight and prevents or delays health conditions such as high blood pressure (McKenzie, et al., 1997; Pica, 2006; Sanders, 2002). The more children can do physically, the more willing they are to interact with other children and to try new and challenging physical tasks (Kim, 2005). This establishes a positive cycle that affects overall learning and health.

PHYSICAL OBJECTIVES

4 Demonstrates traveling skills

5 Demonstrates balancing skills

6 Demonstrates gross-motor manipulative skills

7 Demonstrates fine-motor strength and coordination

There is an important relationship between children's level of motor skill performance and their participation in physical activity. Children with better motor proficiency may find it easier to be physically active and may be more likely to engage in physical activity compared with peers who have poorer motor skill competence. Children with limited motor proficiency may subsequently choose a more sedentary lifestyle to avoid these movement difficulties (Wrotniak et al., 2006).

Motor development is not automatic. If children are to develop physical competence, they need a variety of equipment and materials; planned, appropriate movement experiences; and opportunities to practice and apply previously learned skills (Barbour, 1999; Epstein, 2007; Gallahue, 1995; Manross, 2000; Sanders, 2006).

Objective 4

Demonstrates traveling skills

4

Traveling involves moving the body through space. When an infant rolls over, a toddler takes a few steps, a preschool child rides a tricycle, a kindergarten child skips across the playground, and a second grader dances across the stage, they are traveling. The early years are critical for the development of the large muscles needed for traveling. Basic traveling movements such as running, galloping, and marching can be combined in even more complex movements for dance and sports.

Environmental conditions (e.g., lack of space, weather), the demands of the task, family background, and disabilities influence a child's ability to perform a motor task. Some children with motor impairments achieve traveling movements by using a wheelchair or other adaptive technology. Children without independent mobility may become socially isolated if adults do not support their efforts to participate in ongoing activities (Harper & McCluskey, 2002). The strong desire to play with their peers may motivate children with motor impairments to work toward more independent mobility (Kim, 2005). When children with disabilities achieve greater independent mobility, they show improved social and language development (Charlesworth, 2007; Kim, 2005).

Children learn some motor skills primarily through exploration and discovery. In order to develop more proficient movement skills, children need a combination of unstructured play and appropriate, planned movement experiences (Deli, Bakle, & Zachopoulou, 2006; Manross, 2000; Pica, 1997). Adult guidance is especially important for learning skills such as marching, galloping, and skipping. Verbal cues and modeling can help children learn to perform the skills more successfully (Breslin, Morton, & Rudisill, 2008; Sanders, 2006).

The movement skill of traveling is referenced in the National Association for Sport and Physical Education's (NASPE's) National Standards for Physical Education under Standard 1: "Demonstrates competency in motor skills and movement patterns needed to perform a variety of physical activities" (National Association for Sport and Physical Education, 2004). The standard aims to promote the development of the physical skills children need to enjoy participation in physical activities, with the mastery of movement fundamentals as the foundation for continued skill acquisition. At the lower-elementary level, students achieve mature forms of the basic locomotor skills and vary the manner in which these skills are performed in relation to changing conditions and expectations. At the upper-elementary level, students demonstrate locomotor skills for performance outcomes, using locomotor skills in dynamic and complex environments, as well as in combinations (NASPE, 2004).

Objective 4 Demonstrates traveling skills

Not Yet	1	2	3	4	5	6	7	8	9	10	11	12	13
		Moves to explore immediate environment • Rolls over several times to get toy • Crawls • Cruises • Takes a few steps • Takes steps, pushing a push-toy or chair • Moves from crawling to sitting and back again		**Experiments with different ways of moving** • Walks across room • Uses a hurried walk • Walks backwards • Pushes riding toy with feet while steering • Uses a walker to get to the table • Marches around room		**Moves purposefully from place to place with control** • Runs • Avoids obstacles and people while moving • Starts and stops using wheelchair • Walks up and down stairs alternating feet • Climbs up and down on playground equipment • Rides tricycle using pedals • Gallops but not smoothly		**Coordinates increasingly complex movements in play and games** • Runs smoothly and quickly, changes directions, stops and starts quickly • Steers wheelchair into small playground spaces • Jumps and spins • Moves through obstacle course • Gallops and skips with ease • Plays "Follow the Leader," using a variety of traveling movements		**Uses a variety of traveling movements, varying speed, pathways, and direction** • Gallops quickly in a zigzag line • Hops 15 feet in a straight line, both forward and backward • Skips in a curved line around obstacles, e.g., cones • Walks on two feet and two hands (bear crawl), traveling forward, backwards, and sideways		**Coordinates multiple complex movements while traveling** • Runs down the field with a partner, tossing a football back and forth • Moves around the stage to perform a choreographed dance • Runs while kicking a ball forward • Walks forward while throwing and catching a ball • Jogs forward while dribbling a ball with one hand	

Objective 4 Demonstrates traveling skills

Strategies

- Provide time every day for outdoor play. Make sure there is sufficient space for running, jumping, skipping, and galloping.
- Play music during movement activities. Incorporate dances that may be familiar to families in your program. Model, describe, and suggest ways for children to respond to music by using a variety of movements.
- Use traveling movements to transition children from one activity to another. Invite children to walk slowly, quickly, sideways, or backwards.
- Provide riding toys for children to push with their feet and eventually pedal.
- Provide movement activities that involve all children actively. Avoid activities where children spend much time waiting or watching others participate.
- Include activities that have a range of appropriate ways to participate so that every child is successful most of the time.
- Use movement activities to enhance stories, e.g., encourage a wild rumpus as in *Where the Wild Things Are* or together act out *Going on a Bear Hunt*.
- Set up an obstacle course so children can practice particular skills, e.g., hopping, skipping, running. Help children who need assistance with a skill or to be safe. Adjust the difficulty of tasks to match and slightly challenge children's current ability levels.
- Involve children in traveling games where they start, stop, and change directions quickly, e.g., hopscotch or "Travel, Stop, Change." For "Travel, Stop, Change," call out a traveling movement (e.g., spin, jump, gallop, run). When the whistle blows, children immediately stop that movement and change quickly to the next movement that you call out.
- Use traveling cards with children to direct their movements. For example, the card might indicate, "Gallop six steps, leading with your right foot," "Walk backwards 10 steps," or "Skip to the end of the sidewalk."
- Include activities in which pairs of children take turns being the leader and the follower. Invite the leader to move using a variety of traveling patterns and varying the pathways, directions, and speeds. Encourage the follower to attempt to copy the leader's movements exactly.
- Provide time for children to design and practice a movement sequence consisting of three different traveling skills. Following a practice period, invite children to demonstrate their traveling sequences. Pair each sequence with music to create a dance sequence.
- Have children travel (walk, gallop, skip, jump, hop) to the beat of a drum. Encourage them to travel in different ways as the drum beats slowly and then more quickly. Explain that sometimes the drum will beat in an even rhythm and sometimes it will not. Ask children to determine the best traveling pattern for each rhythm.
- Using instrumental music with a strong beat, have children create dances and follow a partner as they travel to the music. For example, using music with a count of eight, pairs of children could skip forward eight skips, then backward eight skips; do eight slide steps to the right, then eight to the left; gallop forward eight steps, then backward eight steps, etc.

Demonstrates balancing skills

5

Balancing involves movements to help stabilize the body's position when the person is not at rest (Payne & Rink, 1997). Balance is required for an infant to sit unsupported, for a toddler to stoop to pick up a toy and stand up again without tipping over, for a 3-year-old to jump off the bottom step on the climber and land on two feet, and for a first grader to walk across a narrow balance beam.

Turning, stretching, stopping, rolling, jumping and landing, swinging, swaying, and dodging require balance (Sanders, 2002). Balancing is difficult for very young children because of their uneven body proportions. As children become less top heavy, their ability to balance improves.

Balance can be static or dynamic. Static balance involves holding a particular position while the body is stationary, such as standing on one foot or sitting. Dynamic balance requires holding a stable position while the body is moving, such as while jumping and landing (Sanders, 2002).

Children's ability to balance affects their performance of gross-motor tasks (Ulrich & Ulrich, 1985). Appropriate instruction, practice, and safe materials and equipment are needed to help children improve their balancing skills (Bosma, Domka, & Peterson, 2000; Wang & Ju, 2002). Children often use materials in unique and sometimes dangerous ways to help them balance (Berger, Adolph, & Lobo, 2005). It is important to be sure that equipment is stable and in good repair.

Various factors influence children's ability to balance. For example, performance on the balance beam is affected by changes in beam width, length, and height and whether the child is moving (Robert, 1999). Certain disabilities also influence children's balance. Children with Down syndrome, visual impairments, or motor disabilities such as Cerebral palsy may need adaptations to assist them with balancing tasks, or they may need to participate in activities for shorter periods of time (Gould & Sullivan, 1999).

As children move into the elementary grades, they balance on increasingly smaller bases of support while holding the body in inverted positions and in stationary balances on an apparatus. These experiences begin to provide the ingredients for a movement repertoire of balances that may be included in sequences involving traveling and other balances.

As children get older, they combine balancing and transferring weight for a contrast in stillness and action. Experiences include balancing in dynamic environments and transferring weight into stationary, still balances on various bases of support, as well as approaches to and dismounts from apparatus. Tasks that involve sequences of movement on the floor and on apparatus are particularly important and valuable. Children make decisions about the combinations of movements and select and invent ways for one balance or action to move smoothly into another (Graham, Holt/Hale, & Parker, 2010).

Objective 5 Demonstrates balancing skills

The movement skill of balancing is referenced in the National Association for Sport and Physical Education's National Standards for Physical Education under Standard 1 (NASPE, 2004). The standard speaks of children demonstrating control in traveling, weight bearing, and balance activities on a variety of body parts, and being able to participate with skill in gymnastics. Sample performance outcomes for balance include "discovers how to balance on different body parts, at different levels, becoming 'like' a statue while making symmetrical and nonsymmetrical shapes (K–2); balances with control on a variety of objects (e.g., balance board, large apparatus, skates [3–5]); and develops and refines a gymnastics sequence demonstrating smooth transitions (3–5)" (NASPE, 2004).

Objective 5 Demonstrates balancing skills

Not Yet	1	2	3	4	5	6	7	8	9	10	11	12	13	14	15
		Balances while exploring immediate environment • Sits propped up • Rocks back and forth on hands and knees • Sits a while and plays with toys • Sits and reaches for toys without falling		**Experiments with different ways of balancing** • Squats to pick up toys • Stands on tiptoes to reach something • Gets in and out of a chair • Kneels while playing • Straddles a taped line on the floor • Sidesteps across beam or sandbox edge		**Sustains balance during simple movement experiences** • Walks forward along sandbox edge, watching feet • Jumps off low step, landing on two feet • Jumps over small objects • Holds body upright while moving wheelchair forward		**Sustains balance during complex movement experiences** • Hops across the playground • Hops on one foot then the other • Walks across beam or sandbox edge forward and backwards • Attempts to jump rope		**Demonstrates how to balance on different body parts (feet, hands, knees, elbows) at varying levels (e.g., up high, down low) while making different poses** • Balances on different bases of support, e.g., two hands and one foot, one hand and one foot, elbow and knee • Holds balances very still for 3 to 5 seconds • Balances in different body shapes, e.g., round, narrow, wide • Travels and stops in balanced positions • Performs inverted balances, e.g., balances on head and two feet as base of support		**Balances on apparatus with control and stability** • Walks across beam, turns, and walks in different direction • Walks across log on playground or other apparatus, jumps in air, lands, and continues walking • Holds balance on apparatus for 3 to 5 seconds • Moves in and out of different balances by stretching, curling, and twisting		**Designs and performs movements that combine traveling and balance into a smooth, flowing sequence with intentional changes in direction and speed** • Travels, stops, and holds a pose for 3 seconds, then continues to travel • Creates a travel–balance sequence on different bases of support; sequence includes three balances with different bases and at least two different types of traveling movements • Sets travel–balance sequence to music, matching music to movements • Mirrors partner in following a travel–balance sequence	

Objective 5 Demonstrates balancing skills

Strategies

- Modify the environment and learning experiences to accommodate a range of abilities.
- Stay close to catch or support a child if he loses balance. Use soft surfaces, such as rugs or mats, to help cushion falls indoors.
- Encourage children to stop, change directions, or walk up and down low ramps to promote their balance as they walk.
- Place masking tape or brightly colored yarn on the floor and encourage children to practice balancing by walking on it. Coach children about how to hold their arms out to steady themselves. Hold their hands as needed to provide support.
- Encourage children to practice walking with beanbags on different body parts, e.g., on head, shoulder, elbow, or under the chin.
- Introduce balance beam activities to children by offering a wide, low (not more than 4–5 inches off floor) beam. Have children walk with arms out to the side. Increase the challenge by having children walk forward, backwards, or sideways, or walk forward while carrying a light object in their hands. Tilt the beam slightly so children can walk up or down the beam. Provide support as needed, such as holding a hand for the first few times a child walks along the beam.
- Provide opportunities for children to practice static balance. Have children stand on one foot. Give the cue *freeze* when you want the children to hold their positions (for at least 3 seconds). When they can do that, ask them to balance on the other foot or with their eyes closed.
- Create balancing cards that show animals, objects, or people in various positions. For example, you might have a stork standing on one foot, a frog squatting, a toy soldier, an airplane, a person in yoga position, etc. Children select a card and then carry out the act. The other children try to guess what they represent.
- Identify body parts to be used as the base of support (feet, hands, back, bottom) and ask children to create a balance (statue) using that base. Encourage them to be creative in their balances. Note that although children are using the same base of support, the balances may look different.
- Provide opportunities for children to work together to design travel–balance sequences. For example, you might ask children to each devise two different travel patterns and two different balances to add to the group's collective travel–balance sequence.
- Ask children to create drawings of their travel–balance sequences so that they can remember the sequence and practice it again the next time they come to the gym or go outdoors.
- Encourage children to practice the following balance cues by putting them on a poster and hanging it on a wall.
  - Extend your arms for good balance when walking on the beam.
  - Tighten your muscles when performing a stationary balance. Hold your balance perfectly still.
  - Muscular tension is the key to holding your balance.
  - Extend free body parts for stability in your balance.

Objective 6

Demonstrates gross-motor manipulative skills

6

Gross-motor manipulative skills involve giving force to or receiving force from balls or similar objects. A toddler picks up a large ball, lifts it over her head, brings it forward again as fast as she can, and then drops the ball in front of her. A preschool child holds a whiffle ball in one hand, moves the ball back along the side of his head, takes a step while moving his arm forward, and propels the ball. Both of these children are demonstrating their gross-motor manipulative skills by attempting to throw a ball. In addition to throwing, these skills include collecting or catching, bouncing, kicking, and striking. Children can throw at advanced levels before they can catch objects.

The early years are important for the development of fundamental gross-motor manipulative skills. Children should explore and experiment with balls and similar objects of various sizes and weights. Equipment that is proportionate to the sizes and weights of the children is critical to developing mature gross-motor manipulative skills (Payne & Rink, 1997).

Developing competence with basic ball skills increases children's potential for learning more advanced skills such as those used in organized sports. These skills may also have a positive effect on self-concept and social skill development. Previous learning experiences; size, shape, and weight of the ball or object; and the presence of a disability can affect how children perform gross-motor manipulative tasks. Some children with motor impairments may need adaptations to participate in gross-motor activities (Gould & Sullivan, 1999).

When children's movements become more consistent and less haphazard, they are ready for more specific instruction in how to perform a particular gross-motor manipulative task. One way to do this is through the use of cue words or phrases. For example, when helping children learn to catch, you might say, "Watch the ball. Reach with your hands. Pull it into your body." When you tell children discreet actions to take, you help them focus on the skill so they can perform it more efficiently (Breslin et al., 2008; Sanders, 2002). As children play with balls and similar objects, they also need to learn how to maintain their position in relation to people and objects. This is an important safety component (Breslin, Morton, & Rudisill, 2008). Adults are crucial in helping children build a foundation for later skill development and in the safe use of equipment.

The movement skills of kicking and punting, throwing and catching, volleying and dribbling, striking with rackets and paddles, and striking with long-handled implements all are referenced in the NASPE, 2004 standards. The standards speak of younger children demonstrating progress toward achieving mature form in the more complex manipulative skills. Older children then use the skills in dynamic and complex environments and in combinations.

Objective 6 Demonstrates gross-motor manipulative skills

Kicking

Children are introduced to contacting a ball with different parts of the foot—inside, outside, back, and front. They're also given challenges that involve dribbling with either foot, at various speeds, and in different directions. As children mature, they are able to kick for both distance and accuracy. They enjoy and learn from the challenge of one-on-one keep-away situations, which combine the skills of tapping a ball along the ground with the skills needed to dodge an opponent. They can practice in dynamic game situations such as kicking a ball to a target while on the run, kicking for accuracy while trying to maneuver around an opponent, and differentiating high from low kicks (Graham, Holt/Hale, & Parker, 2010).

Throwing and Catching

Sample performance outcomes for throwing and catching include "drops a ball and catches it at the peak of the bounce (K–2); catches a fly ball using mature form (e.g., has eye on ball, moves to position, reaches with hands, catches with hands, bends elbows to pull ball into chest to absorb force (3–5); throws a ball overhand and hits a target on the wall from a distance of 40 feet (3–5); throws a ball overhand to a partner 15 yards away using mature form (3–5)" (Graham, Holt/Hale, & Parker, 2010).

Volleying and Dribbling

Children are able to strike a ball continuously, letting it bounce in their own space (K–2). They are able to control the amount of force that they put into the volley so that they can control the ball in their own space (2–4). As children mature, they are able to control the direction as well as the force of their strikes (3–5) (Graham, Holt/Hale, & Parker, 2010).

Striking With Rackets and Paddles

The standard describes the child's ability to recognize and apply the concept of an appropriate grip to the striking action and the correct biomechanics of the striking action. The sample performance outcome is "identifies and demonstrates key elements of a proper grip when holding a racket to perform a forehand strike (3–5)" (Graham, Holt/Hale, & Parker, 2010). "Generally, striking is the last fundamental motor pattern learned because of the complexity of the hand-eye coordination involved. There are also multiple levels of complexity. Actions that require striking a stationary ball (as in golf) are easier than actions that require the striking of a moving object, as in hockey. Both of these actions are less complex than striking a pitched ball with a bat" (Graham, Holt/Hale, & Parker, 2010).

Objective 6 Demonstrates gross-motor manipulative skills

Not Yet	1	2	3	4	5	6	7	8	9	10	11	12	13	14	15
		Reaches, grasps, and releases objects • Reaches for object • Pushes ball • Drops objects • Grasps a rolled ball or other object with two hands • Bats or swipes at a toy		**Manipulates balls or similar objects with stiff body movements** • Carries a large ball while moving • Flings a beanbag • Throws a ball or other object by pushing it with both hands • Catches a large, bounced ball against body with straight arms • Kicks a stationary ball		**Manipulates balls or similar objects with flexible body movements** • Throws a ball or other object • Traps thrown ball against body • Tosses beanbag into basket • Strikes a balloon with large paddle • Kicks ball forward by stepping or running up to it		**Manipulates balls or similar objects with a full range of motion** • Steps forward to throw ball and follows through • Catches large ball with both hands • Strikes stationary ball • Bounces and catches ball • Kicks moving ball while running		**Manipulates balls or similar objects, propelling them away from the body (throwing) and receiving and controlling them (catching) with increased accuracy** • Catches ball at different levels and places around the body • Watches ball, reaches for it, and pulls it in to complete catch • Kicks for accuracy at target with varying degrees of force • Throws at moving target, e.g., partner • Throws and catches ball over net with partner • Keeps eyes on ball, watching it into the hands		**Manipulates balls or similar objects with accuracy, fluidity, and control** • Contacts ball with foot directly behind center while dribbling around cones • Kicks ball back and forth with partner while traveling • Punts (drop kicks) ball below center to send it upward and forward, watching ball until it contacts foot • Strikes beach ball to partner over low net using hand • Dribbles ball continuously, switching hands • Dribbles while traveling and looking up		**Manipulates and controls balls or similar objects with rackets, paddles, bats, and other long-handled implements, e.g., golf club, hockey stick, lacrosse stick** • Strikes ball with paddle, controlling the ball's direction, force, and pathway • Tosses ball to self and strikes it with bat • While traveling, stops and controls ball with hockey stick • Uses sidearm swinging motion to strike ball forehand or backhand	

Objective 6 Demonstrates gross-motor manipulative skills

Strategies

- Avoid activities that encourage competition or that eliminate children from participating.
- Provide sufficient equipment for each child to participate. Include a variety of shapes, sizes, textures, and weights to encourage experimentation and active participation.
- Ensure children's safety by helping them adjust their position in space in relation to other children and objects. Some children need particular guidance about how to notice and move around other people and objects. Teach the safe use of each piece of equipment.
- Provide balls of various sizes, textures, and grips to explore. Include balls with chimes, bells, and visible items rolling inside.
- Provide opportunities for children to practice releasing balls into targets such as large baskets, buckets, or a small basketball hoop.
- Use scarves or mylar balloons to practice catching. These items are easier to catch than balls because they move slowly and give children time to position themselves for a catch.
- Provide lightweight clubs or mallets and balls of various sizes for children to practice hitting along the ground.
- Provide equipment that is appropriate in scale. Children like to throw and catch large rubber or beach balls. Smaller, softer balls are good for kicking. Also provide yarn balls or beanbags for catching or for throwing against a wall with varying force. Use short-handled, oversized plastic or foam paddles or bats for striking.
- Make modifications for children with disabilities or who have less developed manipulative skills. Use lower targets; provide easy-to-see, bright objects to strike; or reduce the distance between the child and target. Offer balls or similar materials that are lightweight. Hang paper balls for children to hit without having to retrieve them.
- Use specific cues with individual children to help them increase proficiency, e.g., "Look at the target before you throw." Use consistent terminology to avoid confusion.
- Provide children with plastic cups and tennis or foam balls to practice throwing and catching skills. Increase difficulty by having children throw and catch while sitting, standing, crouching, or walking.
- Provide a variety of lightweight balls, bats, rackets, and other equipment for children to use as they practice their skills.
- In a spacious room or gym, set up large targets on the wall at low levels. Provide foam balls. Encourage children to attempt to strike a target by kicking balls toward the wall.
- Provide a variety of balls for children in a large outdoor area. Encourage children to practice kicking a ball along the ground and through the air, challenging themselves to kick farther each time.
- Set up stations in a large outdoor area where children are asked to kick a ball back and forth with a partner. Observe the children as you remind them of the cues for kicking, e.g., contact the ball with the top of your foot, not your toes; contact the ball directly behind center; focus on the ball, not your partner, until the ball leaves your foot.
- Set up cones in a large outdoor area. Ask children to tap or dribble a ball around the cones, increasing and decreasing their speed and moving the ball in different directions, as appropriate.
- Provide a wide-open space and a variety of different sizes and weights of balls. Ask children to punt (drop kick) balls for distance, height, and accuracy. Children who have difficulty with punting can benefit from practicing with a balloon. This helps them understand the concept of dropping, rather than tossing, the object to be punted.
- Encourage children to strike a beach ball at a wall, allow the ball to bounce once on the ground, and then catch the ball. Repeat the "strike, bounce, catch" sequence several times.
- Place a number of plastic balls on cones spaced apart in a large outdoor area. Ask children to alternate using forehand and backhand motions as they strike balls off cones with a racket.
- Play a dribbling tag game. Invite each child to dribble a ball throughout the movement space. Encourage the child to try to tag other players with a free hand while continuing to dribble the ball.

Objective 7

Demonstrates fine-motor strength and coordination

7

Fine-motor skills involve grasping and releasing objects using fingers and hands, as well as using both hands together, and often coordinating these movements with the eyes. They require hand and finger strength and dexterity. An infant who slowly picks up Cheerios® one at a time with his thumb and index finger will become a 2-year-old who scribbles with a crayon. A 3-year-old who squeezes and pounds molding dough will become a 5-year-old who cuts a picture out of a magazine accurately. Dramatic changes occur in what children can accomplish as they gradually gain control of the small muscles in their hands and fingers. Fine-motor skills improve with regular practice and can be supported through routines and play activities.

Fine-motor skills are important in the performance of daily routines and many school-related tasks. The pincer grasp (using the thumb and index finger, or forefinger, in opposition to one another) develops at the end of the first year, enabling the child to manipulate small objects. Fine-motor development progresses slowly during the preschool years. By kindergarten, children who have often experimented with various materials engage in fine-motor activities for longer periods of time and with less frustration than children who have not had opportunities to handle materials.

Despite the growing prevalence of technology in the classroom, written communication skills in the primary grades remain important. The inability to master handwriting can affect proficiency in spelling and composition skills which can lead to long-term negative effects on academic success and self-esteem (Stevenson & Just, 2014; Feder & Majnemer, 2007). Handwriting difficulties are one of the most prevalent causes for school-age children to be referred to occupational therapy (Overvelde & Hulstijn, 2011). In typically developing children, "the quality of handwriting" develops quickly in the first grade and "reaches a plateau" by second grade (Feder & Majnemer, 2007). Handwriting becomes more structured and automated in the third grade (Karlsdottir & Stefansson, 2002).

Hand and finger strength and control also enable children to perform a variety of self-care tasks, such as eating, toileting, dressing, tooth brushing, and nose blowing. These skills give children the experience of doing things on their own and build confidence. Self-care skills are learned gradually and mastered with repetition. Complex skills, such as tying shoes, require children to have an adequate attention span, memory for a series of complex hand movements, and the dexterity to carry them out. Children who have difficulty coordinating the small muscles in their hands have trouble dressing and feeding themselves (Rule & Stewart, 2002).

Objective 7 Demonstrates fine-motor strength and coordination

Gender and family background also affect the development of children's fine-motor skills. Girls tend to be more advanced than boys in fine-motor skills (Sanders, 2006). Some children from at-risk families may have less-developed fine-motor skills. The risk factors were low maternal education, welfare dependency (poverty), only one parent in the home, and having parents whose primary first language was not English (National Center for Education Statistics, 2000).

Children with disabilities and others who have difficulty coordinating the small muscles in their hands may struggle with using pencils, crayons, and scissors (Rule & Stewart, 2002). They may avoid fine-motor activities because the activities are difficult for them, they tire, or they become anxious and give up in frustration. Modification of activities and materials to fit their developmental levels, as well as more structure and guidance, can help children increase fine-motor skills (Stewart, Rule, & Giordano, 2007).

Young children in some cultures perform self-care tasks and family chores that most children in the United States do not perform until they are older, e.g., preparing food (Trawick-Smith, 2006; Whiting & Edwards, 1988; Whiting & Whiting, 1975). Some children are not expected to perform self-care tasks such as dressing themselves until after their preschool years because their families value interdependence (doing things for each other) over personal independence.

Objective 7 Demonstrates fine-motor strength and coordination

a. Uses fingers and hands

Not Yet	1	2	3	4	5	6	7	8	9	10	11	12	13
		Reaches for, touches, and holds objects purposefully • Bats or swipes at a toy • Transfers objects from one hand to another • Releases objects voluntarily • Rakes and scoops objects to pick them up • Picks up food with fingers and puts in mouth • Bangs two blocks together • Crumples paper		**Uses fingers and whole-arm movements to manipulate and explore objects** • Places shape in shape sorter • Points at objects and pokes bubbles • Releases objects into containers • Uses spoon and sometimes fork to feed self • Dumps sand into containers • Unbuttons large buttons • Rotates knobs • Tears paper		**Uses refined wrist and finger movements** • Squeezes and releases tongs, turkey baster, squirt toy • Snips with scissors • Strings large beads • Pours water into containers • Pounds, pokes, squeezes, rolls clay • Buttons, zips, buckles, laces • Uses hand motions for "Itsy Bitsy Spider" • Turns knobs to open doors • Uses eating utensils • Sews lacing cards • Cuts along straight line		**Uses small, precise finger and hand movements** • Uses correct scissors grip • Attempts to tie shoes • Pushes specific keys on a keyboard • Arranges small pegs in pegboard • Strings small beads • Cuts out simple pictures and shapes, using other hand to move paper • Cuts food • Builds a structure using small plastic building bricks		**Uses smooth finger and hand movements** • Stays within the lines while following a maze • Outlines/traces shapes using smooth, even strokes • Pours liquid during science experiment into small opening without spilling		**Manipulates grade-appropriate tools and intricate materials with control and precision** • Cuts complex pictures and shapes, leaving edges smooth • Folds paper to make an origami creature • Uses tiny pieces to make a detailed miniature world for a social studies project • Uses keyboarding skills to compose a short story on the computer	

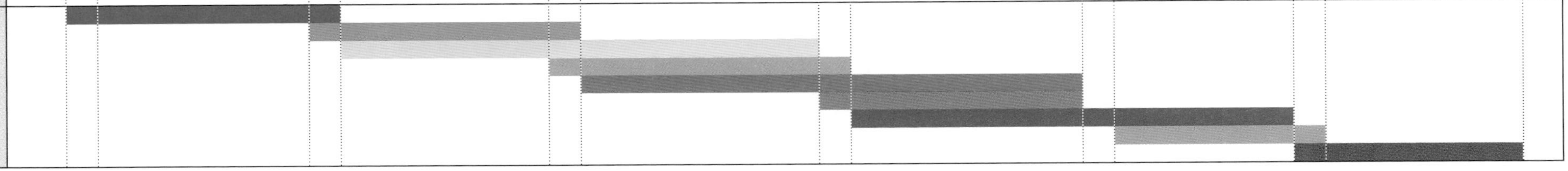

b. Uses writing and drawing tools

Not Yet	1	2	3	4	5	6	7	8	9	10	11	12	13
		Grasps drawing and writing tools, jabbing at paper		**Grips drawing and writing tools with whole hand but may use whole-arm movements to make marks**		**Holds drawing and writing tools by using a three-point finger grip but may hold the instrument too close to one end**		**Uses three-point finger grip and efficient hand placement when writing and drawing**		**Demonstrates control and appropriate pressure when using writing and drawing tools; writes legibly**		**Moves writing or drawing utensils fluidly across the page with increasing speed and accuracy; produces letters and number symbols having accurate formation, size, proportion, slant, and spacing; may use cursive writing**	

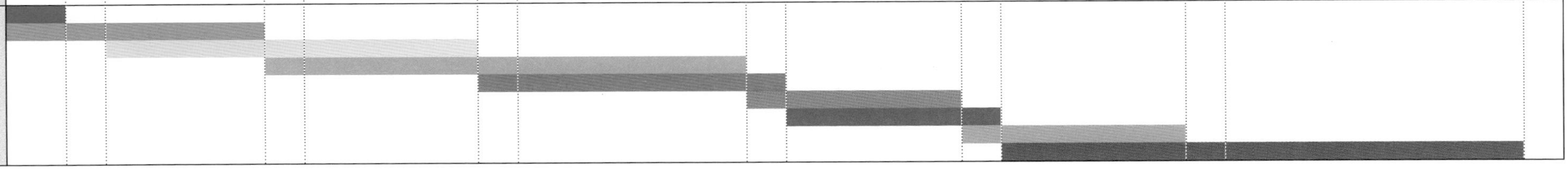

Objective 7 Demonstrates fine-motor strength and coordination

Strategies

- Provide a wide variety of fine-motor activities that interest and appeal to all children in the classroom. Include items that are easy to manipulate by hand and add more challenging activities as quickly as possible without causing frustration.
- Engage children in activities that encourage them to move their fingers individually, e.g., fingerplays, pointing at pictures.
- Provide activities to strengthen the hand grasp and release of toddlers and older children, e.g., using squirt bottles, medicine droppers, punching holes, using clothespins, and handling molding dough.
- Include activities that support eye-hand coordination, e.g., stringing beads on pipe cleaners or laces, picking up objects with tongs or tweezers, placing various sized pegs in holes, and folding paper. Encourage kindergarten students to fold paper into halves, fourths, very small, etc., and/or to create shapes or animals.
- Include activities for that require using two hands together, e.g., tearing paper, opening and closing containers, using wind-up toys.
- Have children watch as you demonstrate a task and describe the steps. Vary your language to accommodate different developmental levels.
- Allow plenty of time for children to explore materials and complete tasks.
- Take advantage of self-care activities (e.g., handwashing and scraping plates) throughout the day to support the development of children's fine-motor skills.
- Give simple, clear, verbal instructions and physically guide, model, or use picture cues to help children perform tasks successfully.

Language

Language is the principal tool for establishing and maintaining relationships with adults and other children. Children's desire to communicate their thoughts, ideas, needs, and feelings with others motivates them to develop language (Epstein, 2007). Learning to understand and use words is complex. Language also involves learning about the structure and sequence of speech sounds, vocabulary, grammar, and the rules for engaging in appropriate and effective conversation (Berk, 2003).

Language development begins at birth, but many children do not receive the ongoing experiences that support this learning. By age 3, differences in children's understanding and use of language are enormous (Berk, 2012; Strickland & Shanahan, 2004). Strong language skills are essential for children's success in school and life (Hart & Risley, 2003; Heath & Hogben, 2004; Jalongo, 2008; Kalmar, 2008). Oral language, including grammar, the ability to define words, and listening comprehension, helps provide the foundation and is an ongoing support for literacy (National Early Literacy Panel, 2008; Strickland & Shanahan, 2004). Children use language to think and to solve problems. Because words represent objects and ideas, language development is closely related to cognitive development. Children with certain types of disabilities face particular challenges in learning to understand and use language effectively.

Family background and culture also affect how children learn language. There are differences in how much mothers talk with their children and what they talk about. Some families focus on social norms such as turn-taking; others discuss what people are thinking and feeling. There are major differences in the kinds of questions they ask (Pena & Mendez-Perez, 2006).

LANGUAGE OBJECTIVES

8 Listens to and understands increasingly complex language

9 Uses language to express thoughts and needs

10 Uses appropriate conversational and other communication skills

Teachers are very important in helping children develop a strong foundation in language. Teachers influence language development through the language they use, the way they set up the environment, and the types of experiences they provide. The opportunities children have for sociodramatic play and the level of that play affects children's language development. Higher levels of play allow for increased language and more complex language structures (Heisner, 2005).

Language continues to be a key factor in children's development and learning as they enter first grade (Dickinson, Golinkoff, & Hirsh-Pasek, 2010). Dramatic increases in children's *metalinguistic awareness* occur during the early elementary years. Children begin to think about the elements of language and to use language to analyze, study, and further understand language (Hulit & Howard, 2002). They have greater ability to use decontextualized language, a highly valued school skill that may ease their transition to formal instruction (Snow, Burns, & Griffin, 1998).

As primary-grade children work collaboratively with others, they use and respond to language as they explain, describe, challenge and defend, and negotiate (Neuman, Copple, & Bredekamp, 1999). The ability to describe the world through language furthers primary-grade children's thinking and their growth in knowledge (Juel, 2006). It also exerts a persistent and indirect influence on later reading, and children who fail to attain grade expectations by third grade are less likely to experience later school success than children with stronger language skills (Morrison, Connor, Bachman, 2006). For children at risk of school failure, early and intensive language support is essential (Dickinson et al., 2010).

Objective 8

Listens to and understands increasingly complex language

8

Children must be able to comprehend what they hear. *Receptive language* includes listening to, recognizing, and understanding the communication of others. An infant turns to the sound of her mother's voice, a 2-year-old answers simple questions, and a kindergarten child follows detailed, multistep directions. To comprehend language, children must focus their attention and listen with a purpose. They must accurately and quickly recognize and understand what they hear (Roskos, Tabors, & Lenhart, 2004). Receptive language starts to develop before expressive language, but they are closely connected (Hirsch-Pasek, Golinkoff, & Naigles, 1996; Strickland, 2006). Expressive language is dependent upon receptive language.

Young children connect what they hear with their background knowledge and experiences (Strickland, 2006). The more children understand about the world around them, the better able they are to make sense of what they hear. Through conversations with adults, listening to stories read aloud, and engaging in meaningful experiences, children develop new concepts and acquire new vocabulary that helps them to understand increasingly complex language.

Some children with hearing impairments may be learning other forms of communication such as sign language or cued speech. Children with receptive language difficulties may have difficulty understanding the meaning of what they hear. They may understand only a word or two and then guess the meaning of the rest of the words.

English-language learners who are not proficient in their first language may find it harder to learn English (Jalongo, 2008; Tabors & Snow, 2001). Environments that are noisy make it even more difficult for them to recognize English words (Jalongo, 2008). Positive language interactions with skillful English speakers are critical to helping them become proficient in English (Piker & Rex, 2008).

Nonverbal communication is an important part of the listening experience and may have different meanings in different cultures. Some people value direct eye contact while listening, and others perceive eye contact as a sign of disrespect (Trawick-Smith, 2006).

Children in the primary grades learn to make contextually sensitive interpretations of the indirect speech acts of others and to draw inferences from what is said (Ackerman, 1978). Inferential processes, knowledge of sentence structure, and background and word knowledge (Senechal, Ouellette, & Rodney, 2006) contribute to their listening comprehension (Snow, Burns, & Griffin, 1998). They take a more analytical and reflective approach to language than they did at younger ages, which helps them understand multiple meanings of words as well as subtle metaphors, riddles, and puns (Berk, 2009).

Oral language comprehension in first grade has been identified as a predictor of later reading comprehension (Fuchs et al., 2012). Children's increasing lexical abilities help them to understand the instructional discourse they encounter in the primary grades.

Objective 8 Listens to and understands increasingly complex language

a. Comprehends language

Not Yet	1	2	3	4	5	6	7	8	9	10	11	12	13	14	15
		Shows an interest in the speech of others • Turns head toward people who are talking • Recognizes familiar voice before the adult enters the room • Looks at favorite toy when adult labels and points to it • Responds to own name		**Identifies familiar people, animals, and objects when prompted** • Picks up cup when asked, "Where's your cup?" • Goes to sink when told to wash hands • Touches body parts while singing "Head, Shoulders, Knees, and Toes"		**Responds appropriately to specific vocabulary and simple statements, questions, and stories** • Finds his favorite illustration in a storybook when asked • Listens to friend tell about cut finger and then goes to the Dramatic Play area to get an adhesive bandage • Responds using gestures to compare the sizes of the three leaves		**Responds appropriately to complex statements, questions, vocabulary, and stories, asking questions when needed; offers opposites for frequently occurring verbs and adjectives; understands the difference between similar action verbs** • Answers appropriately when asked, "How do you think the car would move if it had square wheels?" • Builds on classmates' ideas about how to fix a broken wagon and asks questions in order to better understand plans • Acts out the life cycle of a butterfly after the teacher reads a story about it and demonstrates *sip*, *drink*, and *slurp* to show how a butterfly eats • Plays a "hot, cold" game by giving and following directions with the words *hot* and *cold*		**Checks for understanding of material presented orally by asking questions and making comments; demonstrates understanding of the differences between verbs and adjectives that are somewhat similar; uses context clues (e.g., known words, facial expressions, gestures) to determine meaning of unknown words or phrases from grade-level material** • Watches a webcast of a famous speech and then asks questions about the content during class discussion • Listens to a classmate describe a fossil he found; asks and answers questions about the fossil in a follow-up conversation • Listens to another child explain why she used so many colors in her painting and says to the art teacher, "This one has so many colors. Mine looks kind of plain, but I can add some more paint to make it look exciting."		**Demonstrates understanding of topic by asking clarifying questions and by recounting details from discussions or other information presented orally; indicates differences between closely related verbs and adjectives; determines meaning of unknown words using context clues from grade-level material** • Following a discussion of the weather, writes a story with a classmate, and says, "Since it's a sunny day, we should write that the sun is *dazzling*." • Listens to a tour guide explain a mural on a city building and asks questions about some of the images and the issues they represent; later, shares the ideas in the mural with a peer		**Uses knowledge from discussion to explain ideas and opinions about the topic; explains the main idea when presented with information in a variety of oral formats; uses context to understand literal and non-literal meanings; understands the difference between related words that describe states of mind or degrees of certainty (e.g., *might*, *must*, *will*)** • After watching a video, answers questions concerning the main idea about how robots are used and offers supporting details; asks questions about robots during discussion and elaborates on others' understanding of the topic • When listening to a classmate read, comments that the phrase *had a ball* means they had a great time • After listening to the teacher read a mystery, says, "I suspected the mailman committed the crime, but Luis believed it was the lifeguard."	

Objective 8 Listens to and understands increasingly complex language

b. Follows directions

Not Yet	1	2	3	4	5	6	7	8	9	10	11
		Responds to simple verbal requests accompanied by gestures or tone of voice • Waves when mother says, "Wave bye-bye," as she waves her hand • Covers eyes when adult prompts, "Wheeeere's Lucy?" • Drops toy when teacher extends hand and says, "Please give it to me."		**Follows simple requests not accompanied by gestures** • Throws trash in can when asked, "Will you please throw this away?" • Puts the balls in the basket when told, "Put all the balls in the basket, please." • Goes to cubby when teacher says, "It's time to put coats on to go outside."		**Follows directions of two or more steps that relate to familiar objects and experiences** • Washes and dries hands after being reminded about the hand-washing sequence • Completes a sequence of tasks, "Get the book bin and put it on the table. Then bring the paper and crayons."		**Follows detailed, instructional, multistep directions** • Follows instructions for navigating a new computer program • Follows teacher's guidance: "To feed the fish, open the jar and sprinkle a pinch of food on the water. Then put the lid on the jar and put it back on the shelf, please."		**Asks for clarification in order to understand complex directions; carries out directions with five to six steps** • Follows the steps to set up and play a new board game	

Objective 8 Listens to and understands increasingly complex language

Strategies

- Talk often with children, using rich language to describe objects, events, and people in the environment.
- Walk over to the child instead of speaking from across the room. The child can attend more easily to what you are saying if you are nearby.
- Have the child's attention when you speak. Place yourself face-to-face at the child's level.
- Be clear and specific when making requests and giving directions.
- Use language that is easy for the child to understand, explaining new vocabulary as you use it.
- Use gestures and concrete objects to clarify what you are saying to a child.
- Use the same words and phrases for common classroom activities. This can help English-language learners associate language with meaning, e.g., say, "Hang your painting on the drying rack."
- Give adequate waiting time, so children can process what they hear and take part in discussions.
- Use precise language because young children are very literal thinkers.
- Learn about and respond appropriately to the conversational styles of the children's families.
- Use same-language and different-language peers as social peer resources. Peers can assist dual-language learners in participating in classroom activities and responding appropriately to the teacher's inquires.
- Alert children when giving complex explanations. Tell them what to listen for. For example say, "This is hard to understand. Listen carefully to each step."
- Positively acknowledge when the child follows directions.
- Use multistep and unrelated directions. For example, you might say, "First, take the plastic tablecloth and put it on the table. Next, get the paint, droppers, and six containers off the shelf. Put 10 drops of paint into each container. Put a container and piece of paper at each child's place." Also use multiple directions related to different tasks. For example, "Hang your coat up. Take the books back to the library. When you come back, get out your journal."
- Give children opportunities each day to hear fluent reading (read aloud) from you, in a listening center, or via a Web-based source.
- Do "think-alouds" while reading aloud to children. Talk about what you are thinking about as you are reading a story (e.g., interesting vocabulary words, ways you figured out tricky words in the text, interesting facts you read about, connections you made).
- After you give oral directions to a group, ask a child to repeat the directions in his own words.
- Play "20 Questions" with items in the classroom and have children figure out which item you are thinking about.

Objective 9

Uses language to express thoughts and needs

9

Children all over the world follow the same developmental sequence as they learn to speak. They proceed from cooing and babbling in infancy to forming words and sentences as toddlers and 2-year-olds. As preschool children, they use more adult-like speech, and by the time they have finished third grade, they are using appropriate expression and inflection when telling a story. Children talk to express feelings, make requests, discuss plans, gain information, understand concepts, solve problems, and share ideas and stories. With lots of practice over time, children develop the ability to speak clearly and to use decontextualized language to tell personal stories as they describe objects, people, and events that are familiar but that occurred in another time and place (Nicolopoulou & Richner, 2007; Snow, 1991). This narrative talk or storytelling requires more complex language than is needed for daily conversations (Stadler & Ward, 2005).

The use of language is important to children's literacy development. Children's first writing experiences are usually based on what they learned through narrative talk (Beals, 2001; Dickinson & Tabors, 2001; Hart & Risley, 1995). Later literacy development is influenced by explanatory talk such as discussion of cause-and-effect relationships and connections between ideas, events, and actions (Beals, 2001; Dickinson & Tabors, 2001; Hart & Risley, 1995). Children's later literacy development also is influenced by their ability to define words and their knowledge of grammar (National Early Literacy Panel, 2008).

Children's language skills vary greatly. There are major differences due to family background and income. Family language patterns affect how much speech children use to express their feelings, needs, and ideas (Rogoff, Mistry, Goncu, & Mosier, 1993). Some children speak in complex sentences. Others make brief statements and must be supported to say more about their ideas. Children's narrative topics may be limited to a single focus with a clear beginning, middle, and end. Narratives of other children may flow from one topic into another (Stadler & Ward, 2005). By kindergarten, some children living in poverty have only one fourth of the vocabulary of their middle-class peers (Berk, 2006).

Some children use other forms of communication besides spoken language. They may use sign language or augmentative communication including pictures, switch activated devices, or other mechanisms that can speak for them (Cook, Klein, & Tessier, 2004). It is important to include children's use of these devices when assessing a child's development.

For some children, English is not their first language. They may speak only a little English or none at all. Every language has its own vocabulary and rules for how sounds, words, and larger units of meaning fit together. Many children use the structure of their first language and apply it as they learn English (August & Hakuta, 1998). English-language learners and children with language delays may find it difficult to use language that goes beyond what is familiar (Weitzman & Greenberg, 2002).

Objective 9 Uses language to express thoughts and needs

Children with language delays or hearing or cognitive impairments often speak in short, ungrammatical sentences. Children with language delays may have difficulty retrieving words from memory and may confuse word meanings (Ratner, 2001). Impairments in social interactions may make it challenging for some children with Autism spectrum disorders to learn new words (Parish-Morris, Hennon, Hirsh-Pasek, Golinkoff, & Tager-Flusberg, 2007).

Teachers can influence children's language development (Copple & Bredekamp, 2009). It is important for teachers to engage in conversations with all children, even if they don't yet speak English (Piker & Rex, 2008). Reciprocal, extended conversations with more skilled speakers help children increase their vocabularies, expand their expressive skills, and move toward more conventional grammar. Through participating in extended conversations with adults or mature language users, most children gradually learn adult-like language constructions.

During the early primary years, children's ability to produce mainstream English plays an important role in their academic achievement, and in particular, their reading abilities (Terry & Connor, 2012; Terry, Connor, Petscher, & Conlin, 2012). By the time they enter school, most children can understand and produce a wide range of grammatical forms (Snow, Burns, & Griffin, 1998), although some structures (e.g., gerunds, plurality and tense, adjectives, passive voice) are still developing (Hulit & Howard, 2002). They improve in their ability to master complex grammatical constructions and to apply them in a wider range of situations, including written compositions (Berk, 2009; Snow et al., 1998). As early as first grade, children with more advanced grammatical knowledge produce higher quality written compositions (e.g., more organized, greater sentence flow, more varied sentences) than children with less grammatical understanding (Kim, Otaiba, Sidler, & Gruelich, 2013). During the primary years, children also come to realize that they share responsibility for communicating their thoughts and needs clearly (Hulit & Howard, 2002).

Vocabulary knowledge at school entry and concurrent vocabulary throughout the primary grades and thereafter is important for English-speaking and bilingual children (Swanson, Rosston, Gerber, & Solari, 2008), and is predictive of children's early word reading and of their reading comprehension in third grade and afterward (Juel, 2006). Vocabulary increases tremendously between the beginning and end of elementary school. In addition to conversations with adults and more capable peers, children at this age learn vocabulary through reading (Berk, 2009). Throughout the primary grades, most children not only learn increasingly abstract words, but they also refine the meanings of known words and learn to use them in new ways (Hulit & Howard, 2002).

Specific teaching of vocabulary to primary-grade students is essential (Biemiller & Boote, 2006). While being responsive to teachable moments is helpful, intentional instruction designed to enhance vocabulary is also needed (Neuman & Roskos, 2012). After second grade, the gap between children in the highest and lowest quartile in root word meanings is approximately two grade levels. This gap persists throughout the elementary school years unless teachers take appropriate action to help children build word knowledge.

Objective 9 Uses language to express thoughts and needs

a. Uses an expanding expressive vocabulary

Not Yet	1	2	3	4	5	6	7	8	9	10	11	12	13	14	15
		Vocalizes and gestures to communicate • Coos and squeals when happy • Cries after trying several times to get toy just out of reach • Waves hands in front of face to push away spoon during a feeding • Uses hand gestures to sign or indicate "more"		**Names familiar people, animals, and objects** • Says, "Nana," when grandmother comes into the room • Names the cow, horse, chicken, pig, sheep, and goat as she sees them on the trip to the farm		**Describes and tells the use of many familiar items** • When making pancakes, says, "Here is the beater. Let me beat the egg with it." • Responds, "We used the big, red umbrella so we both could get under it."		**Incorporates new, less familiar, or technical words (acquired through texts and conversations) in everyday conversations; correctly uses new meanings for familiar words** • Uses a communication device to say, "My bird went to the vet. He has a disease. He's losing his feathers." Answers more questions about the bird when asked • After hearing the word in a story, says, "I'm not sure I can put it together. It's *complicated*. What do you think?" • When waiting in line during a jump rope activity, says, "That's funny. We're waiting for our *turn* to *turn* the rope."		**Incorporates new grade-appropriate words (acquired through texts and conversations); clearly describes and explains events, ideas, and feelings using relevant details** • Describes to the teacher how to play the game he learned in speech class earlier that day • Takes a new student to the listening center and shows him how to use the equipment; explains the procedure for signing in		**Incorporates new grade-appropriate words (acquired through texts and conversations); uses several descriptive words to relay detailed and specific information** • Changes the sentence from "The cat was sleeping" to "The gigantic, orange cat was lazily sleeping on the windowsill." • When recounting an event, includes details that help the listener visualize the experience		**Incorporates new grade-appropriate words (acquired through texts and conversations); uses conversational and academic words and phrases; correctly uses abstract nouns** • Says, "I went to my sister's dance recital. She was really nervous, so I gave her lots of *encouragement*." • Gives a persuasive speech about the arts in school after reading a news story that presented two sides of the argument • Writes a poem, and then uses a thesaurus to revise word choice and enhance meaning	

Objective 9 Uses language to express thoughts and needs

b. Speaks clearly

Not Yet	1	2	3	4	5	6	7	8	9	10	11	12	13	14	15
		Babbles strings of single consonant sounds and combines sounds • Says, "M-m-m;" "D-d-d." • Says, "Ba-ba-ba." • Babbles with sentence-like intonation		**Uses some words and word-like sounds and is understood by most familiar people** • Refers to grandma as "Gum-gum" • Asks, "Where bankit?" and a friend brings his blanket to him • Says, "No go!" to indicate she doesn't want to go inside		**Is understood by most people; may mispronounce new, long, or unusual words** • Says, "I saw ants and a hoppergrass" (grasshopper) • Speaks so is understood by the school visitor		**Pronounces multisyllabic or unusual words correctly; speaks audibly** • Says, "Oh, that one has layers, it's a *sedimentary* rock." • Says, "What does *ostracize* mean?" after hearing the word read in *Abiyoyo* • Shares a personal story with classmates during lunch and is clearly heard and understood		**Adjusts volume and rate of speech in order to be clearly understood when speaking to individuals and groups** • Raises volume of voice when sharing an opinion with the group • When asked to speak more slowly, pauses and restates idea at a slower pace		**Speaks clearly when giving a lengthy description of an event or personal experience to an individual or group; adapts word choices to be appropriate to the audience** • Is easily heard and understood by classmates when describing a recent family celebration • Describes each part of a habitat collage to a teacher, and then gives a simpler description to a visiting preschooler		**Uses appropriate expression and inflection when relaying details about a story, personal experience, or specific topic to an individual or group** • During a presentation based on a biography of Bill Peet, engages audience by speaking clearly, loudly, and with inflection • Uses software to create an audiobook by fluently reading a story or poem	

Objective 9 Uses language to express thoughts and needs

c. Uses conventional grammar

Not Yet	1	2	3	4	5	6	7	8	9	10	11	12	13	14	15
		Uses one- or two-word sentences or phrases • Asks, "More?" • Says, "Daddy go." • Uses one word, "Juice," to mean, "I want some juice."		**Uses three- to four-word sentences; may omit some words or use some words incorrectly** • Says, "Bed no go." • Says, "Daddy goed to work." • Responds, "I want banana," when asked what she wants for snack		**Uses complete, four- to six-word sentences** • Says, "I chose two books." • Says, "We are going to the zoo." • Says, "Momma came and we went home."		**Uses long, complex sentences and follows most grammatical rules; uses common verbs and nouns (including plural nouns)** • During class discussion about an upcoming field trip, says, "We are going to the zoo to see the animals. We'll learn where they live and what they eat." • Notices when sentences do not make sense; tries to correct them		**Generates a variety of sentence types; matches correct subject/verb agreement; uses most parts of speech correctly, including nouns (common, proper, and possessive), verbs (past, present, and future), pronouns (personal, possessive, and indefinite), adjectives, conjunctions (e.g., *and, but, or, so, because*), articles (e.g., *a, an, the*), and demonstratives (e.g., *this, these, that*); identifies root words in frequently occurring forms** • Draws a picture and says, "This is what my bike looks like. My sister Julia and I ride our bikes after school every day. Julia's bike is red with blue stripes! My brother only rides his sometimes because he plays baseball, too." • Demonstrates an action word and gives the past, present, and future tense when prompted • When prompted, circles the root word in *baked*, *trying*, and *sees*		**Uses multiple types of less frequently occurring nouns, including collective and irregular plural nouns; uses reflexive pronouns, past tense of frequently occurring irregular verbs, adjectives, and adverbs; rearranges sentences to produce and expand compound sentences** • Says, "I told the dentist that I floss and brush my teeth by myself very carefully. She let me choose a bunch of pretty stickers from the sticker bin." • Cuts and separates the words from a sentence strip and creates a new sentence		**Produces simple, compound, and complex sentences for multiple purposes; identifies and explains the functions of nouns, pronouns, verbs, adjectives, and adverbs in a sentence; uses regular and irregular verbs, plural nouns, and simple verb tenses; uses correct subject/verb and pronoun/antecedent agreement; uses comparative and superlative adjectives and adverbs; uses coordinating and subordinating conjunctions; recognizes differences between written and spoken English** • Says, "I like the water fountain in the cafeteria. It has really cold water. The other fountains at school aren't as good." • Says, "I'm so much taller than my younger sister. It makes sense, though, since she's had the least amount of time to grow." • When given the verb *sing*, is able to produce the phrases, "I sing," "I sang," and "I sung." • Says, "When I wrote a letter to Louis Sachar, I started with, 'Dear Mr. Sachar,' but if I'm walking up to someone, I just say, 'Hello.'"	

Objective 9 Uses language to express thoughts and needs

d. Tells about another time or place

Not Yet	1	2	3	4	5	6	7	8	9	10	11	12	13
		Makes simple statements about recent events and familiar people and objects that are not present • Says, "Got shoes." • Hears helicopter, stops and says, "'copter." • Tells, "Gran lives far away."		**Tells simple stories about objects, events, and people not present; lacks many details and a conventional beginning, middle, and end** • Dictates a simple story with few connections between characters and events • Says, "I've got new shoes. I went to the shoe store."		**Tells stories about other times and places that have a logical order and that include major details** • Tells about past experiences, reporting the major events in a logical sequence • Says, "I went to the shoe store with Gran. I got two pairs of new shoes."		**Tells elaborate stories that refer to other times and places** • Dictates an elaborate story of a recent visit to the bakery, including details of who, what, when, why, and how • Tells many details as he acts out a recent trip to the shoe store		**Tells stories with clear sequence of events, including a climax and resolution** • Tells teacher about a bird's nest and eggs found at home in an outdoor bucket; includes details about how the nest was found, what happened when the mother bird returned, and how her family moved the bucket to keep the birds safe • When recalling a football game, gives details about first- and second-half scores as well as events that took place late in the game		**Accurately and thoroughly retells previously heard stories or information** • After hearing a storyteller on a field trip, retells the story to a younger sibling with accuracy • Listens to a webcast of Robert Munsch telling a story from his childhood, and then shares the story including humorous elements	

Objective 9 Uses language to express thoughts and needs

Strategies

- Serve as a good speech model for children. Speak slowly, and model correct grammar.
- Respect children's communication styles while encouraging them to achieve higher levels of communication. Instead of correcting the child's incorrect pronunciation and grammar, respond by modeling the correct language. Repeat their words with more complete, grammatically accurate, or expanded talk. For example, when the child says, "He goed," say, "Yes, Marcus went to the museum with his aunt and uncle."
- Encourage children to use explanatory talk (explaining and describing) by modeling it. For example, explain, "This jar of paint is hard to open. If I put it under hot water, the cover will expand, and it will be much easier to open."
- Ask open-ended questions that encourage multiple responses. For example, say, "What would happen if...?", "What do you think?", "What else could you do?" Even if children are preverbal, open-ended questions encourage children's thinking, and they benefit from hearing the rich language.
- Have one-on-one conversations with children who are reluctant to speak in a group. Support them in contributing to small-group discussions.
- Provide props that encourage talking, e.g., telephones and puppets.
- Join children's dramatic play to scaffold their storytelling. For example, you might prompt a child by saying, "What did your grandma say after that?"
- Help children connect their everyday experiences and relate the familiar to the unfamiliar. For example, when introducing a new material say, "You can use these new sponge brushes to paint just like you use the big paint brushes. Let me show you."
- Tell children stories without using books. Tell about things that happened in another time and place. For example, you might tell a story about what they did at school earlier in the year. Encourage children to tell their own stories about what they did earlier in the year.
- Include materials to encourage verbal children to tell stories, e.g., wordless picture books, miniature items from a story, and picture story starters.
- Help children increase the richness and diversity of their vocabulary. Introduce children to less common words through books, songs, conversations, discussions, pretend play, firsthand experiences, and in-depth studies.
- Repeat and reinforce new words. Talk about the meanings of new words by providing familiar words with similar meanings. Use new words in different contexts throughout the day.
- Use simple language and speak slowly. Use gestures, pictures, and objects to help children understand meaning.
- Make sure each child can respond to questions, participate in story time, make choices, initiate social conversations, and get your attention when needed. Consider a variety of communication techniques, e.g., gestures, picture boards, and recordable communication devices.
- Ask families about the child's successful communication strategies at home.
- Create "powerful" word charts for words that have synonyms that are more specific or precise. Example: said = cried, exclaimed, yelled, hollered, whispered, croaked, complained, announced

Uses appropriate conversational and other communication skills

10

Conversations involve back-and-forth exchanges. When an infant coos back at his mother while she talks to him, a 2-year-old adds her thoughts when there is a pause in the conversation, a preschool child initiates a conversation with his teacher about a recent vacation, and a kindergarten child takes turns as he engages in a lengthy conversation with several friends, they are all using appropriate communication and conversational skills.

Children acquire vocabulary, other language skills, and background knowledge about many topics by participating in frequent, meaningful conversations with responsive adults. They benefit from conversations that include varied vocabulary and that challenge their thinking (Dickinson & Tabors, 2001). Such conversations contribute to early reading success. In addition, conversations are important to children's cognitive and social–emotional learning (Hart & Risley, 1995). One-to-one, extended, cognitively challenging conversations can be used to engage even reluctant talkers (Snow, Burns, & Griffin, 1998).

Children also must learn the social rules of communicating. This involves being polite, speaking so the listener understands, and turn-taking. The social rules of conversations often vary from culture to culture and from one community to another (Trawick-Smith, 2006).

Social conventions determine how much silent time is expected for thinking and for carefully selecting the right words before making a response (Rowe, 1987). In some families, children may be expected to listen to adult conversations and to speak only when asked to contribute (National Research Council, 1998b). The following list describes differences in several social conventions:

- Turn-taking: Some people engage in conversations where equal turn-taking is not valued; others value it highly.
- Personal space: Some people tend to stand very close together during conversations, while others stand farther apart.
- Eye contact: In some communities, eye contact with an adult is a sign of disrespect or rudeness; in others, eye contact is a sign of respect.
- Touch: A touch, e.g., on the arm or shoulder, may be offensive to some people but considered a friendly gesture by others.
- Gestures: Hand gestures, e.g., making a circle with the thumb and forefinger, may carry different meanings in different cultures.
- Politeness and formality: Some people vary formality and other ways of being polite according to the social status of the person being addressed.

Objective 10 Uses appropriate conversational and other communication skills

During the primary grades, children's communicative competence improves greatly (Berk, 2009; Bjorklund, 2005). They incorporate more socially shared understandings (Hulit & Howard, 2002) and are better able to mentally organize and sequence their information to help maintain a conversational topic. They easily move from one topic to a related topic and introduce new topics. Primary-grade students are better able than younger children to recognize when the conversational partner does not understand and will make multiple attempts to clarify for the listener by simplifying, using other words or gestures, or adding missing information (Hulit & Howard, 2002; Neuman, Copple, & Bredekamp, 1999).

Children in the primary grades better understand and use the social rules of language (e.g., using formal language, taking turns, informing or explaining, making requests, sticking to the topic). They also are better able to use language appropriate for the setting as they become more skillful at register switching, or shifting back and forth between formal and informal language (Trawick-Smith, 2006). Sensitivity to the social expectations of language and communication activities where the child cannot get cues from gestures and facial expressions (e.g., over the telephone) also greatly improve (Berk, 2009). Children with fewer school-like experiences or those from homes where nonstandard English is spoken may have less understanding of the more formal speech used in school, which can interfere with their ability to follow behavioral and academic directions or to read text (Bjorklund, 2005). Instruction is most effective when teachers take into account children's existing social conventions as they help them learn the more formal language that is appropriate for school settings.

Objective 10 Uses appropriate conversational and other communication skills

a. Engages in conversations

Not Yet	1	2	3	4	5	6	7	8	9	10	11	12	13	14	15
		Engages in simple back-and-forth exchanges with others • Coos at adult who says, "Sweet Jeremy is talking." He coos again, and adult imitates the sounds • Shakes head for *no*; waves bye-bye • Joins in games such as pat-a-cake and peekaboo		**Initiates and attends to brief conversations** • Says, "Doggy." Teacher responds, "You see a doggy." Child says, "Doggy woof." • Asks teacher, "Home now?" Teacher responds, "Yes, I'm leaving to go home." • Looks at teacher and points to picture of car. Teacher responds, "No, I'm going to walk home."		**Engages in conversations of at least three exchanges** • Stays on topic during conversations • Maintains the conversation by repeating what the other person says or by asking questions		**Engages in complex, lengthy conversations of five or more exchanges** • Offers interesting comments with communication device • Extends conversation by moving gradually from one topic to a related topic		**Extends conversations by responding to comments and asking questions; asks and answers questions to clarify information during grade-appropriate discussions** • Stays on topic during conversation with another child about weekend plans • Asks questions about how a proboscis works during a small-group conversation about butterflies; offers an explanation to a classmate about how butterflies eat		**Connects others' ideas shared during conversations; asks questions in order to better understand grade-appropriate discussions** • When talking with two friends, says, "I saw that movie, too. What was your favorite part? Oh, that was Paolo's favorite! Mine was the part with the spaceship." • During class discussion about *My Father's Dragon*, asks, "Has the author written any other books?"		**Contributes to a focused discussion on a specific topic, preparing in advance for planned discussions using multiple sources; explains ideas based on both prior knowledge and new information learned from the conversation** • Continues discussion about moon cycles by sharing previously-read information • During science fair, explains to observer how soil helps plants grow; explains lessons learned while completing the experiment	

Objective 10 Uses appropriate conversational and other communication skills

b. Uses social rules of language

Not Yet	1	2	3	4	5	6	7	8	9	10	11	12	13	14	15
		Responds to speech by looking toward the speaker; watches for signs of being understood when communicating • Hears siren and goes to adult pointing, "Fire tuck." • Looks at adult and says, "Ball", repeatedly until adult says, "Ball. You want the ball?"		**Uses appropriate eye contact, pauses, and simple verbal prompts when communicating** • Pays attention to speaker during conversation • Pauses after asking a question to wait for a response • Says "please" and "thank you" with occasional prompting		**Uses acceptable language and basic social rules while communicating with others; may need reminders** • Takes turns in conversations but may interrupt or direct talk back to self • Regulates volume of voice when reminded		**Uses acceptable language and basic social rules during communication with others** • Uses a softer voice when talking with peers in the library and a louder voice on the playground • Says, "Hello," back to the museum curator on a trip		**Listens attentively while taking turns in a discussion, using nonverbal signals to show understanding and interest (e.g., nodding, using appropriate facial expressions)** • Remembers to say "excuse me" when interrupting two teachers who are talking • Waits for turn to speak during group discussion		**Enters discussions in respectful ways (e.g., says, "Excuse me," waits, and signals for a chance to speak); identifies the difference between formal and informal English** • During group work, listens to ideas of others without speaking over them • When listening to a speaker, waits for appropriate moment to ask question, raises hand and says, "Excuse me. I have a question." • Understands the difference between the way she greets the principal each morning and the way she greets her classmates		**Engages politely in conversations in which both speakers present and listen to arguments respectfully** • During a disagreement, listens to other child's viewpoint without interrupting • Invites a classmate to offer an idea about a group project	

Objective 10 Uses appropriate conversational and other communication skills

Strategies

- Build on the child's language. Rephrase what the child says and then add more.
- Learn as much as you can about the communication styles of the families in the program.
- Plan specific experiences where children will be encouraged to talk and to use their communication skills.
- Model appropriate conversational skills, e.g., taking turns, eye contact, speech volume, and using polite words.
- Provide many opportunities for children to hear and use language. Engage in frequent conversations with each child. Listen carefully to what is being said. Children will talk more when they know teachers listen.
- Provide interesting experiences for children to discuss.
- Try to maintain conversations with children for extended exchanges. Listen carefully to what the child is saying. Respond with related comments and open–ended questions that keep the conversation going. Try to get the child to tell you more about the topic.
- Encourage the use of social words in context, e.g., "please" and "thank you." Provide them as options on a child's communication device.
- Use the same communication system as the child, e.g., point to pictures on her picture board to ask if she wants to go outside.
- Place children into groups of three to four children. Pose a "table topic" for the groups to discuss. Initially have children share by taking turns around the circle. Move toward having children listen for pauses in conversations to take their turn sharing.
- Have a child talk about a book or an event. After the child shares his thoughts, have him ask for a peer's opinion.
- Create class rules for great discussions. Start the conversation by asking, "What could we could do to make sure that we have a productive discussion that includes everyone's ideas?"
- Have children talk about something that they know how to do (tie a shoe, make a sandwich, wash the car).
- Create class surveys on a variety of topics (favorite food, favorite ice cream flavor, favorite superhero). Then have the children take turns collecting the data and sharing their findings with the class.
- Teach the children in your class how to introduce themselves to someone they have not met or someone entering the classroom. Designate a child as "class greeter" each week. His job is to introduce himself to persons who enter the classroom and ask them what they need.

Cognitive

Cognitive development, also called intellectual development, is influenced by the child's approaches to learning as well as his biological makeup and the environment. A child's background knowledge, or knowledge base, also affects the way a child thinks. This background knowledge influences the child's information processing, memory, classification, problem solving, language acquisition, and reading and mathematics learning (Bjorklund, 2005; McAfee & Leong, 1994). What and how children learn often varies considerably from culture to culture, and minor variations exist in the ways children within a cultural group perform specific cognitive tasks (Trawick-Smith, 2006). Some children have disabilities that interfere with the development of their conceptual and reasoning skills (Cook, Klein, & Tessier, 2004).

Children who have positive approaches to learning are more likely to succeed academically and to have more positive interactions with peers (Fantuzzo, Perry, & McDermott, 2004; Hyson, 2005, 2008; McWayne, Fantuzzo, & McDermott, 2004; Yen, Konold, & McDermott, 2004). These dispositions and behaviors must be nurtured by effective curriculum and intentional teaching methods (Hyson, 2005, 2008; Hyson, Buch, Fantuzzo, & Scott-Little, 2006).

The physical environment of the classroom and the kinds of interactions children have with adults and other children influence the way children approach learning and influence other aspects of their cognitive development. Play is important for learning; researchers have found many connections between cognitive competence and play, particularly high-quality dramatic play. The benefits of play include self-regulation; memory development; divergent thinking; problem solving; language development; and academic skill development in literacy, math, social studies, and science (Bergen, 2002; Bodrova & Leong, 2004; Charlesworth, 2007; Fantuzzo & McWayne, 2002; Howes & Matheson, 1992; Klein, Wirth, & Linas, 2004; Krafft & Berk, 1998; Newman, 1990; Nourot & Van Hoorn, 1991; O'Reilly & Bornstein, 1993; Smilansky & Shefatya, 1990; Steglin, 2005).

COGNITIVE OBJECTIVES

11 Demonstrates positive approaches to learning
12 Remembers and connects experiences
13 Uses classification skills
14 Uses symbols and images to represent something not present

Notable shifts occur in the cognitive abilities and processes of children in the primary grades. They become more flexible and multidimensional in their thinking, solve a wider range of problems, mentally and symbolically manipulate concrete concepts, and think about their own mental activities (Berk, 2009; Bjorklund, 2005; Tomlinson, 2012).

As children progress to higher grades, more is required of them, and the ways they approach learning become increasingly important (Li-Grining, Votruba-Drzal, Maldonado-Carreño, & Haas, 2010). During the school day, they use self-regulatory skills to focus on tasks, remain in their seats, and cooperate with classmates (Blair, 2002; Li-Grining et al., 2010; Raver, 2002). Their socialization to the school environment nurtures the development of goal orientation, focused attention, resourcefulness, initial engagement, and the ability to plan (Chen, Masur, & McNamee, 2011).

Objective 11

Demonstrates positive approaches to learning

When children have a positive approach to learning, they are likely to want to learn more. There are five dimensions to this objective: attention and engagement; persistence; problem solving; curiosity and motivation; and flexibility and inventiveness.

Attention, Engagement, and Persistence

As children mature, they demonstrate an increasing capacity to concentrate, to persist, and therefore, to become deeply involved in what they are doing, despite distractions and interruptions. The ability to resist distractions, remain positively engaged, and persist at learning tasks is related positively to children's academic achievement, cognitive development, and peer interactions (Blair, 2003; Deater-Deckard, Petrill, Thompson, & DeThrone, 2005; Duncan et al., 2007; Fantuzzo, Perry, & McDermott, 2004; Howse, Lange, Farran, & Boyles, 2003; Hyson, 2008; Jablon & Wilkinson, 2006; Ladd, Birch, & Buhs, 1999; Normandeau & Guay, 1998).

There are variations among children's levels of attention, engagement, and persistence. Bilingual children may sometimes be more likely to attend to relevant details during attention-demanding tasks than their monolingual peers because they have had experience attending to one language while ignoring the other language (Bialystok & Martin, 2004). In general, children show greater persistence on tasks that are challenging for them (tasks that are not too easy or too difficult). They are likely to be more attentive, interested, and engaged when they make choices about their learning (Brophy, 2004; Kohn, 1993).

Some children with particular disabilities may be less likely to become engaged in activities or may show engagement in ways that are different from those of typically developing children. Children with attention deficit disorders (ADD, ADHD) may find it difficult to persist with classroom performance tasks. Children with Autism spectrum disorders may repeat behaviors, continuing to do the same things again and again. They may do this even if their strategies are not successful. Children living in poverty may find it hard to regulate their attention and persist with challenging tasks if they are hungry, sick, or sleepy (Howse, Lange, Farran, & Boyles, 2003; Hyson, 2008).

Positive evaluative feedback from adults helps children persist with difficult tasks (Berk, 2003; Burhans & Dweck, 1995; Kelley, Brownell, & Campbell, 2000). Children who are distracted easily may need to work with only a few materials and choices at one time. Sometimes a task must be presented in smaller steps so that the child can understand what to do (Gargiulo & Kilgo, 2007; Lewis, 2003).

Engagement is often grouped into three classes: cognitive, behavioral, and emotional (Fredricks, Blumenfeld, & Paris, 2004). Students in primary grades must maintain and expand chains of thought for a prolonged amount of time (cognitive engagement), actively participate (behavioral engagement), and be interested in/connected to material (emotional engagement) so that they may persist. When teachers provide students with specific feedback as opposed to vague, broad remarks, it helps foster their perseverance (Copple & Bredekamp, 2009).

Objective 11 Demonstrates positive approaches to learning

Problem Solving

Children solve problems by using available information, resources, and materials to overcome obstacles and achieve a goal. An infant cries when hungry. A toddler backs down steps consistently once he has been taught to go down backwards. A preschool child tries several strategies, modifying them as he goes along. A kindergarten child works with peers trying various suggestions for attaching new pieces to a sculpture. A third grader bargains with a friend to make an advantageous baseball card trade. In order to use relevant information to solve problems, children need to have organized what they know and be able to retrieve it. Very young children independently discover many ways to solve problems as they explore their bodies and interact with materials and people.

Children become increasingly selective in and adept at using problem-solving strategies. With experience, they become better at selecting and monitoring strategies and applying them in new situations (Berk, 2002, 2003; Bjorklund, 2005). Even after using a more efficient strategy, children often return to using a less effective strategy. This switching among strategies aids cognitive development. It allows children to reason about their choices, comparing more and less effective strategies.

Play gives children many opportunities to solve problems. In particular, sociodramatic play fosters children's problem-solving skills (Bergen, 2002; Fisher, 1992). Research shows that there are cultural and individual differences in the ways children approach problem-solving tasks. Some children interact with others to solve problems. Some children watch how others work with materials before beginning to use them. Other children solve problems independently, handling materials to figure out how they work. (Bergen, 2002; Berk, 2002, 2003; Trawick-Smith, 2006). One way is not necessarily better than another.

As students advance to the primary grades, they become more adept at choosing the most applicable strategy to solve a given problem, and they do so with increasing efficacy (Lemaire & Lecacheur, 2011). It remains important for teachers to model constructive attitudes toward problem solving so that students internalize positive approaches to resolving problems (Copple & Bredekamp, 2009).

Curiosity and Motivation

Young children want to know more about themselves and the world around them. An infant explores a block by putting it in his mouth and banging it on the ground. A toddler turns the water handle repeatedly to make the water start and stop. A 2-year-old repeatedly asks, "Why?" A preschool child who is interested in airplanes asks an adult to read a nonfiction book about how jets are made. A second grader searches for a library book on homes in the Arctic to support a group research project on types of shelter. These children are all demonstrating their curiosity and motivation to learn.

Curiosity promotes cognitive, social–emotional, and physical development throughout life by stimulating exploratory behaviors (Reio, Petrosko, Wiswell, & Thongsukmag, 2006). By responding to children's questions and providing safe environments that encourage active exploration, adults foster children's curiosity and motivation to learn. When children are motivated, they have a desire to continue with challenging tasks. Most children find new learning self-motivating (Hyson, 2008). Giving them rewards (e.g., food items, smiley faces, stickers) may diminish their curiosity and motivation to pursue the activities in the future (Arnone, 2003; Deci, Koestner, & Ryan, 2001; Elliot & Dweck, 2005; Katz & Chard, 1995; Stipek, 2002).

All children do not show their curiosity or motivation to learn in the same ways, and teachers may interpret some children's behaviors as a lack of interest and motivation. Some children are taught not to ask questions of adults, and some watch how others use materials rather than explore them actively. Some children with particular cognitive disabilities demonstrate little apparent curiosity or motivation, and they need a great deal of adult support.

In primary school and beyond, students tend to be more motivated in learner-centered classrooms, which promote critical thinking skills and focus on student-initiated study topics (Cornelius-White, 2007). When students feel a sense of agency in their education, they exercise their curiosity to learn something new. They feel competent and more motivated to learn when teachers use scaffolding to meet individual learning needs (Daniels & Perry, 2003).

Objective 11 Demonstrates positive approaches to learning

Flexibility and Inventiveness

Cognitive flexibility is important for children's academic achievement (George & Greenfield, 2005; Hyson, 2008). Children who are flexible in their thinking consider alternative possibilities, find their own ways to resolve conflicts, and solve problems with tools and materials. When a 2-year-old tries a block and then uses a broom handle to reach a toy under a bookshelf and when a preschool child makes up new lyrics to a familiar song, they are approaching tasks with flexibility and inventiveness.

Flexible thinking is critical to children's development of sorting and categorization skills, understanding of concepts, problem-solving skills, reasoning skills, divergent thinking, and inventiveness. Children need unhurried time to explore topics in depth and to complete activities; space that inspires them to create; a varied collection of found, recycled, and purchased materials and props; an encouraging classroom atmosphere that supports risk-taking, acceptance of mistakes, and innovation; and opportunities to express their innovative thinking through creative products (Pope & Springate, 1995).

Flexibility requires children to shift focus from one topic to another, recognize relevant information, and change their strategies to match changing task demands. There are age differences in children's cognitive flexibility. Infants become increasingly able to shift attention from one object or person to another (Berk, 2002). A developmental spurt in children's cognitive flexibility occurs between 3–5 years of age (Deak, 2003; Smidts, Jacobs, & Anderson, 2004). Children who are bilingual may show enhanced cognitive flexibility as they switch between languages (Bialystok, McBride-Chang, & Luk, 2005). Some children with particular disabilities, such as autism spectrum disorders, may have difficulty with flexible thinking and may need specific activities to encourage flexibility of thought (Carruthers, 1996; Gould & Sullivan, 1999; Lewis, 2003).

As students enter elementary school, more cognitive flexibility is required of them as they encounter numerous varied tasks. Reading in particular is a skill that entails high cognitive flexibility, as it involves many simultaneous components such as phonological and semantic processes. Students must possess the ability to simultaneously classify printed stimuli along phonological and semantic dimensions in order to read successfully (Cartwright, 2002).

Objective 11 Demonstrates positive approaches to learning

a. Attends and engages

Not Yet	1	2	3	4	5	6	7	8	9	10	11	12	13	14	15
		Pays attention to sights and sounds • Watches the teacher walk across the room • Turns head toward sound of mother's voice		**Sustains interest in working on a task, especially when adults offer suggestions, questions, and comments** • Takes small blocks from adult and continues to drop them into a container • Continues ring stacking when the teacher says, "You're putting the biggest ones on first." • Continues the play about going to a restaurant after the teacher offers a menu		**Sustains work on age-appropriate, interesting tasks; can ignore most distractions and interruptions** • Makes relevant contributions to group discussion about class pet • Focuses on making a sign for a building while others are rolling cars down a ramp nearby		**Sustains attention to tasks or projects over time (days to weeks); can return to activities after interruptions** • Returns to block construction over several days, adding new features each time • Pauses to join in problem-solving discussion at adult's request, then returns to art project		**Selectively focuses attention based on task difficulty and shifts attention toward teacher's goal; demonstrates concentrated effort** • Concentrates to sound out unknown words • Notices the loud construction work outside but focuses attention back to the task at hand when reminded by the teacher		**Concentrates on tasks for extended periods but may become restless, especially during activities viewed as less interesting; repeatedly practices activities thought to be enjoyable** • Focuses attention as classmates read aloud • Attends at the beginning of the school program, but begins to wiggle as the program becomes less interesting • Plays a long board game until its conclusion • Practices playing kickball in order to improve skills		**Directs attention based on previous performance and concentrates on activities that require additional study** • Looks up unfamiliar words that require more information for understanding • Begins doing math work first because that is the most difficult for him • Systematically scans reading material looking for key words	

Objective 11 Demonstrates positive approaches to learning

b. Persists

Not Yet	1	2	3	4	5	6	7	8	9	10	11	12	13
		Repeats actions to obtain similar results • Repeatedly shakes a rattle to produce noise • Hits a toy on a play gym accidentally; then waves arms to hit it again • Puts objects in a wagon and then dumps them out over and over again		**Practices an activity many times until successful** • Stacks blocks again and again until tower no longer falls • Uses shovel in many ways to fill small bucket with sand • Chooses the same puzzle every day until he can insert each piece quickly and easily		**Plans and pursues a variety of appropriately challenging tasks** • Keeps looking through all of the magnetic letters for those that are in her name • Works with others to learn how to use a new software program		**Plans and pursues own goal until it is reached** • Keeps building sand structure, trying multiple ways to get the bridge to hold • Returns from lunch with a different idea about what to add to her story • Reads own writing about autumn to small group, then makes changes based on questions from peers		**Plans and completes grade-appropriate tasks and projects with minimal adult assistance** • Works methodically to independently create a bridge from different types of materials • Says, "I need to plan this out and do it right so it will look good when I give it to the teacher." • After writing a paragraph about polar bear habitats, revisits the piece in order to correct spelling and punctuation errors and to evaluate word choice		**Finishes long assignments and projects that last for days or weeks; may briefly give up on difficult tasks but returns to complete them** • Works for several days gathering information and collecting and assembling materials to complete a diorama • Becomes frustrated when trying to put together a complex puzzle, stops for a brief time, and then works with resolve until it is completed • Creates a story outline before writing a mystery about a missing bicycle; later revises and edits story for content and writing mistakes	

Objective 11 Demonstrates positive approaches to learning

c. Solves problems

Not Yet	1	2	3	4	5	6	7	8	9	10	11	12	13
		Reacts to a problem; seeks to achieve a specific goal • Grunts when cube gets stuck in shape sorter • Reaches for a toy that is just out of reach • Blows on warm cereal after seeing someone blow on cereal		**Observes and imitates how other people solve problems; asks for a solution and uses it** • Seeks help opening a stuck cap; pulls one end as teacher pulls the other • Asks another child to hold his cup while he pours milk		**Solves problems without having to try every possibility** • Looks at an assortment of pegs and selects the size that will fit in the hole • Tells another child, "Put the big block down first, or the tower will fall down."		**Thinks problems through, considering several possibilities and analyzing results** • Considers new information before trying a strategy: "If I put this box on top, I can see if they are the same size." • Thinks about a book character's problem and suggests solutions • Thinks of different ways to hang a paper chain in the doorway and then tries the best idea		**Solves a wide range of problems using a variety of strategies; attempts to solve problems independently before asking for assistance from adults or peers** • Uses a board as a lever to lift a heavy object • Makes a reasonable estimate of the answer to a math problem, thinks aloud, and then works backward to obtain the correct answer • Repeats an experiment several times to see if the results are the same		**Plans, considers various alternatives, and combines skills and strategies needed to solve problems** • Makes alphabet tabs to help organize the books so they are easier to locate • Thinks through the process and then makes a list of the steps needed to conduct the experiment • Bargains and trades cards with a friend to get the ones needed for a collection	

Objective 11 Demonstrates positive approaches to learning

d. Shows curiosity and motivation

Not Yet	1	2	3	4	5	6	7	8	9	10	11	12	13	14	15
		Uses senses to explore the immediate environment • Turns in direction of a sound • Moves closer to touch an object • Shakes or bangs a toy to make it work		**Explores and investigates ways to make something happen** • Enjoys taking things apart • Turns faucet on and off • Tilts a ramp to find out if a car will go down faster		**Shows eagerness to learn about a variety of topics and ideas** • Seeks answers to questions about the storm • Shows interest in learning how the firefighter's clothes protect him		**Uses a variety of resources to find answers to questions; participates in grade-appropriate research projects** • Locates informational book on insects to identify butterfly seen outside • Asks visiting musician clarifying questions about her instrument • Explores a number of Mercer Mayer books; works with others to write opinions about the books		**Shows enthusiasm for learning new things and looks for opportunities to gain new knowledge and skills; asks open-ended questions about surroundings and everyday events** • Shows excitement when the silkworms arrive and eagerly observes and documents changes over time • Requests that the music teacher help the class learn a new dance • Asks *What would happen if...?* questions when listening to an expert speak about nutrition		**Shows interest in an increasing range of phenomena outside of direct experiences by generating questions and researching the topic** • Makes observational drawings of different cloud formations seen while on the play yard • Asks questions, looks for books in library, and seeks information from other sources after a family from Iceland moves in next door • Contributes to group writing project about the Amazon rainforest after reading multiple books on the subject		**Asks thoughtful and increasingly complex questions; builds knowledge through research projects; contributes to discussions by applying previously gathered information about a topic** • Spends time taking apart discarded objects to see what is inside and how they work • Plans a research project after watching a video about how a potter creates his pottery and reading a book about Native American pottery • Participates in discussion about local volunteer opportunities after researching a community service project that distributes coats during winter	

Objective 11 Demonstrates positive approaches to learning

e. Shows flexibility and inventiveness in thinking

Not Yet	1	2	3	4	5	6	7	8	9	10	11	12	13	14	15
		Imitates others in using objects in new and/or unanticipated ways • Notices another child reach a toy with the broom handle; then tries • Imitates a friend, putting a basket on head to use as a hat		**Uses creativity and imagination during play and routine tasks** • Strings wooden beads into a necklace as part of dramatic play • Uses a table, sheets, and towels to build a tent		**Changes plans if a better idea is thought of or proposed** • Accepts idea to use tape instead of glue to fix the tear • Suggests building on a hard surface when structure keeps falling down		**Thinks through possible long-term solutions and takes on more abstract challenges** • Offers ideas about how to make the Block area larger for building • Creates board game; thinks of how to play it from start to finish		**Exhibits creative ways to complete tasks; uses own perspective when describing directions or rules** • Begins with one art medium and then combines several different media to create a unique product • Participates in a movement activity mirroring the leader rather than using the correct (left/right) hand		**Accepts last-minute changes and requires less detailed instructions; experiments with invention** • Assumes additional responsibility easily when a group member suddenly cannot complete his part of the project • Looks at basic instructions on how to put together the airplane and completes it without help • Experiments with different materials outdoors and "invents" a new type of snowshoe		**Reverses thoughts mentally; understands directional perspectives other than his or her own** • When solving a fraction problem, reverses mentally from the whole to parts and back to the whole • Gives accurate left/right directions to another child using the viewpoint of the other child	

Objective 11 Demonstrates positive approaches to learning

Strategies

- Use the child's name to get his or her attention, e.g., say, "Look, Juan!" as you begin to speak.
- Help the child stay focused by singing about an activity if it is helpful to the child, e.g., sing, "This is the way we stack the blocks, stack the blocks, stack the blocks...."
- Provide children with time, space, and a variety of interesting materials for play.
- Provide recyclable as well as new materials that can be used in a variety of innovative ways, e.g., boxes, tubes, spools, containers.
- Provide many opportunities for children to make choices from interesting materials that are familiar and challenging, and encourage children to use them in many ways.
- Rotate materials regularly to maintain children's interest. Provide materials that build on those already familiar to the children.
- Interpret and expand on what children do and say. Model deliberate, strategic engagement in activities and self-talk to help children stay engaged and persist with challenging tasks.
- Provide opportunities for children to observe others solving problems and to work with other children and adults to solve problems together.
- Support children's efforts during challenging tasks by providing specific, positive verbal feedback or physical support while encouraging them to come up with solutions, e.g., "Keep turning the puzzle piece to figure out how it fits."
- Describe children's problem-solving strategies, e.g., "You tried reaching into the jar to get the balls out, and then you turned the jar over and dumped them out."
- Limit directions to three steps at a time. Reinforce the directions visually by demonstrating the activity, by using pictures, or by using picture and word cues.
- Encourage children to learn from their mistakes. Encourage them to make and test predictions and to examine their thinking.
- Respond to children's explorations and discoveries with enthusiasm and encouragement rather than by providing rewards like stickers or prizes.
- Support children's spontaneous interests, e.g., their examinations of the locust shells found in the play yard, in addition to offering teacher-directed activities based on the children's interests.
- Encourage children to solve problems for themselves when appropriate. Be available to offer support, encouragement, and new ideas when needed.
- Demonstrate, explain, and engage children in trying different ways of doing things. Discuss whether the strategies worked well.
- Take time to answer *why* questions, offering explanations that the child can understand.
- Encourage children's inclination to ask questions and wonder. Help them refine their questions and support them in finding answers.
- Play games that support children's curiosity and internal motivation, such as "Mystery Bag." Hide an object inside a bag. Give verbal clues about its identity. Let children feel, describe, and guess what it is before looking at it.
- Encourage children's imaginations by finding images in clouds or puddles. Discuss pictures in which part of an object is hidden.
- Nurture children's curiosity by providing thought-provoking, hands-on, investigatory experiences that motivate them to apply their developing skills and prior knowledge and that challenge them to think.
- Ask children open-ended questions such as, "What do you think would happen if you...? What else could you do with...? Can you think of another way to...?"
- Point out strategies children used successfully in similar situations, e.g., prompt, "Yesterday you used the broom to get the dishes from behind the sink. I wonder if it would work to get the puzzle piece that dropped behind the shelf?"
- Organize the play environment to encourage sociodramatic play, including props, utensils, and tools to support different roles. Create new settings for dramatic play, e.g., a post office, clinic, grocery store, bakery, or campsite. Serve as a sensitive play tutor, engaging in play while following the children's leads.
- Plan so that children can spend days or weeks investigating interesting objects in their environment, seeking answers to their questions, and finding solutions to problems.
- Provide well-defined boundaries for children who need support in order to focus, e.g., use freestanding cardboard dividers for table activities and colored tape to define workspaces on the floor. Limit the number of choices they are given.
- Model flexibility by changing an activity to incorporate children's interesting ideas. To help children consider different perspectives or solutions, explain why the activity is being changed.
- Emphasize the process children use to come up with possible approaches to tasks instead of focusing on finished products and answers.
- Guide children in doing in-depth, long-term, and open-ended studies and explorations.
- Encourage children to think of multiple ways to create something using the same materials. For example, they might see how many different ways they can make a boat using milk cartons, paper, foil, craft sticks, etc.
- Be mindful to create "real world" problems for the children to solve. "What can we do to make sure that we have enough snacks for everyone this week?"
- Set up multi-day projects in the classroom. Projects that require "wait time" (e.g., art projects that must dry, wood projects involving glue that must set, cooking projects that must cool) between steps help students practice persistence.

Objective 12

Remembers and connects experiences

12

Memory involves complex cognitive processes. To remember, children must attend to the important aspects of information so that it can be stored and later retrieved and used. Children store information in long-term memory if the information is meaningful to them, if they are able to connect it to something they already know, and if they sense its importance. When toddlers name common objects, preschool children talk about something they did yesterday, and first graders retell a story in detail, they are remembering and connecting information and experiences.

When children determine whether something is the same as, similar to, or different from what they have encountered before, they are using *recognition memory*, e.g., the child recognizes a book he or she has heard before. *Recall memory* is harder; children must imagine something that is not present, e.g., recall foods eaten by the hungry caterpillar without looking at the pictures. Cues improve children's free recall memory (Berk, 2002; Bjorklund, 2005).

As children develop their abilities to attend and to use memory strategies, their learning is enhanced. They use their existing knowledge and understanding as the basis for making new experiences, ideas, and concepts meaningful.

Making links between new and known information may be challenging for some children. Children with learning disabilities may find it hard to attend to relevant information or to organize information so it can be retrieved (Trawick-Smith, 2006). English-language learners must remember words and their meanings in more than one language.

Adults play an essential role in helping children improve their memory skills. Adults help children connect new experiences to prior knowledge and revise their previous thinking to fit with new experiences. Adult scaffolding, or support, helps children attend and use memory strategies such as categorizing (Barry, 2006; Larkina, Guler, Kleinknect, & Bauer, 2008; McAfee & Leong, 2007; Mussen, Conger, Kagan, & Huston, 1990).

Children from different families and communities may depend on different senses to help them obtain and retain information. Some children retain information that they hear for a longer time, while other children more easily remember information they obtained from drawings, photographs, or other graphics (Bjorklund, 2005; McAfee & Leong, 1994; Trawick-Smith, 2006).

As students enter primary school, they draw upon information stored in long-term memory to help them solve increasingly complex problems. They use the information along with input received into their short-term or working memory as they engage in multifaceted tasks (Berk, 2009; Bjorklund, 2005), such as learning to read (Bjorklund, 2005) and solve mathematical problems (Raghubar, Barnes, & Hecht, 2010).

Primary-grade students use a growing number of comprehension strategies to make connections in everyday life as well as when they read. These approaches include "activating prior knowledge, predicting, organizing, questioning, summarizing, and creating mental pictures" (Dougherty Stahl, 2004). Mental imagery and illustrations can serve as cues to help students comprehend text better and recall more details (Gambrell & Jawitz, 1993).

Objective 12 Remembers and connects experiences

a. Recognizes and recalls

Not Yet	1	2	3	4	5	6	7	8	9	10	11	12	13	14	15
		Recognizes familiar people, places, and objects; looks for hidden object where it was last seen • Looks for food dropped from high chair • Uncovers bear after adult covers it with a blanket • Says or signs names of common objects when sees them		**Recalls familiar people, places, objects, and actions from the past (a few months before); recalls one or two items removed from view** • Looks for horse used a few months ago in bin of toy animals • Identifies one or two objects taken away while playing "What's Missing?" • Shows fear of a bee after having been stung		**Tells about experiences in order, provides details, and evaluates the experience; recalls three or four items removed from view** • Identifies four objects taken away while playing "What's Missing?" • Says, "We went to the baseball game. We sat way up high. We ate peanuts and drank lemonade. I really liked it a lot but my sister didn't."		**Uses a few deliberate strategies to remember information** • Creates an observational drawing of a fire truck and then refers to it later while building with blocks • Tells the teacher, "I'm putting my book in my backpack so I'll remember to take it home."		**Begins to use rehearsal strategies, but may need adult prompts/cues; is able to describe details of people, places, things, and events from memory** • Repeats the message to the principal over and over after the teacher says, "You may repeat it quietly to yourself while you walk down the hall." • Outlines the shape of the word as he says the word • When talking about a nearby community center, includes details about the people who work there, the games they play, and the books and toys that are available		**Uses rehearsal strategies spontaneously to remember information; uses awareness of routines to think ahead; remembers about five pieces of information at a time** • Spells the words over and over until she has them memorized to use later as she writes her story • Tells the group, "We need to be finished with our project before lunch because the Spanish teacher comes today and we won't have time in the afternoon to finish." • Follows directions for a simple five-step science experiment • Retells a Tomi DePaola story including relevant and descriptive details but omitting unnecessary parts of the story		**Begins to use semantic grouping strategies to help remember, but may need adult cues or instruction on how to be efficient; recognizes inconsistencies and incompleteness of information** • Tells his friend, "This is something we'll need to remember later to finish our work. I'll write it down where we have things about mammals." • After reading science text, groups new words into previously known categories to help remember meanings • States, "This paragraph doesn't make sense. They left out what the people eat and how they get and prepare their food." • Reads a book about the Iditarod and determines which information to include in an oral report on the subject	

Objective 12 Remembers and connects experiences

b. Makes connections

Not Yet	1	2	3	4	5	6	7	8	9	10	11	12	13	14	15
		Looks for familiar persons when they are named; relates objects to events • Turns head toward door when her teacher says, "Bethany, Mommy is here." • Throws paper away when teacher says, "Please put this in the trash."		**Remembers the sequence of personal routines and experiences with teacher support** • Goes to attendance chart with parent upon arrival • Gets a paper towel after teacher says, "What do we do next, after we wash our hands?"		**Draws on everyday experiences and applies this knowledge to a similar situation** • After hearing *A Chair for My Mother* read aloud says, "My Nana has a chair like the one Rosa and her family bought." • Uses traffic-directing signals on the bike track after seeing a police officer demonstrate them • Divides crayons into "fair share" groups after watching a teacher do it the day before		**Generates a rule, strategy, or idea from one learning experience and applies it in a new context** • Proposes a one-way sign for entering and exiting the cubby area after a neighborhood walk where children discussed one-way street signs • Tallies friends' favorite ice cream flavors after learning how to make tally marks to count how many people wear shoes with buckles		**Connects the past with the present using general time estimates between events; connects time with specific daily events and salient events with the months and seasons** • Places his first birthday, learning to ride a tricycle, going to kindergarten, and attending first grade in the correct sequence on the timeline • Says, "My birthday is in the spring, in April. Sometimes it's cool on my birthday and sometimes it's kind of warm." • Says, "We always have music in the afternoon, except on Wednesdays, and then we have music in the morning."		**Provides general descriptions of events to occur in the future; links material learned previously and in other contexts** • Tells about the major family events planned for the summer • Says, "We won't do that again for five more days." • During a class discussion of Mars, shares information learned from a book and from a guest speaker		**Associates people and events with the past, present, and future; begins to organize and compile information from multiple sources to create a useful document connecting events** • Completes a timeline of transportation in the past, present, and future • Says, "Remember Samson? He was in second grade with us." • Writes a short report on past and present life in the local community using information from books, photographs, maps, videos, web sites, and interviews	

Objective 12 Remembers and connects experiences

Strategies

- Talk about the child's home experiences and use the child's first language (if possible) to help her relate old and new experiences.
- Demonstrate and explain how different experiences relate, e.g., "Your sweater goes over your head, just as your T-shirt goes over your head."
- Use gestures and language to draw attention to particular features of objects and people.
- Give cues involving many senses, not just verbal cues, to help children remember and learn particular information.
- Use photos and objects to talk about the child's past experiences.
- Involve children in "Remember when..." games and discussions, e.g., ask, "Do you remember the elephant we saw at the zoo yesterday?" Talk with toddlers about events in the immediate past, and talk with preschool and kindergarten children about events that took place in the more distant past.
- Expand on children's fragmented recollections by asking varied questions, adding information to children's statements, and commenting about events.
- Encourage children to represent events in multiple ways. For example, after a trip to the fire station, follow up discussions by making a class book with photos and drawings of the trip. Place photos of the trip in the Block area so children can re-create the fire station or fire truck. Develop a list with children of new props to include for dramatic play. Read books or look on the internet for information about firefighters, and compare the information with what the children experienced on their trip.
- Give children enough time to think and make connections before expecting an answer.
- Play memory games like "What's Missing?" Display a few items, remove one, and invite children to tell which one is missing. Display and remove more items with older children.
- Guide children to make analogies. Help them to see ways in which things they learned about earlier are similar to other things. For example, after studying turtles, they may notice that crabs, crawfish, and lobsters also have shells that help protect them.
- Play games like, "What do they have in common?" Show children pictures of various animals, people, and/or objects and have them communicate ways in which they are alike.
- Play memory games with children.
- Sing songs with students that help them learn to count by 2s, 5s, and 10s.
- Play games like "Simon Says" using two- and three-step directions.
- Read a book aloud. After reading, tell children that you are going to retell the story but that you are going to get one part wrong. Ask them to listen closely to your retelling and then discuss with a classmate the part you got wrong. Then have the whole class discuss it.
- Read books that are part of a series and ask children what kinds of things carry over from book to book (e.g., say, "I remember from the last book that his little sister is afraid of water. That's probably why she doesn't want to go to the lake in this book").

Objective 13

Uses classification skills

13

Classification refers to the grouping and organizing of objects, pictures, words, or ideas on the basis of particular criteria. When a toddler tries to put a key in a doorknob, a 2-year-old puts all of the beads in a container with a bead label, and a preschool child explains why he put the snake and lizard picture cards in one pile and the birds in another, they are using classification skills.

Children initially identify broad categories, e.g., food. Next they develop subcategories, e.g., fruit. They then differentiate further and identify additional subcategories, e.g., apples (Pauen, 2002). Exploration of objects, expanding knowledge of the world, and increased language skills contribute to children's ability to classify (Berk, 2002; Gelman & Coley, 1990). When children classify, they organize their experiences and manage enormous amounts of information that can be retrieved later. The ability to classify is important for learning and remembering (Larkina, Guler, Kleinknect, & Bauer, 2008). It supports the development of logical thinking.

Children's earliest classifications are based on their sensory perceptions (Berk, 2003). By the end of the first year their classifications become more conceptual, based on common functions or behaviors. When children are particularly knowledgeable about a topic, they are likely to categorize at a more mature level (Bjorklund, 2005; Gelman, 1998).

Adults help children classify more accurately and think more deeply about categories by naming categories and by talking with children about pictures and objects (Gelman, 1998; Gelman, Chesnick, & Waxman, 2005; Gelman, Coley, Rosengren, Hartman, & Pappas, 1998).

When an adult reads a picture book and explains that chickens and ducks are both birds, children begin to understand that particular similarities group them together despite their differences. Teachers can assess children's classification skills during conversations with them and as they observe children sorting and re-sorting spontaneously, e.g., grouping all shades of blue crayons together while drawing or sorting by properties suggested by someone else, e.g., "Give me all of the blue teddy bears."

Cultural unfamiliarity makes it harder for children to classify accurately and at higher levels (Lin, Schwanenflugel, & Wisenbaker, 1990). Without the support of language, some English-language learners may find sorting and classifying tasks more challenging than their English-speaking or bilingual peers. Some children with learning disabilities develop classification skills more slowly than their typically developing peers, and some may not be able to develop high-level classification skills (Trawick-Smith, 2006).

Classification skills are further developed in elementary school. Students in the primary grades have a stronger comprehension of part/whole relationships. They also are able to classify using more than one characteristic and understand that an object can be a part of more than one group at the same time (Copple, 2012). While adults tend to classify objects based more on function than physical similarity, students in the primary grades give equal consideration to function and appearance when classifying (Diesendruck, Hammer, & Catz, 2003).

Objective 13 Uses classification skills

Not Yet	1	2	3	4	5	6	7	8	9	10	11	12	13
		Matches similar objects • Puts one sock with another sock • Gathers all the vehicles from a shelf • Picks out and eats only the animal crackers • Puts only blue pegs in pegboard; leaves red and yellow pegs to the side		**Places objects in two or more groups based on differences in a single characteristic, e.g., color, size, or shape** • Puts all the red beads together and all the blue beads together • Pulls out all the trucks from the vehicle bin • Identifies fabric pieces as being scratchy or soft • Puts pictures into piles of babies, older children, and grown-ups		**Groups objects by one characteristic; then regroups them using a different characteristic and indicates the reason** • Says, "These buttons are blue, and these are red"; then re-sorts buttons into big and little • Points to groups of animals and says, "These are zoo animals because they live at the zoo"; then sorts the zoo animals into those with stripes and those without stripes		**Groups similar objects by more than one characteristic at the same time; switches sorting rules when asked and explains the reasons** • Organizes a sticker collection into groups and subgroups and explains why and how; then creates a new grouping when the teacher makes a suggestion • Creates four piles of shapes; big red triangles, small red triangles, big blue triangles, small blue triangles. Switches when asked to form two groups of all the big and small triangles		**Groups objects and words in multiple ways based on physical attributes, functions, and semantic or conceptual associations** • Before putting the art tools away, sorts them into different categories based on their function • Defines *market* as a place where people go to buy things such as food or clothes. • When asked to create sorting rule for list of spelling words, creates two lists: words that end in *ack* and words that end in *ick*		**Forms simple hierarchical classifications** • Completes a hierarchical classification chart of Mammals: Zoo Animals (Large and Small) and Farm Animals (Large and Small) by placing animal pictures in the appropriate categories and subcategories or by writing animal names in the appropriate categories and subcategories • Arranges sports trading cards into the global category based on type of sport (baseball and football) and then into subcategories (position played in each sport)	

Objective 13 Uses classification skills

Strategies

- Model sorting and classifying, and provide opportunities for children to practice, e.g., prompt and model, "Let's pick up all the toys that are trucks."
- Sing, recite fingerplays, and read books that focus on colors, shapes, machines, animals, or other categories.
- Play sorting and matching games, using materials that are familiar to the child. Think about the child's family background, neighborhood, and community as you choose familiar materials, e.g., toys, clothing, utensils, food labels.
- As children sort objects, name the categories and use gestures and statements to point out the similarities of the items in each group. Ask children about the groups, e.g., ask, "Why do these things belong together?"
- Provide children with opportunities to arrange collections into groups by using various rules that you and the children make together.
- Use "mystery boxes" to help children develop classification skills. Put one item into the box. Have each child ask one *yes* or *no* question about what is in the box, e.g., "Is it an animal? Is it brown? Does it have four legs?" Support children's efforts by periodically summarizing what is known about the object, e.g., "We know it is a brown animal with four legs. What else do we need to know?"
- Record children's ideas about each of two groups, e.g., cats and dogs. Ask them to find similarities between the two groups. Present their ideas in a Venn diagram.
- Set up a sorting station in your classroom. Collect small containers of different kinds of objects, some related (buttons, shapes) and some random (small objects). Have children sort the objects and record their categories. Note that when objects are random, children need more time to sort them and will likely come up with creative categories.
- Give the same set of objects to multiple groups of children. Ask them to record all the ways they can sort the objects. Challenge groups to see who can come up with the most.
- Enlist children's help with organizing the Library area. Ask, "How can we organize this collection of books?"
- Give a child several pictures of cartoon characters or famous people. Ask him to think of all the ways the pictures could be sorted.

Objective 14

Uses symbols and images to represent something not present

14

Children engage in symbolic thinking when they use representations of objects, events, or persons that are not present. A toddler points to a picture of a cow when an adult asks, "Where's the cow?" A preschool child builds an elaborate structure with blocks and announces, "The dragon lives in this castle!" Both of these children are engaging in abstract thinking. As children mature, they use substitutes that are increasingly different in form and/or function from what they symbolize. Thinking symbolically is necessary for language development, problem solving, reading, writing, mathematical thinking, and participating fully in society (Deloache, 2004; Younger & Johnson, 2004).

Children younger than age 3 have trouble understanding and maintaining the distinction between a symbol and what it represents (Berk, 2002; DeLoache, 1987; Fletcher & Sabo, 2006). Before children can effectively use symbols such as letters, numbers, or maps, they must understand implicitly that symbols represent other things (DeLoache, 1991). By about 18 months of age, children begin treating pictures symbolically rather than as objects to explore manually by hitting, rubbing, patting, scratching, etc. (Preissler & Carey, 2004). This marks an important point in their development of symbolic thinking (DeLoache, 2004; Fletcher & Sabo, 2006). Tools such as webs, graphs, and concept maps are symbolic representations that help preschool and kindergarten children organize and visually represent what they know and think (Birbili, 2006).

As students age, symbols become even more significant as they allow learners to attain information without "direct experience" (DeLoache, 2004). This is just one of the many important elements of symbolic thinking. As the push to incorporate algebraic thinking in elementary school increases, students must have a strong grasp on symbols in primary school so that they can later use them to represent and solve problems (Carpenter & Levi, 2000).

Dramatic play, sometimes called symbolic, pretend, make-believe, fantasy, or imaginative play, is an important vehicle for development and learning (Bergen, 2002; Klein, Wirth, & Linas, 2004; Nourot & Van Hoorn, 1991; Similansky & Shefatya, 1990; Steglin, 2005). Dramatic play contributes to children's development of abstract thinking and imagination and supports their school adjustment, memory, language, and self-regulation abilities (Bodrova & Leong, 2004; Fantuzzo & McWayne, 2002; Krafft & Berk, 1998; Newman, 1990).

Objective 14 Uses symbols and images to represent something not present

Sociodramatic play is a complex, abstract type of dramatic play that involves more than one child playing together. Advances in cognition and language allow children to use more involved play themes and story lines. Sociodramatic play has several important elements (Similansky & Shefatya, 1990): role-play (pretending to be someone else); props (use of real or imaginary objects); verbal make-believe (substituting speech for actions and situations); interaction (agreeing on roles for two or more children and relating to one another from the perspectives of their roles); verbal communication (interacting verbally about the play situation and roles); and persistence (remaining at play for a sustained period). As children act out their roles, they arrive at a shared understanding of the rules for behavior (Bodrova & Leong, 2004). The type of props influences children's pretend play. Children act out more familiar, everyday roles when realistic props are provided. They engage in more fantasy roles when nonrealistic props are offered (Berk & Winsler, 1995).

There are cultural differences in the ways children play. Children from some family backgrounds do not engage in dramatic play unless the classroom environment resembles their home environment (Heisner, 2005; Levy, Wolfgang, & Koorland, 1992; Trawick-Smith, 1998a). English-language learners or children with language delays may find it difficult to engage in elaborate, verbal negotiations and to make their ideas about pretend themes and roles clear (Bergen, 2002; Casby, 1997). Disabilities may also affect children's dramatic play. Children with visual or hearing impairments may seek adults, rather than peers, as play partners. Some children with Autism spectrum disorders do not engage readily in sociodramatic play (Trawick-Smith 2006).

In the primary grades, sociodramatic play becomes more elaborate as students take on more intricate roles and better understand the complementary roles of multiple players (Berk, 2009). Students also engage in other types of play with increasingly complex rules (DeVries, 2006). Their heightened capabilities allow them to participate in more difficult board and computer games as well as physical activities (Manning, 2006). The activities in which children participate in middle childhood can affect roles they take on in adolescence (McHale, Crouter, & Tucker, 2001; Scarr & McCartney, 1983). As an example, the student who is engrossed in strategic board games in the primary grades is likely to become a member of the chess club in high school.

Objective 14 Uses symbols and images to represent something not present

a. Thinks symbolically

Not Yet	1	2	3	4	5	6	7	8	9	10	11	12	13
		Recognizes people, objects, and animals in pictures or photographs • Touches the cow in the illustration when an adult reads, "And the cow jumped...." • Points to photograph and says, "Mommy." • Identifies a duck in a variety of different photos and illustrations		**Draws or constructs, and then identifies what it is** • Draws various shapes and says, "This is my house." • Glues red yarn on paper and says, "I made spaghetti."		**Plans and then uses drawings, constructions, movements, and dramatizations to represent ideas** • Sees a dump truck outside and plans how to draw it • Says, "Let's pretend to be seeds growing like in the book."		**Represents objects, places, and ideas with increasingly abstract symbols** • Makes tally marks • Makes and interprets graphs with teacher's help • Attempts to write words to label a picture		**Shows increasing ability to interpret and record ideas and thoughts and to solve problems without concrete points of reference** • Makes detailed drawings, writings, and notations, and engages in complex discussions reflecting on a trip to the computer store • Solves a math problem several different ways (pictures, numbers, written sentences) • Asks questions and then explains her thinking back to the teacher • Solves a simple word problem comparing two amounts without relying on manipulatives		**Mentally manipulates information and uses logical arguments with increasing regularity; needs concrete points of reference for complex concepts and text; reflects on her work** • Reasons that if one object (A) weighs more than a second object (B), and B weighs more than a third object (C), then A must weigh more than C • Mentally organizes symbolic concepts (e.g., thirty-seven, 37, 37 pounds, 37 years of age, 37 points scored, the 37th in line) • Uses simple map icons to locate and represent landmarks and/or people (e.g., airplane shape for airport, open circle for cities, colored lines for rivers)	

Objective 14 Uses symbols and images to represent something not present

b. Engages in sociodramatic play

Not Yet	1	2	3	4	5	6	7	8	9	10	11	12	13	14	15
		Imitates actions of others during play; uses real objects as props • Holds a toy phone to ear • Wraps a blanket around a doll and then rocks it		**Acts out familiar or imaginary scenarios; may use props to stand for something else** • Puts beads in a muffin tin, places tin in oven, and asks, "Who wants some cupcakes?" • Uses a short rope as a fire hose • Pretends to be the birthday boy at the party and blows out the candles on the pegboard "cake" after others sing "Happy Birthday"		**Interacts with two or more children during pretend play, assigning and/or assuming roles and discussing actions; sustains play scenario for up to 10 minutes** • Pretends to be the bus driver, and tells the other children, "You can be the passengers. Give me your tickets, and I will give you change."		**Plans and negotiates complex role-play; joins in detailed conversation about roles and actions; play may extend over several days** • Joins in elaborate play about taking a dog to the veterinarian, assigning roles, switching roles, creating props, and returning to the play day after day		**Creates rich dialogue, props, costumes, scenery, and sound effects to support role-play** • Role-plays characters who have moral dilemmas and story lines with organized plots • Creates masks, scenery, and sound effects that convey an ominous feeling to use during an enactment of *Jack and the Beanstalk*		**Composes a complex play and uses body, voice, and/or technology to communicate characters' personal thoughts, feelings, actions, and sounds; uses symbolic play themes or props to create games with rules** • Records thunder, drum beats, and clapping to use as sound effects in a dramatization • Evolves playing "store" into playing a "money bags" game with mutually agreed upon rules		**Acts out real-life (including social issues) and fanciful scenarios through improvised and planned dramatic play and performances; manages and directs play during student-created dramatizations** • Creates and directs a performance (skit, puppet show, or story dramatization with make-up and disguise) for the kindergarten class • Improvises a pantomime skit and asks friends to describe what it is about	

Objective 14 Uses symbols and images to represent something not present

Strategies

- Provide many opportunities for children to learn about diverse symbols and their functions, such as language, gestures, letters, numerals, photographs, drawings, models, maps, graphs, webs, and video images.
- Provide books appropriate for the age and abilities of the child.
- Point to pictures during story reading, calling attention to what the pictures mean.
- Show children common objects and encourage them to think about how to use them to represent something different.
- Collect data about the classroom routines of children, e.g., attendance, transportation to school, or snack choices. Graph or otherwise present the information by first using concrete objects, then pictures, and then abstract symbols.
- Schedule adequate time for pretend play to take place indoors and outdoors.
- Match play props to the family backgrounds and developmental characteristics of the children.
- Model pretending, e.g., pretend to take a bite of a plastic apple or rock a baby doll to sleep.
- Provide familiar household items for children to use during pretend play, e.g., a toy broom for sweeping and empty food boxes representative of the foods children eat at home.
- Arrange the environment and introduce props that will encourage play. Observe children while they are playing to gather information about what props to include and what suggestions to make. Decide whether to sustain play by participating or by not intervening.
- Offer both highly realistic and less realistic props for pretend play to accommodate the range of developmental levels.
- Provide multipurpose, open-ended props that can represent many things, e.g., blocks and boxes. Encourage children to use gestures and descriptive language as they dramatize.
- Encourage children to pretend without props as another way of engaging in dramatic play.
- Describe what children are doing, offer suggestions, and make modifications for children with disabilities.
- Ask open-ended questions to extend children's imaginative play and expressive language.
- Extend children's pretend play by interacting with them. Imitate what they are doing; comment and ask questions; or take a role, using a play voice and gestures.
- Plan specific activities to enhance children's knowledge of the world and the roles of people in various settings, e.g., field trips, book reading, visitors. Talk about people's roles.
- Encourage older children to make their own props to use in play or to support their learning, e.g., number lines, word walls, alphabet books, etc.
- Teach children a few basic signs from American Sign Language.

Literacy

The early years are critical for literacy development. Children who do not learn to read and write by the end of the primary grades are at risk for school failure. Children who are especially likely to have difficulty learning to read in the primary grades are those who begin school with less prior knowledge, verbal abilities, phonological sensitivity, familiarity with the basic purposes and mechanisms of reading, and letter knowledge (National Early Literacy Panel, 2008; Snow, Burns, & Griffin, 1998). The level to which a child progresses in reading and writing is one of the best predictors of whether the child will function competently in school and in life (Neuman, Copple, & Bredekamp, 1999).

Literacy learning begins at birth. During the early childhood years, children engage in emergent reading and writing behaviors that form the foundation for conventional literacy, but many children do not receive the ongoing experiences that support this learning. By age 3, differences in children's understanding and use of literacy skills are enormous. Children's literacy development may be negatively affected by factors including poverty; limited English proficiency; visual, hearing, and language impairments; cognitive deficiencies; and parents who have difficulty reading (National Early Literacy Panel, 2008; Snow et al., 1998).

Reading aloud to children appears to be one of the most important activities for building the understandings and skills needed for reading success (Neuman et al., 1999). Children from middle-class families have been read to for about 1,000 hours before beginning kindergarten. Children from families living in poverty have been read to for about 25 hours (Berk, 2006; Neuman, 2003). When children enjoy having books read to them, and when they are excited about what they are hearing and learning, they are motivated to learn to read, and later, to read to learn (Heroman & Jones, 2004).

LITERACY OBJECTIVES

15 Demonstrates phonological awareness, phonics skills, and word recognition

16 Demonstrates knowledge of the alphabet

17 Demonstrates knowledge of print and its uses

18 Comprehends and responds to books and other texts

19 Demonstrates writing skills

Listening, speaking, reading, and writing develop interdependently in children, and each contributes to development of the other. Effective instruction can have a large impact on children's literacy development. Children who would otherwise be most at risk for school failure stand to benefit the most from high–quality experiences (Campbell, Ramey, Pungello, Sparling, & Miller-Johnson, 2002). Through thoughtful planning and developmentally appropriate literacy instruction, teachers can inspire children to want to read, write, and learn (Neuman et al., 1999).

During the primary grades, most children make the transition to becoming real readers. They learn to decode unknown words, read with fluency, comprehend various types of text, and read for specific purposes and for pleasure (Roskos & Neuman, 2013; Shanahan, 2015; Tomlinson, 2009). Exposure to a wide variety of levels and text types (e.g., literature, poetry, informational texts, reports, journals, blogs) furthers students' reading abilities as they learn strategies for decoding and comprehending the various genres (Fountas & Pinnell, 1996; McLaughlin, 2012). They use cues at the word, phrase, sentence, and story or text level to monitor their understanding and confirm or reject their attempts at interpreting print (Hughes, 2007; Iaquinta, 2006; McLaughlin, 2012).

Reading shares a close relationship with writing (Kim, Al Otaiba, Sidler, & Gruelich, 2013), and most students' reading and writing abilities improve greatly over the primary years. As students become more proficient at reading, they begin to read more closely and to compare, analyze, and reason about what they read. They learn to write collaboratively and independently for different purposes, audiences, and to support their learning (McLaughlin & Overturf, 2012). These skills are important for students' success in school and in the workplace (Graham & Harris, 2015; Neuman & Gambrell, 2013).

Achieving literacy may be more challenging for some students (Kim, Puranik, & Al Otaiba, 2015; Snow et al., 1998). Teachers must be aware of how particular disabilities, native language, contexts, learning environments, social interactions, cultural practices, and cultural tools inform and shape reading and writing (Hull & Moje, 2013; Kim et al., 2015). Readers bring to print their understanding of word order, meaning, and the sounds of spoken language (Fox, 2003). It is important to be cognizant of these interactions for native English speakers and for children for whom English is not their first language (Espinosa, 2005, 2015; Olson, Scarcella, & Matuchniak, 2015).

Teachers need to understand the similarities and differences between a student's native language and English. English is more difficult to learn to read than many languages (Juel, 2006; Vaughn, Linan-Thompson, Pollard-Durodola, Mathes, & Hagan, 2006). Phonemic awareness skills can be particularly challenging to master. In general, the same principles that are effective for native English speakers are beneficial to students learning English, but adjustments to instructional practices are necessary (August & Shanahan, 2010; Olson et al., 2015). Similarities between a child's native language and English, and his proficiency in the native language and in English, influence the amount and type of instructional adjustment needed for him to learn English successfully (August & Shanahan, 2010; Snow et al., 1998). For children with disabilities, special instructional practices or intervention may be required (Snow et al., 1998).

In their journey towards literacy, all students need a literacy-rich, supportive environment where teachers provide appropriately challenging instruction and numerous opportunities for practicing newly developed skills (Snow et al., 1998; Tomlinson, 2009). Students need ample time to read and write for multiple purposes in order to achieve fluency and use metacognitive strategies (National Reading Panel, 2000). As they mentor and collaborate with peers and demonstrate their understandings, they contribute to a literate classroom environment (Roskos & Neuman, 2013).

Demonstrates phonological awareness, phonics skills, and word recognition

15

Phonological awareness, or phonological sensitivity, is the ability to discern the sounds and patterns of spoken language. As this awareness develops, children learn to hear the separate sounds of oral language that are blended in ordinary speech. For some children, distinguishing the parts of spoken language is difficult because it requires them to attend to the sounds of speech separately from meaning.

Phonological awareness is an important skill in learning to read. Children typically begin to demonstrate this awareness by about age 3, and their skills improve gradually over many years (Snow, Burns, & Griffin, 1998). Phonological sensitivity is a strong predictor of later reading, writing, and spelling ability (National Early Literacy Panel, 2004, 2008). Instruction that strengthens children's phonological awareness has been shown to contribute to later reading success (Ehri et al., 2001; National Early Literacy Panel, 2008). Children become phonologically aware through experiences such as reciting poems, singing, and clapping the syllables of chanted words (Adams, 1990, 2001; Carroll, Snowling, Hulme, & Stevenson, 2003; Strickland & Schickedanz, 2004). Phonological awareness skills are typically learned in a particular order (Anthony, Lonigan, Driscoll, Phillips, & Burgess, 2003). However, children acquire these skills in an overlapping sequence rather than by mastering one level before the next (Dickinson & Neuman, 2006).

Children who are learning two or more languages must learn very different sound systems (Gonzalez, 1998). They must distinguish English phonemes that may not be part of their native languages. A child may therefore have difficulty hearing and/or producing the sounds of English.

In primary school, teachers help children further their phonemic awareness and support them as they learn decoding and phonics skills, word structure analysis, and recognition of frequently occurring sight words (Florida Center for Reading Research, n.d.). The focus on rhyme and alliteration in the earlier years builds to the process of decoding words in elementary school. Children's ability to use phonological awareness and phonics skills is critical in learning to decode unknown words (Snow, Burns, & Griffin, 1998). Phonological processing predicts children's later reading comprehension and reading disability status (Fuchs, Compton, Fuchs, Bryant, Hamlett, & Lambert, 2012). Students' failure to use phonemic decoding skills and to master word recognition hinders their ability to comprehend text (Snow, Burns, & Griffin, 1998).

The ability to consciously focus on the structure of words such as base words and inflections (morphological awareness) is also important as primary-grade students learn to read. Morphological knowledge facilitates decoding as students decompose multi-morphemic words into familiar root words and known affixes (Kruk & Bergman, 2013). Students' abilities to utilize morphological processes support a variety of literacy skills, including word identification, reading fluency (Green, 2009; Wolter, Wood, & D'zatko, 2009), and reading comprehension (Apel, Wilson-Fowler, Brimo, & Perrin, 2012).

Objective 15 Demonstrates phonological awareness, phonics skills, and word recognition

a. Notices and discriminates rhyme

Not Yet	1	2	3	4	5	6	7	8	9	10	11
		Joins in rhyming songs and games • Hums along and joins in random words in rhyme • Sings with a group, "One, two, buckle my shoe..."		**Fills in the missing rhyming word; generates rhyming words spontaneously** • Completes the rhyme in the phrase, "The fat cat sat on the ____ (mat)." • Chants spontaneously, "Me, fee, kee, tee, lee, bee."		**Decides whether two words rhyme** • "Do *bear* and *chair* rhyme? What about *bear* and *goat*?" • Matches rhyming picture cards		**Generates a group of rhyming words when given a word** • Says, "Bat, sat, lat," when asked, "What words rhyme with *cat*?"		**Generates rhyming words without a prompt word; identifies rhyming words in written text; uses rhyme to decode text** • Makes the word *bat* with the plastic alphabet letters and then changes the first letter to create the words *cat*, *hat*, *mat*; reads each one and says, "I made a lot of rhyming words." • Identifies all the rhyming words after reading a simple story told in rhyme	

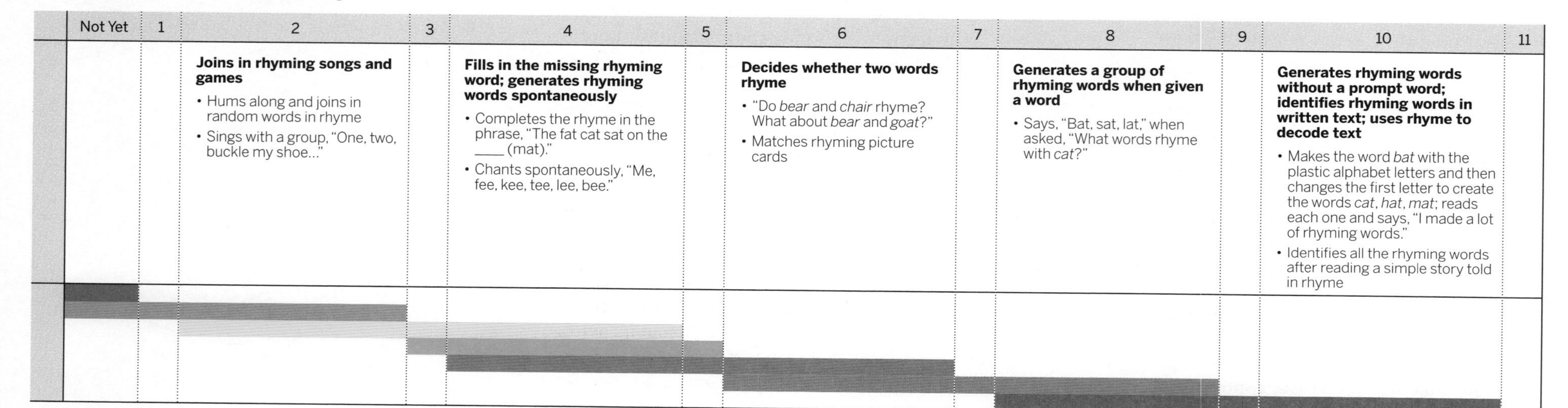

b. Notices and discriminates alliteration

Not Yet	1	2	3	4	5	6	7	8	9
		Sings songs and recites rhymes and refrains with repeating initial sounds • Sings, "I'm bringing home a baby bumble bee..."		**Shows awareness that some words begin the same way** • Says, "*Max* and *Maya*...our names start the same!"		**Matches beginning sounds of some words** • Groups objects or pictures that begin with the same sound • Picks up a toy bear when asked, "What begins the same way as *box*, *baby*, and *bike*?"		**Isolates and identifies the beginning sound of a word** • Says, "/m-m-m/," when asked "What is the first sound of the word *milk*?" • Responds, "/t/," after being asked, "What's the beginning sound of *toy*, *toe*, and *teeth*?"	

Objective 15 Demonstrates phonological awareness, phonics skills, and word recognition

c. Notices and discriminates discrete units of sound

Not Yet	1	2	3	4	5	6	7	8	9	10	11	12	13	14	15
		Shows awareness of separate words in sentences • Joins in clapping each word while chanting, "I like ice cream." • Jumps upon hearing a specified word in a story		**Shows awareness of separate syllables in words** • Claps each syllable of name, *Tri-na* and *Chris-to-pher* and counts the syllables in each • Puts together *pen* and *cil* to say *pencil* • Puts together *foot* and *ball* to say *football*		**Verbally blends and separates onset and rime in one-syllable words** • Says, /c/ake, and /r/ake when the teacher says "cake" and "rake." • Points to Mick and Jill when the teacher plays a game and asks, "Where is _ick? Where is _ill?"		**Verbally blends, separates, and adds or substitutes individual sounds in simple, consonant-vowel-consonant (CVC) words; reads common high-frequency sight words** • Claps each phoneme of *hat*: /h/ /a/ /t/ • Says, "Hat," after hearing /h/ /a/ /t/; changes the middle sound to make /h/ /o/ /t/ • Accurately reads *you*, *here*, *my*, *are*, and *sad* in *My Friend Is Sad*		**Distinguishes short from long vowel sounds in one-syllable words; reads grade-appropriate irregularly spelled words; uses word families to read unknown words** • While playing a "stand up, sit down" game, correctly stands for long vowel sounds in words and sits for short vowel sounds • Recognizes *said*, *does*, and *were* • Breaks the word *her* into parts as he says, "/h//er/"; says /ch/e/s/t/ for the word *chest*		**Reads grade-appropriate irregularly spelled words; uses word families and analogy of known sight words to read unknown words** • Reads words such as *great*, *eight*, *sound*, and *would* without pausing to sound them out • Says, "I think this word is *brother* because it looks like *mother*."		**Reads grade-appropriate irregularly spelled words** • Reads words such as *doesn't*, *young*, and *straight* without pausing to sound them out • Recognizes *fountain* because it has a similar spelling to the known word *mountain*	

Objective 15 Demonstrates phonological awareness, phonics skills, and word recognition

d. Applies phonics concepts and knowledge of word structure to decode text

Not Yet	1	2	3	4	5	6	7	8	9	10	11
		Shows understanding that a specific sequence of letters represents a spoken word • Says, "You have to put the letters in the right order when you write my name." • Says, "I made an invitation. Can you please write the letters to spell the word party?" • Writes *cts* to represent the word cats		**Deciphers a few words using the letter-sound associations of most consonants and the five major vowels (short and long sounds); notices different letter sounds in similarly spelled words** • Reads the words *map, egg,* and *fun* when told they have short vowel sounds • Sounds out *pit* while reading and says, "This looks like *pat*, except *pat* has an /ă/ sound, not an /ĭ/ sound." • Draws a picture for a friend and writes, "I luv yu."		**Deciphers regularly spelled one- and two-syllable words (after breaking into syllables) using letter-sound associations (including common consonant digraphs and final-e and vowel teams), common roots, and inflectional endings; breaks words into syllables based on the number of vowel sounds heard** • Sounds out, /c/ /a/ /m/ /p/ and says, "Camp. When you add *ing*, the word is *camping*!" • Sounds out *churn* and *chirp* using digraph knowledge • Reads *rainbow* and says, "It has two syllables because I hear a long *a* and a long *o*." • Says, "I know this word is *tape* not *tap* because the *e* on the end makes the vowel sound long."		**Deciphers regularly spelled two-syllable words using letter-sound associations and common affixes** • After learning about the prefix *un*, reads *undo, untie*, and *unhappy* • Reads *playing, teams, flame,* and *hikes* using vowel teams • When asked, student explains why the word *sunshine* has a short vowel in the first syllable and a long vowel in the second		**Deciphers multisyllable words by applying letter-sound associations, derivational and Latin suffixes, roots, and contractions** • Decodes words such as *bakery, familiar,* and *bottomless* • Reads *can't, won't,* and *aren't* in the paragraph when the teacher asks her to find the contractions that mean *cannot, will not,* and *are not* • After learning about the suffixes *-ish, -less, and -ly*, adds the words *brownish, motionless,* and *honestly* to the word wall	

Objective 15 Demonstrates phonological awareness, phonics skills, and word recognition

Strategies

- Know each child's level of phonological awareness and provide appropriate experiences. Plan specific activities to help children attend to rhyme, alliteration, and smaller and smaller units of sound.
- Encourage children to listen to sounds in the environment. Record different sounds for children to identify.
- Use songs, stories, and rhymes that play with language. Informally, but intentionally, draw children's attention to the sounds of language.
- Encourage children to play with words and to make up their own rhymes.
- Have children fill in rhyming words in a verse. For example, "The cat wore a____ (hat). He slept on a ____ (mat). He played with a _____(bat)."
- Play games that focus on alliteration (initial sounds). For example, have children think of words that begin with the same sound as another child's name (Bonito, Betty, baby, bath, buttons, etc.).
- Clap or tap rhythm sticks to mark the syllables of preschool and kindergarten children's names as you say them.
- Draw children's attention to the phonemes in spoken words during daily routines. For example, dismiss children to go to lunch by saying, "If your name begins with the /m/ sound like Matthew, you may go to lunch."
- Plan activities with children that focus on onset and rime. For example, have children group words by their beginning sounds (*rake, rat, rose*) or create word families that emphasize the ending sounds (*ring, sing, king*).

Objective 16

Demonstrates knowledge of the alphabet

16

Knowledge of letters and words is an important component of literacy. It involves more than reciting the alphabet song or recognizing individual letters. Children must understand that speech can be recorded in print and that words in print can be spoken. Readers must understand that a letter is a symbol that represents one or more sounds. A more complex level of understanding requires knowing that these symbols can be grouped together to form words and that words have meanings. The idea that written words are composed of letters that represent sounds is called the *alphabetic principle*. Children's understanding of the alphabetic principle is a predictor of future reading success.

Young children's alphabet knowledge, especially their ability to rapidly name letters and numerals in random order, is a strong predictor of later reading, writing, and spelling ability (Adams, 1990; National Early Literacy Panel, 2004, 2008; Stevenson & Newman, 1986). In addition, preschool children's letter knowledge is a unique predictor of growth in phonological sensitivity across the year (Burgess & Lonigan, 1998). There is a high correlation between knowing the names of the letters and knowing the letter sounds. These appear to be overlapping skills (Lomax & McGee, 1987; Richgels, 1986; Worden & Boettcher, 1990). Children's knowledge of the alphabet is also closely related to their comprehension skills by the end of second grade (Cats, Fey, Zhang, & Tomblin, 2001).

By the end of the kindergarten year, most students will have a strong sense of alphabet knowledge, as this is the year during which they can begin to use uppercase and lowercase letters to create morphemes and words (Ehri, 2005). As the year progresses, students become adept at using letters as the building blocks for their writing (Ritchey, 2008).

Knowledge of the alphabet plays a role in later literacy development (National Early Literacy Panel, 2008). Students can use their alphabet knowledge strategically to identify unknown words. This gives them the confidence and freedom to read a variety of texts on their own (Fox, 2003).

Objective 16 Demonstrates knowledge of the alphabet

a. Identifies and names letters

Not Yet	1	2	3	4	5	6	7	8	9
		Recognizes and names a few letters in own name		Recognizes and names as many as 10 letters, especially those in own name		Identifies and names 11–20 upper- and 11–20 lowercase letters when presented in random order		Identifies and names all upper- and lowercase letters when presented in random order	

b. Identifies letter–sound correspondences

Not Yet	1	2	3	4	5	6	7	8	9
		Identifies the sounds of a few letters		Produces the correct sounds for 10–20 letters		Produces at least one correct sound for each letter in the alphabet		Produces short and long vowel sounds and most frequent sounds for each consonant	

Objective 16 Demonstrates knowledge of the alphabet

Strategies

- Focus on letters as part of meaningful activities. Point out particular letters as you take dictation, compose messages, and read stories. Call attention to the letter-sound relationship. For example, you might say, "That word begins just like Tamika. It begins with the letter T."
- Display the alphabet at the child's eye level. Make smaller versions for children to use as references. For example, provide alphabet strips or alphabet cards in the Library area. Children can refer to these as they read or write.
- Use the children's names to help them learn the alphabet letters and their sounds. For example, have children place cards with their photos and names printed on them underneath alphabet letters posted around the room. Talk about whose names are under each letter and the sound the letter makes.
- Sing the alphabet song. Sing each letter slowly so children can hear each letter. Point to each letter on a large alphabet chart as you sing.
- Read alphabet books. For example, *Chicka, Chicka Boom Boom* (Bill Martin, Jr.) and *The Alphabet Tree* (Leo Lionni) are good for group reading. Talk about the letters, their shapes, and the names of the pictured objects that begin with the letter.
- Place alphabet books in the Library area and in other interest areas. Select books that include words with a single letter sound (snake), rather than a blend (*sh*ip) to avoid confusion.
- Encourage sensory exploration of the alphabet. Offer children a variety of ways to explore the alphabet: by using sandpaper or felt letters, salt trays, clay, magnetic letters, and by forming letters with their bodies.
- Create an alphabet word wall that features words and pictures that are relevant to the children in the classroom. Begin by posting photos of the children with their names, and add photos and words related to the current study topic, e.g., if studying trees, words might include acorn, pinecone, bark, etc.
- Provide environmental print in the language(s) spoken by the children in the group. Encourage children to identify letters.
- As you read a suspenseful story, pause and emphasize the sound of the beginning letter of the word you are reading, e.g., "And then, behind the tree, she saw the /b/, /b/, /b/. What starts with the /b/ sound? Yes! She saw the /b/ bear!"

Demonstrates knowledge of print and its uses

17

Long before they learn to read, young children try to make sense of the print around them. Children see print in their homes, in their schools, on street signs, and elsewhere throughout their communities. They see it in books, on grocery lists, and on food containers. Knowledge of print and its uses includes understanding that print carries a message and that print is organized and read in particular ways. Through print-rich environments and scaffolding by adults, children learn about the many functions of print; how books are handled; and features of print, such as punctuation. Children need these skills to be successful readers and writers.

Young children's concepts about print are a good predictor of later reading, writing, and spelling ability (National Early Literacy Panel, 2004, 2008; Clay, 1979a, 1979b; McCormick & Mason, 1986; Wells, 1985). Understanding that print is meaningful is one of the first steps children take in learning to read and write (Mason, 1980). Children learn much about print from what is included in the environment, e.g., signs and labels, and from including print in their play (McGee, Lomax, & Head, 1988; Neuman & Roskos, 1993). They learn the uses of written language before they learn its forms (Gundlach, McLane, Scott, & McNamee, 1985; Taylor, 1983). Although the first stages of reading and writing are predominately about function, children develop an interest in print conventions. However, children do not systematically progress from one stage to the next (Morrow, 2005).

Becoming a proficient reader involves reading different types of materials for a variety of purposes. Students therefore begin to read a much larger repertoire of text types during the primary years. As they approach each new piece of writing, students understand what they read based on their own knowledge and personal experience (Fox, 2003).

To become skilled readers, students in the primary grades are taught to use story and text structures to help them comprehend texts. Their capacity to recognize and use text structures has been shown to increase reading comprehension, to affect how much students remember, to enhance the learning of content, and is considered to be a valuable reading strategy (Hess, 2011).

In addition to understanding a variety of text structures, students learn about the specific features (e.g., table of contents, glossary, subheadings, bold font) of each type of text. These features assist the reader in organizing the information presented by the text and thus, aid in comprehension (Dymock & Nicholson, 2010).

Objective 17 Demonstrates knowledge of print and its uses

a. Uses and appreciates books and other texts

Not Yet	1	2	3	4	5	6	7	8	9	10	11	12	13	14	15
		Shows interest in books • Gazes at the pages of a book • Brings book to adult to read		**Orients book correctly; turns pages from the front of the book to the back; recognizes familiar books by their covers** • Hands teacher book and says, "Let's read *Corduroy*!"		**Knows some features of a book (e.g., title, author, illustrator, front and back covers); connects specific books to authors** • Says, "I want to read this Dr. Seuss book today." • Says, "Eric Carle wrote this book. He is the author." • Selects a book in the library and talks to the librarian about the front and back cover; points out the title page when prompted		**Uses various types of books for their intended purposes** • Selects a nonfiction book about insects to identify the butterfly seen on the playground		**Explains differences between types of texts; locates information in text using basic text features (main headings, table of contents, glossaries, electronic menus, icons)** • Selects a simple storybook to read when finished with an assignment • Checks the glossary when teacher suggests using it to find out the meaning of *gill* while looking at a book about sharks • Determines that a classmate's book is fiction because it has a talking dog. Says, "My library book is also about dogs, but it's nonfiction. The dogs don't talk."		**Locates information using text features (captions, bold print, subheadings, glossaries, indexes, electronic menus, icons) and dictionaries; understands story structure** • Selects a book of jokes from the e-books menu to read so she can tell a joke to the teacher • Independently checks the glossary to determine the meaning of a bolded word in science text • During a class discussion of *James and the Giant Peach*, describes the basic story structure		**Uses text features and search tools (keywords, sidebars, hyperlinks) proficiently to locate information related to a specific topic; explains parts of stories, poems, and dramatic plays (chapter, verse, scene, act, etc.) and how they work together** • Reads a grade-appropriate newspaper article about construction of a new recycling center • Uses key words and follows hyperlinks when searching the Web for information related to a class project • When writing about a poem he has read, uses the word *stanza* to refer to particular text	

Objective 17 Demonstrates knowledge of print and its uses

b. Uses print concepts

Not Yet	1	2	3	4	5	6	7	8	9	10	11
		Shows understanding that text is meaningful and can be read • Points to the words on the sign by the fish bowl and says, "Just one pinch!"		**Indicates where to start reading and the direction to follow** • Points to beginning of text on the page when pretending to read and moves finger left to right as she continues down the page		**Shows awareness of various features of print: letters, words, spaces, upper- and lowercase letters, some punctuation** • Points to the word *hippopotamus* and says, "That's a long word." • Says, "That means stop reading," as he points to a period at the end of a sentence		**Matches a written word with a spoken word, but it may not be the actual written word; tracks print from the end of a line of text to the beginning of the next line** • Touches each word on the page while reciting the words from *Brown Bear, Brown Bear, What Do You See?* • Picks up finger and returns it to the beginning of the next line when pretend reading		**Distinguishes features of a sentence, including capitalization and punctuation** • Says, "I think there are four sentences in this passage because I see four periods." • Reminds friend to look at the ending punctuation to know whether it stops, shows excitement, or asks a question	

Objective 17 Demonstrates knowledge of print and its uses

Strategies

- Create a print-rich environment. Include print that is meaningful, functional, and interesting. Avoid displaying so much print that it clutters the room.
- Display print at the child's eye level. If you place print too high, children will not be able to see it or attend to its features.
- Support children's play with print as they imitate real-life situations. For example, offer books, newspapers, or magazines to add to the doctor's office. Supply paper and markers for making signs, writing checks, or creating appointment books.
- Write signs, charts, recipes, labels, and other classroom materials in the children's presence. Describe the process as children watch you write. Call attention to the features of print such as individual letters, words, spaces, upper- and lowercase letters, and punctuation.
- Distinguish between children's drawing and writing. Use the words *drawing* and *writing* when making comments about their products. For example, you might say, "You *drew* a rainbow. I see you *wrote* your name and Toben's name next to your picture."
- Point out the title, author, and illustrator as you read books with older children.
- Draw children's attention to the conventions of print. For example, when you record a child's dictation, talk about where you are starting to write, why you are beginning the sentence with an uppercase letter, and what the punctuation mark means at the end of the sentence. As you read, move your finger under the words to help children learn directionality.
- Use story and informational books and planned writing experiences to teach about print. Intentionally read books aloud to individuals, small groups, and large groups of children. Place both fiction and nonfiction books in various interest areas so children can find the information they need and discover purposes for print. For example, you might include books about plants in the Discovery area if you have plants there.
- Talk with children about the many ways print is used around them. For example, look on the Internet to check the day's weather. Read the lunch menu. Read aloud a card to be sent to a sick classmate.
- Talk about concepts about books when you read to children. Talk about where the writing starts on the page and which way to proceed when reading.

Comprehends and responds to books and other texts

18

Comprehension, the process of finding meaning, is the goal of reading instruction. Comprehending text involves connecting what is heard and read with background knowledge and experiences. The more the language and meaning of the text relates to a person's prior knowledge, the easier it is to make sense of what is read. Comprehension of oral language and simple texts is essential to future reading success; children learn to process what they hear and read (Teale & Yokota, 2000). Children who engage in frequent activities with books have larger, more literate vocabularies. These children learn to read better than children who have few book experiences (Dickinson & Tabors, 1991; Wells, 1986). Although most children are not reading before they enter kindergarten, the development of listening comprehension skills is important. Through meaningful language activities, children develop and integrate comprehension skills.

Children follow a typical progression in learning to read storybooks. Initially they point to and label pictures in a book, treating each page as a separate entity. As they pretend to read, the story they tell does not flow from page to page. Next, they begin to talk about the pictures and follow the story across the pages. Their language transitions from sounding like "talk" to a more reading-like intonation. Finally, they begin using different strategies (known words, knowledge of letters and sounds, patterns in text, picture and context clues) to make meaning of the text (Sulzby, 1985).

Dramatic play relates to comprehension in powerful, complex ways (Christie, 1983; Pellegrini & Galda, 1982; Saltz, Dixon, & Johnson, 1997; Silvern, Williamson, & Waters, 1983). Metaplay, in which children assume a role and negotiate what will happen next, has been shown to increase story comprehension (Trawick-Smith, 1998a). Retelling stories also helps children develop a sense of story structure and other understandings about language that contribute to their comprehension of text (Morrow, 1985). Children who speak a dialect or who are English-language learners may retell a story using the grammar of their dialect or first language. Their use of standard English grammar increases over time as they gain more experience with listening and responding to stories (Schickedanz, 1999).

Reading is much more than word calling and decoding. In the primary grades, students interpret the meaning behind the words they read using the context of the word as well as their personal vocabularies (Fountas & Pinnell, 2011).

In addition to linguistic skills, students also use cognitive skills to process and give meaning to texts (Florida Center for Reading Research, n.d.). Students in the primary grades enact several comprehension strategies when reading. These include "activating prior knowledge, monitoring comprehension, generating questions, answering questions, drawing inferences, creating mental imagery, identifying the text structure the writer has used, and creating summaries" (Dymock & Nicholson, 2007).

Objective 18 Comprehends and responds to books and other texts

Teachers can help students "think about their thinking" through the use of metacognitive strategies. A particularly effective way to increase students' metacognitive strategies is to invite them to explain the processes they used (Pressley & Block, 2002). Discussing text is especially helpful for students to build meaning, as it allows them to see where they have misunderstood something and substantiates what they have understood correctly (Hammond & Nessel, 2011).

During the primary-school years, students are asked to assert their own opinions as they read. They are exposed to authors' views and asked if they agree or disagree, and are then asked the reasons for their opinions. Students are challenged to "move beyond passively accepting the text's message to question, examine, or dispute the power relations that exist between readers and authors" (McLaughlin & DeVoogd, 2004).

As the use of technology gains ground in more and more primary schools, students encounter additional types of texts, as well as varied media in which they explore these texts. In these "blended" learning environments, students engage in online forums, create blogs, and use e-book readers, gaining digital literacy skills as they navigate the online world and learn to read, write, and communicate within it (Hull & Moje, 2013).

Objective 18 Comprehends and responds to books and other texts

a. Interacts during reading experiences, book conversations, and text reflections

Not Yet	1	2	3	4	5	6	7	8	9	10	11	12	13	14	15
		Contributes particular language from the book at the appropriate time • Says, "You're not big enough," when teacher pauses in *The Grouchy Ladybug*		**Asks and answers questions about the text; refers to pictures** • Responds, "He was mad. He threw his hat down."		**Identifies story-related problems, events, and resolutions during conversations with an adult** • When prompted, says, "George got put in jail. He ran out the open door and got out."		**Engages in teacher-led reading activities using emergent reader books and other simple texts; focuses on major characters, events, and information; describes relationships between text and illustrations; makes comparisons, infers, and draws conclusions; identifies the author's supporting points** • Shares the illustration of Camilla looking like a pill from *A Bad Case of Stripes* and talks about what happened and why it's funny • Says to a friend, "In this book, Olivia needs help, but in the other book, she's helping someone else." • Says, "I think the author drew the illustrations using bright colors because he's describing spring, when flowers bloom and the grass turns green." • After reading a new version of *The Three Little Pigs*, makes props and retells the story incorporating the major details and differences between the new and older versions		**Uses print and illustrations in first-grade-level texts to describe and compare individuals, events, ideas, narration, connections, and information** • Says, "I like roller coasters, so I'm like Junie in the book, not like her brother, who's afraid of roller coasters." • Says, "The chart on page 10 shows us why it's good to recycle at school." • Says, "The author likes winter time even though it is very cold. She says building a snowman is fun so we will like winter." • Chooses a phrase from a poem and talks about the emotions it conveys		**Uses second-grade-level texts to make comparisons and connections; identify the main focus/main points, ask and answer who, what, where, when, and how questions about key details; describe characters' points of view and responses to events; explain how words, phrases, or images/illustrations supply meaning** • During Readers' Theater, reads aloud using different voices to reflect different settings, characters, and characters' emotions • Discusses similarities and differences between/among versions of *Jack and the Beanstalk* that were written by authors from Iceland, Egypt, and Vietnam • After reading a science selection, contributes to group writing of a step-by-step procedure for the science experiment		**Uses third-grade-level texts to ask and answer questions referencing appropriate illustrations and specific text; makes comparisons between texts by the same author or on the same topic; explains how characters' actions contribute to events; differentiates own viewpoint with those in text** • Discusses information about the moon's surface, atmosphere, and key events of the astronauts obtained from a website and from a science text Presents similarities and differences, referring to specific text and photos in the two sources • Compares the settings of two *Boxcar Children* books by saying, "This story takes place in a candy factory, and this one happens at a baseball game." • After reading a biography of Dr. Martin Luther King, Jr., creates a timeline of his life and related historical events • After reading a book about the rainforest, answers questions about the author's reasons for and opinions about saving the rainforest	

Objective 18 Comprehends and responds to books and other texts

b. Uses emergent reading skills

	Not Yet	1	2	3	4	5	6	7	8	9
			Pretends to read a familiar book, treating each page as a separate unit; names and describes what is on each page, using pictures as cues		**Pretends to read, using some of the language from the text; describes the action across pages, using pictures to order the events; may need prompts from adult**		**Pretends to read, reciting language that closely matches the text on each page and using reading-like intonation**		**Tries to match oral language to words on page; points to words as he reads**	

Objective 18 Comprehends and responds to books and other texts

c. Retells stories and recounts details from informational texts

Not Yet	1	2	3	4	5	6	7	8	9	10	11	12	13	14	15
		Retells some events or information from a familiar story or other text with close adult prompting • Says, "The pig builds a house from it," when the teacher asks, "What does the first little pig do with the straw?" Then says, "The wolf blows it down," when the teacher asks, "What does the wolf do to the house?" • After hearing the teacher read *Sam Helps Recycle*, says, "Sam got in the car to go to the recycle place."		**Retells familiar stories and recounts details from a nonfiction text using pictures or props as prompts** • Retells the basic events of *The Three Little Pigs* using felt pieces on a felt board • While recounting the story, looks at the photos in *Sam Helps Recycle* to remember the process of sorting bottles and cans		**Retells a familiar story and recounts an informational text in proper sequence, including major events and characters, as appropriate** • Retells *The Three Little Pigs*, starting with the pigs saying good-bye to their mother, remembering the correct order in which the pigs build their houses, and ending with the wolf climbing down the chimney and falling into the pot of hot water • Retells *Sam Helps Recycle* by recounting the process of recycling from beginning to end		**Retells stories and recounts informational texts with many details about characters, events, ideas, and story lines** • Retells *The Three Little Pigs* and includes details about how the mother felt about her children leaving home, the pigs' personalities, and why building a house from bricks is better than building a house from straw or sticks		**Paraphrases grade-appropriate literature and informational texts and includes the major points and central message** • Reads and then retells a story in own words, including the important details about the setting, plot, events, and characters and their feelings • Reads a simple informational book on dolphins and then explains how they hunt for food		**Summarizes the major points and central message in grade-appropriate literature and informational texts; makes interpretive comments about text** • Reads a multi-paragraph folktale and tells the main topic, what each paragraph is about, and the moral of the story • Reports on reptiles after reading an informational book on the topic		**Summarizes the major points, central message, and underlying themes in grade-appropriate literature and informational texts; indicates how key points support the central idea** • Reads a biography on Abraham Lincoln and explains how what is read relates to historical events • Explains the steps in an experiment after reading the instructions • After reading *Lulu and the Brontosaurus*, talks about how Lulu changes after the brontosaurus makes her his pet and gives examples to show what Lulu learned about how to treat others	

Objective 18 Comprehends and responds to books and other texts

d. Uses context clues to read and comprehend texts

Not Yet	1	2	3	4	5	6	7	8	9
		Uses different strategies to make meaning from print (determines patterns in text; uses known words; asks questions; sounds out words; uses frequently occurring affixes and inflections) • Looks at the illustrations before beginning reading and predicts what the passage will be about • Notices the same phrases over and over again as she reads the repetitive text • Reads the root word *big* in *bigger* and sounds out the rest of the word		**Uses various strategies to make meaning when reading first-grade-level content (monitors for understanding; asks and answers questions; uses sentence-level clues; uses known affixes)** • Reads, "The dog *bigs* for his food," and says, "That doesn't make sense." Looks carefully and rereads, "The dog *begs* for his food." States, "Now it makes sense!" • Asks for clarification of the word *hibernation* when reading a book about polar bears in order to understand the passage • Says, "I think the horse will get away. I see the prefix *un* before the word *tied*. If the horse is untied, he is going to run when it storms."		**Uses various strategies to make meaning when reading second-grade-level content (monitors for understanding; uses sentence-level clues; uses known affixes, roots, and individual words in compounds)** • Rereads the preceding several sentences to infer the meaning of a new word • Looks at additional information in a diagram when reading a passage about different types of exercise		**Uses various strategies to make meaning when reading third-grade-level content (monitors for understanding; uses sentence-level clues; uses known affixes, roots, and individual words in compounds; distinguishes literal from non-literal content)** • Records specific questions to help guide his study of the science text • Uses a dictionary to find the meaning of the word *cerebral* after reading it in a book about the brain • While reading a story, says, "I think this means he might get into trouble about the way he is talking" after reading, "That boy is skating on thin ice." • Reads a sentence over to get the meaning of a word	

Objective 18 Comprehends and responds to books and other texts

e. Reads fluently

Not Yet	1	2	3	4	5	6	7	8	9
		Reads and comprehends emergent reader texts and other print materials • Reads part of an emergent reader text proficiently, requesting teacher help with words not understood • Reads the names of the children in the class from the teacher's attendance roster		**Fluently reads and comprehends first-grade-level texts** • Reads a simple text about sea turtles easily and with understanding on successive readings • Reads and answers a simple word problem during math instruction		**Fluently reads and comprehends second-grade-level texts** • Uses a smooth, conversational style while reading a familiar e-book to friends • Reads a school newspaper article about the proposed new playground		**Fluently reads and comprehends third-grade-level texts** • Reads a poem aloud, reflecting the mood portrayed in the selection • Reads an informational book on inventors after independently reading a chapter storybook about the life of Thomas Edison	

Objective 18 Comprehends and responds to books and other texts

Strategies

- Provide high-quality children's literature from a variety of genres. Include picture books, poetry, and informational books. Call attention to how ideas are presented in different ways in different types of books.
- Prepare children for reading by taking a *picture walk*. Introduce the story by previewing the pictures. Ask children to predict what the story is about by looking at the cover. Turn the pages slowly as you *walk* through the book so children can make predictions about the story.
- Provide opportunities for children to talk about stories before and after they are read. Encourage them to ask questions and to make predictions.
- Support children's use of language from books. Introduce and discuss new words in meaningful contexts.
- Engage children in helping you read repeated phrases in books. For example, from *The Very Busy Spider* (Eric Carle) they might "read" with you as you point to the words, "The spider didn't answer. She was very busy spinning her web."
- Help children connect new information and ideas to what they already know. For example, you might say, "Does this remind you of _________?" "How is _____ like _____?" "Have you ever________?"
- Facilitate story retellings. Use simple pictures, puppets, costumes, or props to help children recall the story. For example, for the story *Jump Frog, Jump*! (Robert Kalan), you might use a toy fly, frog, fish, snake, turtle, net, and basket as props.
- Support story retellings by taking turns telling parts of the story. Have children tell more of the story as they are able.
- Provide repeated readings of the same book so children can focus on different aspects of the book each time, e.g., story line, details, specific vocabulary words.
- Read chapter books with children.
- Model using different strategies for making meaning from print. Show children how to use picture cues, context, sounding out words, and known (high-frequency) words.

Demonstrates writing skills

19

Writing is an important aspect of emergent literacy. Writing letters or name writing is a predictor of later literacy (National Early Literacy Panel, 2008). Writing begins with making a mark. Then, when children are given the time, opportunities, and materials to practice, their writing skills continue to advance. Children begin to understand that writing is recorded speech. As their phonological awareness advances, children write a few letters that represent sounds in words. Their writing gradually becomes more conventional, typically as they enter the elementary grades.

Writing originates from drawing and is supported by make-believe play. Children learn to associate symbols with meaning (Vygotsky, 1997). To write, children need to understand that letters are symbols. By exploring writing, children learn about letters, sounds, and the meaning of text (Schickedanz & Casbergue, 2009). Understanding the mechanics of the writing system (letter naming and letter–sound correspondences) has a moderate correlation with reading in the primary grades (Stuart, 1995).

Writing letters requires children to know how each letter looks and how to put line segments together to form them. They must also know the orientation of letters and learn the particular order of the letters in each word (Schickedanz, 1999). Reversed letters are very common in preschool and kindergarten children's writing (Schickedanz & Casbergue, 2009) and are not a cause for concern. Because fine-motor skills are necessary to control writing tools, it is helpful to know that markers are easiest for children to use; followed by chalk; then crayons; and, last, pencils (Charlesworth, 2007). Hand dominance, which usually develops between 1 and 2 years of age, may not develop fully until around age 7.

Writing is a purposeful part of children's everyday life. It is a versatile tool for maintaining personal relations, creating imaginary worlds, sharing information, influencing others, and learning (Graham, Gillespie, & McKeown, 2013). Many educators have described the stages that students move through as they progress toward formal writing (e.g., Baghban, 2007b; Schickedanz & Casbergue, 2009). As primary-grade students move into the "standard spelling" phase of writing, they spell most words correctly and develop an understanding of root words, compound words, and contractions (Gentry, 2008). They may move back and forth between writing stages and may initially use drawing, along with writing, as inspiration for producing longer, more complex stories (Baghban, 2007b).

During the primary years, students also are developing a set of skills that help them write for a variety of purposes. They are taught to use six writing traits to compose pieces that convey precisely what they intended: main message, organization of the piece, diction, voice, conventions, and sentence fluency (Education Northwest, n.d.).

Teachers play a critical role in furthering children's writing development (Graham et al., 2013). The substantive quality of children's writing (i.e., ideas, organization, word choice, and sentence flow) is related to teachers' responsiveness during writing experiences (Kim, Otaiba, Sidler, & Gruelich, 2013). It is vital for students to see that their writing is important and worthwhile (Calkins, 2001). Research underscores the importance of providing a classroom environment where students are supported to write frequently and for a variety of purposes (Graham et al., 2013). Conventions of writing should be taught within the context of a student's own writing, rather than in isolation (Ehrenworth & Vinton 2005).

Objective 19 Demonstrates writing skills

a. Writes name

Not Yet	1	2	3	4	5	6	7	8	9	10	11	12	13	14	15
		Makes scribbles or marks • Scribble writes deliberately • Makes marks that appear to adults to be in random order		**Makes controlled linear scribbles** • Scribbles lines, circles, or zigzags in rows • Often repeats action and forms		**Writes mock letters or letter-like forms** • Writes segments of letter forms, e.g., lines, curves • May use too many segments to create a letter, e.g., five horizontal lines on the letter *E* • May not orient letter segments correctly		**Writes letter strings** • Writes some letters correctly • Writes letters in unconventional order		**Writes partially accurate first name** • Writes all the letters of own name, although some may not be sequenced correctly • Writes all the letters of own name, but some of the letters are not formed or oriented correctly		**Writes accurate first name** • Writes all the letters of own name in the correct sequence, form, and orientation • Uses uppercase or lowercase letters (or a combination of both) when writing name		**Writes accurate first and last name**	
		Carolyn		Lilly		Paula		Emma		Vicky		Brooke		Abraham	

Objective 19 Demonstrates writing skills

b. Writes to convey ideas and information

Not Yet	1	2	3	4	5	6	7	8	9	10	11	12	13	14	15	16	17	18	19
		Uses drawing, dictation, and scribbles or marks to convey a message • Scribble-writes deliberately • Makes marks that appear to adults to be in random order		**Uses drawing, dictation, and controlled linear scribbles to convey a message** • Scribbles lines, circles, or zigzags in rows • Often repeats action and forms		**Uses drawing, dictation, and mock letters or letter forms to convey a message** • Writes segments of letter forms, e.g., lines, curves • May use too many segments to create a letter, e.g., five horizontal lines on the letter *E* • May not orient letter segments correctly		**Uses drawing, dictation, and letter strings to convey a message** • Writes strings of letters • Writes some letters correctly • Writes letters in unconventional order • Begins to separate groups of letters with spaces • May copy environmental print		**Uses drawing, dictation, and early invented spelling to convey a message** • Uses first letter of word to represent whole word • Writes initial and/or final sounds of a word to represent the whole word **Note: In Spanish, early invented spelling may consist primarily of vowels.*		**Produces very simple compositions (narrative, informative/explanatory, and opinion) using writing, drawing, and dictation to supply information about a topic and narrate an event, incorporating feedback from others as needed** • Writes a simple opinion piece about a favorite book, adding suggestions from the teacher • Writes about a visit to a pet store using drawing, writing, and dictation • Adds information to a class poster about chicks after reading about them on a science website		**Produces simple compositions (narrative, informative/explanatory, and opinion) to supply information about a topic and narrate a sequence of events that include key components (reasons for opinions, facts, some closure), incorporating feedback from others as needed** • Writes and illustrates a story in her journal about going on a fishing trip; describes the sequence of events, provides basic details, and includes an ending • Writes an informative text about how to care for a pet, including basic facts and an appropriate closure • Composes an opinion piece, "Why We Need Longer Recesses," introducing the topic, stating his opinion, offering a simple rationale, and providing a sense of closure • Works with others to create research project about trees		**Produces longer, more detailed compositions (narratives, informative/explanatory, and opinion pieces) that have a clear structure (beginning, middle, and conclusion), revising and editing by incorporating feedback from others as needed** • Writes a narrative story that has a clear beginning, middle, and end, and adds an illustration; revises story to focus on topic and corrects punctuation after hearing feedback from classmates • Writes a fantasy story and says, "I can't make this story too scary because it's for the preschool class." • Composes a well-structured report on bees by working with others and reading multiple texts on the topic; includes facts and details about life cycle and habitat		**Produces more complex and lengthy compositions (narratives, informative/explanatory, opinion pieces, and research projects) using vocabulary and sentence structure appropriate to composition type and audiences; plans, revises, and edits writing by incorporating feedback from others as needed; writes over short and extended time frames as appropriate for the task and purpose** • Takes several days to write a "chapter book" about school to share at kindergarten orientation • Composes an article, a poem, and a cartoon to include in the school newspaper, incorporating feedback from classmates • Uses multimedia writing tools to create a nonfiction text based on information gathered online, including text, pictures, and diagrams; says, "I have to think and write quickly because this is due soon."	

Objective 19 Demonstrates writing skills

c. Writes using conventions

Not Yet	1	2	3	4	5	6	7	8	9
		Prints many upper- and lowercase letters; writes a letter or combination of letters for most consonants and short vowel sounds; uses basic capitalization (first word in a sentence and the pronoun "*I*"); writes simple words phonetically based on knowledge of sound-letter relationships • Makes an alphabet chart, including pictures and both upper- and lowercase letters • Starts a sentence with an uppercase "I" when writing in a journal • Uses phonetic spelling to label the buildings created in the Block area		**Prints all upper- and lowercase letters; uses basic capitalization and punctuation; spells using learned spelling, phonemic awareness, and spelling conventions; makes simple edits to drafts** • Uses capitals for names of people and dates; uses commas for words in series and dates; applies appropriate ending punctuation • Says, "I need to make a few edits so everyone can read my story."		**Uses capitalization and punctuation with increasing accuracy; spells using learned spelling, phonemic awareness, word families, and basic affixes and syllable patterns; makes edits using suggestions from others or after proofreading** • Uses capitals when writing about holidays, branded products, and geographic names; uses commas in letter greetings and closings; uses apostrophes for word contractions and to indicate common possessives • Makes edits using writing software		**Uses increasingly complex capitalization and punctuation; spells most words accurately or with a close approximation; clarifies and edits own writing during and after composing to create a fairly polished final draft** • Capitalizes appropriate words in titles, uses commas when writing addresses, and adds quotation marks as needed • Edits as she writes and then proofreads and makes final changes	

Objective 19 Demonstrates writing skills

Strategies

- Provide ample time, materials, and space for children to write throughout the day. Offer unlined and lined paper of different sizes and shapes, pencils of various sizes, crayons, markers, and white boards, magic slate, and other writing supplies.
- Provide specific opportunities to write outdoors. For example, write letters in the dirt or sand with fingers or small sticks or write on the sidewalk with chalk or water. Encourage children to make meaningful signs to use during outdoor activities, e.g., "STOP" or "detour" for a puddle of water.
- Include activities that give children reasons to write their names. For example, they may write their names on drawings, letters, greeting cards, sign-up sheets for a popular activity, or attendance sheets upon arrival each day.
- Provide accurate models of children's names. Print clearly using upper- and lowercase letters. Make names available for children to use as resources as they write.
- Plan specific activities that focus on writing. For example, with older children you might write the story of the day on chart paper.
- Model writing with children. Talk about what you are doing as you write. For example, you might say, "I'm making a sign to let people know the toilet is out of order." As you write "Out of order," say each word slowly and spell it. Call attention to each phoneme by saying the sound aloud as you write the letter(s).
- Encourage children to write words that are important to them as they create drawings, messages, greeting cards, lists, signs, menus, or books.
- Support the writing efforts of children. Say words slowly, emphasizing each sound so children can write the sounds they hear. Talk about directionality and letter shapes as you form the letters.
- Provide opportunities for children to write their own books using their own illustrations or photos. Provide word banks of common words for children to refer to as they work.

Mathematics

Children slowly construct informal mathematical knowledge, beginning in the first few months of life. First-hand exploration is important for learning mathematics. As infants, children begin to use their everyday experiences to construct a variety of fundamental mathematical concepts and strategies. The knowledge children acquire informally provides the foundation for the concepts and skills that they later learn formally in school. Through the essential process skills of problem solving, reasoning, communicating, making connections, and representing, children learn mathematics content (Copley, 2000; Geist, 2009).

Research has made a clear link between early math skills and later school reading and math achievement. An analysis of six longitudinal studies showed that early math skills have the greatest predictive power, followed by reading and then attention skills (Duncan et. al., 2007). Children's knowledge at kindergarten entry is considered predictive of future mathematics success throughout their years in school. Evidence shows that high-quality early childhood education programs can make a difference in children's mathematical learning (Clements & Sarama, 2009).

Regardless of social class, culture, or disability, most children develop mathematical skills. However, there are gaps in some children's informal knowledge that make it difficult for them to understand school mathematics (Benigno & Ellis, 2004; Klein & Starkey, 2004).

Language plays a central role in teaching and learning mathematics. For a child with a disability, the environment or materials may need to be adapted, routines adjusted, or an activity modified. The teacher's role is to determine what special supports a child needs to participate fully (Copley, Jones, & Dighe, 2007).

Adults play a significant role in helping children learn mathematical vocabulary, concepts, and process skills. If children are to develop the knowledge needed for later formal learning, they need frequent practice with materials in play settings and adult-guided activities that include meaningful discussions and applications (Varol & Farran, 2006).

MATHEMATICS OBJECTIVES

20 Uses number concepts and operations

21 Explores and describes spatial relationships and shapes

22 Compares and measures

23 Demonstrates knowledge of patterns

"More so than in other subject areas, mathematics is a sequential discipline in which earlier understandings provide an essential foundation on which later skills and concepts build" (Tomlinson, 2009). Children who enter first grade with mathematical learning gaps or those who struggle with mathematics in first grade will likely continue to have problems unless steps are taken to help them to be successful (Baroody, Lai, & Mix, 2006; Clements & Sarama, 2009). One of the major sources of learning difficulties is disconnected formal instruction that does not build on children's existing knowledge or strengths (Baroody et al., 2006; Geary et al., 2009).

Early identification is key for learners who struggle with mathematics (Baroody et al., 2006; Jordan, 2007), and identifying children's procedural and conceptual knowledge is important for understanding their mathematical development (Canobi, 2004; Siegler et al., 2010) and for planning appropriate instruction. Helping children understand the overarching, connected concepts of mathematics (the "big ideas") can assist them in solving applied mathematics problems presented in various contexts (Baroody et al., 2006; Clements & Sarama, 2009; Cross, Woods, & Schweingruber, 2009). Appropriate technology integrated into everyday classroom experiences can be an important tool in enhancing mathematics instruction for young children (Clements, 2004b; Linder, 2012).

Objective 20

Uses number concepts and operations

20

Children's understanding of counting, number symbols, and number operations is fundamental to their success with more complex mathematics (Ginsburg & Baroody, 2003; Zur & Gelman, 2004). When an infant signs more to request another bite of applesauce, a young child proudly announces, "I 2 years old," and a preschool child counts out 18 napkins at snack time, they are using number concepts and operations. Teachers play a critical role in helping children develop an understanding of number concepts and operations through intentional teaching during planned activities and daily routines.

To count well, children must learn: 1) the verbal number sequence; 2) one-to-one correspondence, i.e., that one number name is matched to a single object in a set being counted; and 3) cardinality, i.e., that the last number named when counting objects tells how many. Children can look at a small group of objects and identify the quantity without counting, e.g., counters or domino patterns. This is subitizing. From this children explore concepts of more and less, how many, and parts and wholes (Clements & Sarama, 2009). As they learn to discuss mathematical ideas, they learn ordinal counting: how to indicate the position of something in a sequence, e.g., first, second, third, and so forth. Over time children develop strategies such as counting on from a quantity (rather than beginning at one), counting back, or counting by groups (skip counting), e.g., by 2s, 5s, or 10s.

Through everyday experiences and planned learning activities, young children begin to construct understandings about the number operations of separating (subtracting) and combining (adding). Taking away is a common separating operation that makes a collection smaller and answers the question "How many are left?" Children can often solve subtraction problems before they can solve addition problems (Copley & Hawkins, 2005). Addition problems involve combining sets of objects to find out "How many in all?" Young children typically use fingers or other objects to solve problems involving combining or separating, (Baroody, 2004). Physical objects that are directly related to the problems being solved are best (Clements & Sarama, 2009).

In the primary years, learning a variety of mental math strategies such as counting on and making 10 gives students the skills they need to develop their own strategies and solve more complex math equations. Many kindergarten students begin to invent and use mental strategies for single-digit addition, such as beginning with the larger addend and counting on from there (Baroody, 1987a). Students' use of invented strategies for multidigit addition and subtraction in the primary grades has been found to enhance their understanding of base-ten number concepts (Carpenter, Frank, Jacobs, Fennema, & Empson, 1998).

Objective 20 Uses number concepts and operations

Young children also must learn to connect quantities with their written number symbols, or numerals. Displaying numerals with representations of their quantities helps children associate the amount with the numeral (Copley, 2000; Payne & Huinker, 1993). Before children can connect quantities with numerals they must develop a mental image of each numeral and its spoken name. Children sometimes confuse numerals that are similar in appearance, e.g., 2 and 5, and 6 and 9. Numerals that are easily confused should be taught side by side so the teacher can point out how they differ (Baroody, 1987b). Some children benefit from handling three-dimensional numerals with textured surfaces (Charlesworth, 2005).

Number sense early in first grade has been found to be related to later first- and third-grade mathematics achievement (Jordan, Glutting, & Ramineni, 2010). Throughout the primary grades, students' number and operation sense becomes much more complex (Witzel, Ferguson, & Mink, 2012). Their informal mathematical knowledge helps them transition to formal mathematical understandings (Purpura, Baroody, & Lonigan, 2013) that involve representing number in various ways, including fractions, place value, number operations, and mathematical equations. It is important for students to be presented with numerous and varied examples and to hear and use less common comparative terms used to measure quantities with numbers (Cross et al., 2009).

As with younger children, math should be meaningful and connect to children's daily lives and background knowledge (Burton, 2012). Teachers should encourage students to collaborate with peers, to express their understandings through various means of representation (Whitin & Piwko, 2012), to use invented strategies (Carpenter, Franke, Jacobs, Fennema, & Empson, 1998), and to discuss and reason about their understandings (Baroody, Lai, & Mix, 2006; Carpenter et al., 1998). Further, students should be presented with a variety of problem types and use relational thinking (Jacobs, Franke, Carpenter, Levi, & Battey, 2007) as they explore mathematical equivalence situations in different problem formats (McNeil, Fyfe, Petersen, Dunwiddie, & Brletic-Shipley, 2011). Conceptual understandings that undergird mathematical processes are essential so that students do not simply memorize facts without the ability to generalize and apply their understandings in new situations and in different contexts (Baroody et al., 2006; Carpenter et al., 1998; Siegler et al., 2010; Witzel et al, 2012). Along with a deep understanding, much meaningful practice is required to develop the fluency students need to support adaptive, flexible performance (Cross et al., 2009).

Objective 20 Uses number concepts and operations

a. Counts

Not Yet	1	2	3	4	5	6	7	8	9	10	11	12	13	14	15
		Verbally counts (not always in the correct order) • Says, "One, two, ten," as she pretends to count		**Verbally counts to 10; counts up to five objects accurately, using one number name for each object** • Counts to 10 when playing "Hide and Seek" • Counts out four scissors and puts them at the table		**Verbally counts to 20; counts 10–20 objects accurately; knows the last number states how many in all; tells what number (1–10) comes next in order by counting** • Counts to 20 while walking across room • Counts 10 plastic worms and says, "I have 10 worms." • When asked, "What comes after six?" says, "One, two, three, four, five, six, seven...seven."		**Uses number names while counting to 100 by 1s and 10s; counts 30 objects accurately; tells what number comes before and after a specified number up to 20** • Counts 28 steps to the cafeteria • When asked what comes after 15, says, "Sixteen. That's one larger, and 17 is one larger than 16." • When asked what comes after 16, says, "Seventeen" without beginning at one		**Counts to 120 to determine how many; uses skip counting by 2s, 5s, and 10s; begins counting forward at any number between 1 and 120; counts backward from 20** • Says, "I can count to 50 really fast: 10, 20, 30, 40, 50!" • Accurately counts from 115 to 120 beginning at 115 when asked to do so		**Counts to 1,000 to determine how many; uses skip counting (2s, 5s, 10s, and 100s); begins counting at any number between 1 and 1,000; switches between skip counts** • Counts to 1,000 by 100s: "100, 200, 300...700, 800, 900, 1,000!" • When asked to count to 200, begins counting by 2s but then changes to counting by 10s when she realizes it is taking too long		**Counts to more than 1,000 using number word patterns (e.g., tens, teens) and skip counting; uses skip counting by 2s, 4s, 5s, 6s, 10s, and 100s** • Begins counting, "999, 1,000, 1,110, 1,120, 1,130...1,180, 1,190, 2,000." • Groups objects into sets of four and then counts them: "Four, eight, twelve, sixteen, twenty, twenty-four, twenty-eight, thirty-two...."	

Objective 20 Uses number concepts and operations

b. Quantifies

Not Yet	1	2	3	4	5	6	7	8	9	10	11	12	13	14	15
		Demonstrates understanding of the concepts of *one*, *two*, and *more* • Says, "More apple," to indicate he wants more pieces than given • Takes two crackers when prompted, "Take two crackers."		**Recognizes and names the number of items in a small set (up to five) instantly; combines and separates up to five objects and describes the parts** • Looks at the sand table and says instantly, without counting, "There are three children at the table." • Says, "I have four cubes. Two are red, and two are blue." • Puts three bunnies in the box with the two bears. Counts and says, "Now I have five."		**Makes sets of 6–10 objects and then describes the parts; identifies which part has more, less, or the same (equal); counts all or counts on to find out how many** • Says, "I have nine cars in a row. I only need one more to get to 10!" • Says, "I have eight big buttons, and you have eight little buttons. We have the same." • Tosses 10 puff balls at the hoop. When three land outside, says, "More went inside." • Puts two dominoes together, says, "Five dots," and counts on: "Six, seven, eight. Eight dots all together."		**Solves simple equal share problems; makes sets of 11–20 objects and then describes the parts** • Cuts a banana in half and says to a friend, "Now, we each have a fair share because we each have the same." • Uses two-sided counters to determine different number combinations for 14 • Counts the students in the circle, and says, "There were 12 of us from Mrs. Holt's class, and four more kids came. That means there are 13, 14, 15, 16 of us playing dodge ball."		**Answers *how much* questions about wholes partitioned into equal-size shares of two and four; verbally labels each part and describes its relationship to the whole** • Cuts a paper pizza into two equal parts; gives one part to a friend and says, "We have equal amounts. We each have half of the pizza." • Divides a clay length into four equal parts when asked by the teacher to make fourths Signs, "It's three fourths" when asked what three pieces of the whole represent		**Answers *how much* questions about wholes partitioned into equal shares of two (halves), four (fourths), and three (thirds); verbally labels each part and describes its relationship to the whole** • Divides a rectangle into two rows and two columns of equal size; colors in one part when asked to represent one fourth, colors in another part to show one half • Says, "When I put these four quarter pieces together, I have one whole. Four fourths equal a whole." • Provides the correct response when the teacher shows pictures representing two thirds, two fourths, one half, etc.		**Compares fractions and explains them using physical models, pictorial representations, and number lines** • Partitions the space on a number line from 0 to 1 into six equal parts Puts a red dot to indicate 4/6, a green dot to indicate 2/6, and a blue dot to indicate a whole. Signs, "That's six sixths." • Given a plate divided into eighths, shows one piece for 1/8, three pieces for 3/8, and four pieces for 4/8. Then says, "Hey, these 4/8 are equal to one half because they are the same size!"	

Objective 20 Uses number concepts and operations

c. Connects numerals with their quantities

Not Yet	1	2	3	4	5	6	7	8	9	10	11	12	13	14	15
		Recognizes and names a few numerals • Points to the 1 when the teacher says, "Where is the numeral 1?" • Notices numerals around the room and calls some of them by name		**Identifies numerals to 5 by name and connects each to counted objects** • Says, "Five" as she attaches five clothespins to the 5 card • Tells her friend, "That's a 3, and there are three puppies on this page."		**Identifies numerals to 10 by name and connects each to counted objects** • Shouts, "Seven," and jumps seven times when the teacher holds up the number 7 card • Says, "I put nine buttons in the 9 box."		**Identifies numerals to 20 by name and connects each to counted objects; represents *how many* by writing one-digit numerals and some two-digit numerals** • Says, "I drew 15 flowers to go on page 15 of our number book." • Types in the numerals *1*, *8*, and *3* when sets of one, eight, and three figures appear on the computer screen • Counts out 16 bears and writes *16* on its corresponding card		**Represents *how many* by writing one-, two-, and three-digit numerals to 120; uses relational symbols (<, >, =) to indicate relationships between whole numbers** • Counts out 63 crayons, writes *63*, and signs, "I have 63 crayons." • Writes *118* when the teacher says, "There are 118 marbles in this jar. Write the number of marbles as a numeral." • Indicates the appropriate relational symbol when the teacher writes number pairs (e.g., 3 _ 7, 4 _ 4, 95 _ 77)		**Represents *how many* by writing one-, two-, three-, and four-digit numerals to 1,000; uses relational symbols to compare and order whole numbers** • Counts the grouped pictures on the computer screen and types *384* to indicate *how many* • Writes *276 > 249*, *248 > 100*		**Represents fractional quantities as parts of a whole (a/2, a/3, a/4, a/6, a/8); uses relation symbols (<, >, =) to show fractional comparisons** • Indicates 1/8 when the teacher holds up one part of a region partitioned into eight equal pieces; indicates 8/8 to represent the whole • Colors in two sixths of a paper pie and writes *2/6* to indicate the amount eaten • Looks at the number line, and says, "Two fourths is the same as one half," and then writes in words and symbols, *two fourths is equal to one half*; *2/4 = 1/2* • Compares two number lines with unequal partitions and indicates that 2/6 of one is smaller than 2/4 of the other	

Objective 20 Uses number concepts and operations

d. Understands and uses place value and base ten

Not Yet	1	2	3	4	5	6	7	8	9
		Indicates base-ten equivalents for numbers 11–19 using objects and drawings; may use simple equations • Snaps cubes into one group of ten and seven ones and says, "I made one ten and seven ones. That's 17." • Draws 10 dots enclosed in a circle (one ten) and nine single dots (nine ones) when the teacher says, "Make 19 using tens and ones." • Counts out groups of 11–19 objects and tells how many tens and how many ones are in each group		**Uses place-value understanding to represent and write two-digit numbers, add one- and two-digit numbers (within 100), and subtract multiples of 10 from multiples of 10 (10–90)** • Accurately responds when asked, "What does the numeral 1 stand for when I write *13*? What does it stand for when I write *31*?" • Says, "Fifty-four is the same as five tens and four ones. Forty-five is four tens and five ones. Fifty-four is bigger because it has more tens." • Working with a classmate, combines her six tens and five ones with his two tens and seven ones. As she writes *92*, says, "Now we have eight tens and twelve ones. We can trade in ten ones to make another ten. Now we have nine tens and two ones."		**Uses place-value understanding to represent and write three-digit numbers (including expanded form); adds up to four two-digit numbers; adds and subtracts three-digit numbers (within 1,000)** • Takes bundles of tens and puts together 10 of them. Says, "This bundle is 100. I can write *100* to stand for one hundred, zero tens, and zero ones." • Types *267 = 200 + 60 + 7* (expanded form) • Looks at the numeral 723 and says, "That's the same as seven hundreds, two tens, and three ones; and three ones, two tens, and seven hundreds. If I add another hundred, it's 823." • Calculates and explains 24 + 32 + 16 by recomposing the ones into one ten and two ones (carrying)		**Uses place-value understanding to represent and write four-digit numbers; multiplies one-digit whole numbers by 10s (10–90); rounds three-digit whole numbers to the nearest ten or hundred** • Correctly fills in the missing numbers: 1,000 = 1,000 ones 1,000 = 100 tens 1,000 = 10 hundreds • Writes *5 x 10 = 50* when asked to solve the problem, "If you had five groups of 10, how many would you have? • Writes *230* when asked to round 228 to the nearest ten; writes *700* when asked to round 657 to the nearest hundred	

Objective 20 Uses number concepts and operations

e. Applies properties of mathematical operations and relationships

Not Yet	1	2	3	4	5	6	7	8	9
		Solves addition and subtraction word problems of whole numbers within 10 using a variety of strategies (counting objects or fingers, counting on, counting back); makes number pairs within 10 • Uses counters to represent the problem, "Kalinda had six crayons. She shared two with Sam. How many crayons does Kalinda have left?" • Draws seven flowers and then draws two more, and says, "Now I have nine. Seven plus two more equals nine." • Plays the "Spill the Six Beans" game and records the number combinations 6 = 2 (red sides) + 4 (white sides); 6 = 5 (white sides) + 1 (red side)		**Solves three-number word problems with answers within 20 using addition properties (associative, commutative, and additive); solves addition and subtraction equations of different types with unknowns in various positions for amounts up to 20** • Solves the problem using drawings, "Grady had three marbles and then he bought some more. Now he has 12 marbles. How many more marbles did he buy?" • Demonstrates an understanding of the commutative property of addition by saying, "I know that 8 + 5 = 13 because 5 + 8 = 13." • Accurately completes the equation 7 + __ = 11; checks the answer using counting chips • Plays the "True or False?" game, accurately identifying addition and subtraction equations within 20 as true or false (e.g., 7 = 5 – 2; 19 = 19; 18 = 19 – 1)		**Solves one- and two-step word problems of various types using addition and subtraction (within 100) and explains strategies; uses repeated addition to find the number of objects presented in rectangular arrays (up to five rows and five columns)** • Counts and records the number of markers at each table; adds the numbers together and then subtracts the dried-out markers from the total • Solves the word problem, "The bookshelf is 30 inches wide. The books already on it take up 10 inches of the space. How much space is left to put other books on the shelf?" • Makes four rows of five cubes each and writes *5 + 5 + 5 + 5 = 20* to represent the arrangement and sum of the equal addends		**Solves, represents, and explains two-step word problems of various types (equal-sized groups, arrays, measurement quantities) using properties of whole number operations and multiplication/division inverse relationships; uses estimation strategies (mental number line, rounding) to determine if answers are reasonable** • Solves multiplication problems using the commutative property of multiplication ($a \times b = b \times a$) and the associative property of multiplication ($[a \times b] \times c = a \times [b \times c]$) • Correctly writes the equation for and solves the word problem, "Rudy has 20 inches of yarn. How long must he cut each piece if he gives five friends equal lengths?" ($20 \div 5 = n$) • When shown six groups of eight stars, writes the equation 6 x 8 = 48	

Objective 20 Uses number concepts and operations

f. Applies number combinations and mental number strategies in mathematical operations

Not Yet	1	2	3	4	5	6	7	8	9
		Adds and subtracts whole numbers fluently within five • Adds numbers within five quickly as they appear on the whiteboard • Plays *Spills the Beans* (using five beans) and rapidly adds the number of black beans and white beans to get a total number		**Adds and subtracts whole numbers fluently within 10 using mental strategies (counting on, making ten, decomposing/recomposing, addition/subtraction relationship, and easier equivalent known sums)** • Responds readily to "say it fast" (to 10) challenges (e.g., 2 + 8 = __; 9 – 2 = __; 7 + 3 = __) • Uses decomposing and recomposing as he states, "Figuring out 4 + 5 is easy because I can use a doubles plus one. It is 4 + 4 = 8 and 1 more is 9."		**Adds and subtracts whole numbers fluently within 20 using previously learned mental strategies; knows all the addition combinations of two, one-digit numbers from memory** • Tosses three dice and quickly adds the numbers by counting on • Uses known one-digit sums to add the number of steps to move forward in a board game		**Adds and subtracts whole numbers fluently within 1,000; multiplies and divides whole numbers fluently within 100 using previously learned mental strategies, the relationships between addition/subtraction and multiplication/division, and algorithms based on place value; identifies the products of all one-digit numbers from memory** • Uses fluent knowledge of multiplication and addition to determine the total number of wheels on the cars that pass the play yard • States, "If 7 x 9 = 63, then 63 ÷ 9 = 7," and proceeds to show thoughts using a grouping illustration	

Objective 20 Uses number concepts and operations

Strategies

- Provide a variety of materials to help children develop an understanding of quantity. Offer buttons, bottle caps, keys, sticks, beans, cubes, counting bears, and other materials for children to count and compare. Model comparison vocabulary. Use words like *more*, *most*, *less*, *fewer*, *least*, *same as*, or *equal*.
- Recite fingerplays or rhymes and sing songs about numbers. Read stories that include numerals and items to count.
- Observe children to determine their counting skills. For those just beginning to count, display a few identical items in a straight line. As children gain skills, change the arrangement of objects. Gradually add more and varied objects to count.
- Use everyday activities as opportunities to count. Talk aloud as you count to solve problems. For example, you might say, "I wonder how many glue sticks we need to put out so everyone at the table has one. Let's count the children to find out."
- Model counting strategies. Touch or point to each object as you count slowly, saying the number name. Show how to keep track of the objects counted. For example, you might physically move the objects toward you as you count each one. Count on from an amount, e.g., "How much is four and three more? Four...five, six, seven. Seven."
- Practice counting in ways that involve multiple learning styles and representations. Involve the senses as children touch, hear the spoken number, see the numeral, or physically move their bodies.
- Include materials and activities that associate numerals with sets.
- Use everyday situations to illustrate combining and separating. For example, when a child leaves the Dramatic Play area, you might say, "We had three children in the Dramatic Play area. Tommy went to play in the Block area. How many children are left?"
- Encourage children to tell *how many* stories. For example, they might tell how many children are on the climber or how many markers they have after a friend gave them more or put some away.
- Provide various materials for children to make number combinations. For example, use colored counters to make combinations for the numeral 4 (e.g., one red bear, three green bears; two blue bears and two yellow bears, or four bears of the same color).

Objective 21

Explores and describes spatial relationships and shapes

21

Understanding spatial relationships and shapes helps children build the foundation for understanding geometry. Spatial awareness, how objects are oriented in relation to one another, develops as children begin to explore the relationship between their bodies and the things around them. As they learn to navigate their environment, they learn about direction, perspective, distance, symbolization, and location. The awareness of spatial relationships develops as infants see faces from different positions and perspectives. Toddlers try to fit their bodies into boxes of different sizes. Preschool children walk around block structures to see which sides they want to draw, and kindergarten children attempt to give directions to particular locations. Children who have a strong spatial sense do better in mathematics (Clements, 2004).

Positional words describe spatial relationships and help children deepen their understanding of those relationships. Directional words describe *which way*, e.g., up, down, forward, and backward. Distance words tell *how far*, e.g., near, far, and close. Location words specify *where*, e.g., on, off, under, and over. Children from a variety of cultures generally understand the spatial terms of *in*, *on*, and *under* before they understand *next to* or *by* (Plumert & Hawkins, 2001).

Young children explore two- and three-dimensional shapes long before they can name and describe them. In addition to square, rectangle, triangle, and circle, preschool children can learn the three-dimensional shapes of cube ("like a box"), rectangular prism ("like a box"), cylinder ("like a can"), and sphere ("like a ball") (Copley, Jones, & Dighe, 2007). Typically, young children form a visual prototype that they use to classify shapes by their overall appearance (Clements, 2004). For example, they say that a triangle is a triangle because it "looks like one" (Van Hiele, 1986). It is important to provide a wide variety of models of each shape so that children do not perceive that a particular shape looks only one way, e.g., think all triangles must have a point on top in the middle (Clements, Battista, & Sarama, 2001). Many types of squares and rectangles should be presented to help children understand that a square is a special type of rectangle. Double-naming, as in *square-rectangle*, may be helpful (Clements & Sarama, 2009). Shapes should be rotated into different positions (e.g., on their sides or upside down), and examples should be provided for comparison (Charlesworth, 2005).

Children do not develop their ideas about shapes by simply looking at them. They need to manipulate, draw, compare, describe, sort, and represent the shapes in a variety of ways (Charlesworth, 2005; Clements, 1999). Infants, toddlers, and twos explore shapes as they fit a circle into the matching hole on a shape sorter; work shape puzzles; and blow bubbles outdoors, saying "Lots of balls!" Older preschool and kindergarten children can combine shapes to produce composite shapes, e.g., using two triangles to produce a square (Clements, Wilson, & Sarama, 2004). This is an important process that helps children understand and analyze shape (Clements, 2004).

Objective 21 Explores and describes spatial relationships and shapes

Primary-grade students' understandings of spatial relationships (Clements, 2004a; Clements & Sarama, 2009) and shapes differ from those of younger children and adults (Sera & Millett, 2011). They rely more on the essential attributes of different shapes than they did previously, with categorical understanding of some shapes, such as circles, emerging before those of others shapes, such as triangles and pentagons (Cross et al., 2009). Knowledge of abstract properties of and knowledge of shape naming may play an important role in the development of shape perception and children's ability to ignore certain irrelevant aspects of shape similarity (Sera & Mullett, 2011). Opportunities to move, subdivide, and combine shapes can enhance children's spatial thinking and the formation of spatial-numeric connections needed to develop the background for measurement (Tomlinson, 2009), solve geometric problems, and use array models for multidigit multiplication (Clements, Battista, Sarama, & Swaminathan, 1997).

Objective 21 Explores and describes spatial relationships and shapes

a. Understands spatial relationships

Not Yet	1	2	3	4	5	6	7	8	9
		Follows simple directions related to position *(in, on, under, up, down)* • Follows teacher's directions to put the trash *in* the can • Raises hands *up* and *down* as the song directs		**Follows simple directions related to proximity (*beside, between, next to*)** • Follows teacher's direction to put the cup *next to* the plate • Sits beside her friend when he says, "Sit *between* me and Laura."		**Uses and responds appropriately to positional words indicating location, direction, and distance** • Says, "Look for the surprise *behind* the tree." • Moves game piece *backward* when playmate gives directions		**Uses and makes simple sketches, models, or pictorial maps to locate objects** • Constructs a map of the play yard using landscape toys • Uses a map of the classroom to find the hidden treasure	

Objective 21 Explores and describes spatial relationships and shapes

b. Understands shapes

Not Yet	1	2	3	4	5	6	7	8	9	10	11	12	13	14	15
		Matches two identical shapes • Puts a circular puzzle piece in the circular space • Places shapes in a shape-sorting box		**Identifies a few basic shapes (circle, square, triangle)** • Looks at a wheel and says, "A circle." • Names shape pieces as he puts them on a shape lotto card		**Describes basic two- and three-dimensional shapes by using own words; recognizes basic shapes when they are presented in a new orientation** • Says, "It's a ball 'cause it rolls." • Puts hand in feely box and says, "It has three sides and three points. It's a triangle."		**Shows that shapes remain the same when they are moved, turned, flipped, or slid; breaks apart or combines shapes to create different shapes and sizes** • Says, "It's still a triangle no matter how I turn it." • Cuts apart a rectangle to make two squares and says, "Both of these squares have four sides."		**Distinguishes essential attributes of triangles, rectangles, squares, trapezoids, half circles, and quarter circles; visualizes and creates known shapes** • Recognizes cardboard shapes in the feely bag by touch, describes their defining characteristics, and asks others to guess the shape • When asked to make a square, quickly puts together two right triangles		**Uses essential attributes to label and create quadrilaterals, pentagons, hexagons, and cubes; visualizes and predicts the results of combining and taking apart two-dimensional and three-dimensional shapes** • Using a geoboard, creates a "mystery shape" (pentagon) by following teacher's verbal directions; when complete, indicates the shape is a pentagon and tells why • Tells friend, "I think it will make a hexagon if I put these six triangles together. Let's try it and see. Hey, it works! Now let's see what shape it makes if I add six more triangles, one on each side."		**Classifies known shapes into higher and subordinate categories; provides rationale for classifications; divides shapes into parts with equal areas and expresses the parts as unit fractions** • Uses essential attributes to generate examples and non-examples of known two-dimensional shapes • Creates Venn diagrams that show relationships between different quadrilaterals (e.g., squares, rectangles, rhombuses); explains the classifications • After dividing a rectangular "farm" into three equal parts, says, "The farmer has corn planted in one third of the area of his farm. He likes potatoes the best, so he used two thirds of the area to plant potatoes."	

Objective 21 Explores and describes spatial relationships and shapes

Strategies

- Label shapes with correct names as the children use them. For example, when a child says, "I got a round one," when describing a sphere, you might say, "Yes, it is round. It looks like a ball. It's called a sphere."
- Guide children's explorations of shapes. Discuss the features as children explore. Use the word *not* as you talk about a shape. For example, you might say, "This is *not* a circle because it does not have curved lines."
- Present shapes that differ in size and orientation. For example, so that children will not think that all triangles have equal-length sides, present narrow triangles, wide triangles, and triangles rotated in various positions.
- Encourage children to create new shapes from other shapes. Use computer software that allows children to manipulate shapes and see the results as they move and combine pieces.
- Model and encourage the use of positional words as children climb in, out, on, or through objects. For example, you might say, "Lars crawled *over* the box and *under* the rope. Now he is *in* the tunnel."
- Use maps or other representations with children to help them think spatially. For example, provide a simple map with easily found landmarks and specific clues about the location of the hidden object or photograph classroom materials and activities from different positions. Discuss where in the classroom the materials or activities are located and where you stood to take the photo.
- Encourage children to represent shapes in various ways. For example, they might draw shapes and then recreate them on a geoboard or with tangram pieces.
- Read books that feature positional relationships and encourage children to act out the movements in the story, e.g., *Going on a Bear Hunt* (Helen Oxenbury and Michael Rosen).
- Use shape names and positional words when giving children instructions, e.g., "Billy, can you find the towel with the red squares? I think it's under the round yellow plate.

Objective 22

Compares and measures

22

Young children frequently compare measurement as they interact. They say, "I want so much grapes, not little bit grapes!" "I'm bigger!" or, "Joe has the longest one!" They understand that there are different ways of measuring. They begin to recognize the attributes of *length*, *height*, and *width* (how long, tall, and wide something is), *capacity* (how much something holds), *weight* (how heavy something is), *area* (how much space is covered), and *time* (sequence and duration). Time is a difficult measurement concept for children to learn because it is not a physical attribute of objects. In fact, telling time does not develop well until after kindergarten, but preschool children develop an understanding of the passage of time as they go through predictable daily routines (Geist, 2009).

Children's initial ideas about size, quantity, and seriation involve comparisons related to their play materials and books. They know about the differently sized beds and bowls in *The Three Bears*. Young children experiment first by lining up objects; then they can begin to connect number to length as they use nonstandard measurement tools, e.g., links, blocks, rods (Clements & Sarama, 2009). Experimenting with tools that give different results, e.g., sometimes measuring an object with links and later measuring the same object with rods, is an essential step to understanding why standard tools, e.g., rulers, measuring tape, are important for comparing measurements.

In addition to nonstandard measurement tools, children can benefit from exploring and using tools with uniform units, e.g., rulers and centimeter cubes, as their measurement ideas and skills are developing (Clements, 2003; Sarama & Clements, 2006). Actual measurement involves associating a numeral with an attribute of an object, e.g., "This box is 9 inches long." Understanding how to measure accurately is a skill that takes many years to learn (Mix, Huttenlocher, & Levine, 2002).

During the primary grades, students increase their abilities to make comparisons and learn to measure using a standard unit (Clements, Sarama, & DiBiase, 2004; Clements & Stephan, 2004). They measure time, money, length, volume, mass, and area. However, meaningful measurement is not a set of simple skills, but rather a complex combination of skills and concepts that develop gradually over years (Clements & Stephan, 2004; Fuson, 2004). In measuring length, for example, students need to understand *unit iteration* (not leaving space between consecutive units), *correct alignment* (with the measurement tool), and the *zero-point concept* (point where measurement begins) in addition to counting and appropriate tool selection (Clements & Stephan, 2004).

Students in the primary grades may collect, report, and interpret their measurement findings and other relevant ideas on simple graphs of various types and complexities as they use the information to make comparisons and answer questions (Burton, 2012; Clements, 2004b; Friel, Curcio, & Bright, 2001). As with measurement skills, making sense of graphs is a complex process, and children's graphing abilities develop gradually (Friel et al., 2001). Teachers must observe students as they engage in comparison activities, interpret their understandings, and ask questions of varying degrees of difficulty that will lead students to develop important conceptual knowledge (Burton, 2012; Clements & Stephan, 2004).

Objective 22 Compares and measures

a. Measures objects

Not Yet	1	2	3	4	5	6	7	8	9	10	11	12	13	14	15
		Makes simple comparisons between two objects • Pours sand or water from one container to another • Indicates which ball is bigger when shown a tennis ball and a beach ball		**Compares and orders a small set of objects as appropriate according to size, length, weight, area, or volume** • Puts blocks side by side in order of length • Lays two short blocks on top of a long block to see if it's the same length • Holds a dry sponge and a wet sponge and determines which weighs more		**Uses multiples of the same unit to measure; uses numbers to compare; knows the purpose of standard measuring tools** • Measures by using paper clips, cubes, string, hands, feet or other objects • Measures block tower with linking cubes and says, "I made mine 15 cubes high!" • Stands on scale while pretending to be in a doctor's office		**Uses measurement words and some standard measurement tools accurately** • Says, "We need two cups of flour and one cup of salt to make dough." • Says," If I add three more tiles to this side of the scale, they'll be the same."		**Measures length accurately and expresses the measurement in whole numbers** • Compares the length of several objects using cardboard strips, carefully placing them with no gaps and overlaps • Measures using the meter stick and says, "This is 5 centimeters long."		**Measures and compares the length of two objects using standard length units** • Estimates that the table will fit into a space, but when she measures the space, says, "It won't fit. The table is 1 foot and 3 inches too long."		**Solves one-step word problems related to measurement of liquid volume, mass, area, and perimeter** • Solves the problem, "If Gilberto had 12 liters of water, how many more liters would he need to buy to have 26 liters?" • Uses centimeter grid paper to indicate a 3 by 4 and a 4 by 3 square area; multiplies and says, "The area of both is 12 units because I multiplied one length by the other length." Counts the squares and says, "See, both of them are 12."	

Objective 22 Compares and measures

b. Measures time and money

Not Yet	1	2	3	4	5	6	7	8	9	10	11	12	13
		Knows usual sequence of basic daily events • Says, "We go outside after lunch."		**Relates time to daily routines and schedule** • Says, "I go to auntie's house every morning before school." • Looks at the teacher's watch and asks, "Does it say it's time to go outside?" • Moves the daily schedule marker to the time block that indicates Large Group		**Uses some time measurement words and tools** • Says, "We have music this afternoon at 1:00." • Looks at the clock and begins to put away materials for lunch at noon • Goes to the calendar to see how many more days until the field trip • Notices and asks about the differences between an analog and digital clock		**Tells and writes time in hours and half-hours using both analog and digital clocks; makes amounts using pennies (P), nickels (N), and dimes (D)** • Records the time as the teacher sets the time first on the analog clock and then on the digital clock • Counts four dimes, saying, "Ten, twenty, thirty, forty."		**Tells and writes time to the nearest five minutes; indicates a.m. and p.m.; solves word problems involving coins (P, N, D, Q) and dollar bills, and expresses the answer using currency symbols** • Says and then writes, "I go to bed at 9:15 p.m." • Writes 8:30 a.m. when asked to write the time the opening school bell rings. • Writes the correct answer to the problem, "If you had $4.00, and the book cost $5.50, how much more money would you need?"		**Solves one-step word problems related to time to the nearest minute** • Makes a daily schedule chart by writing the times each activity occurs; compares how long between time periods	

Objective 22 Compares and measures

c. Represents and analyzes data

Not Yet	1	2	3	4	5	6	7	8	9	10	11
		Knows a few ordinal numbers • Responds, "I'm first to use the computer. Then you're next." • Says, "I was first. Justin was last." • Says, "I sat in the biggest chair first, then the middle-size chair and the little chair third. I'm like Goldilocks."		**Creates and reads simple graphs; uses simple comparison and ordinal terms to describe findings** • Looks at a picture graph and says, "Most kids like grapes. It has nine people. Apples are second. Eight kids like apples." • Tallies the number of classmates who have shoelaces on their shoes and the number who have Velcro®		**Organizes, represents, and analyzes data with up to three categories; uses simple numerical summaries (counts, tallies) and ordinal terms to describe findings** • Surveys the class and makes a graph indicating favorite yogurt flavors (vanilla, blueberry, or strawberry) • Reads a simple bar graph and says, "The trucks are first because they have the most; there are 14 trucks. The cars are the second most because there are 13. SUVs are third. There are only 10 of them."		**Organizes, represents, and interprets data with up to four categories; describes data points; asks and answers questions related to the total data set and to its parts** • Measures the length of four objects and creates a four-row horizontal graph to represent the information. Explains what the graph represents; asks and answers questions related to the total data set and its parts • Works with several classmates to make 'snakes' of different lengths using whole-unit cubes. Measures each 'snake' and records the lengths on a number line (line plot). Later, tells the class the lengths referring to the line plot.		**Reads and creates scaled picture or bar graphs where each picture/bar represents more than one data point; uses the graph to ask and answer questions** • Looks at a scaled picture graph (one picture = two persons) and indicates 12 persons in total, 10 of whom ride the train and two of whom drive cars • Creates a bar graph where each bar represents 10 individuals; colors in three bars and says, "There were 30 people who liked cats best and 20 who liked dogs. That's 10 more people who like cats."	

Objective 22 Compares and measures

Strategies

- Take advantage of daily opportunities to talk about comparing and measuring. Extend children's visual comparisons of length, height, weight, and area. For example, when children debate about who found the longest rope or who has the biggest leaf, encourage them to compare by laying them side by side or placing one on top of the other.
- Provide many opportunities for children to measure using non-standard measures. For example, offer plastic snap cubes, plastic chains, paper clips, blocks, paper strips, straws, plastic cups, or large spoons. Encourage children to think of other materials they can use to measure.
- Plan activities that allow children to compare measuring with non-standard and with standard measures. For example, make a small batch of molding dough using cups and spoons from dramatic play. Make another batch using standard measuring cups and spoons. As children compare the products, guide them to discover the advantages of standard measuring tools.
- Encourage children to use measuring tools in their own ways during measurement activities and during dramatic play. Model the conventional use of measuring tools during class activities. Explain tools and methods as you engage in real measurement activities. Use measurement vocabulary to describe the process.
- Offer a variety of standard measuring tools for children to investigate and use. Include rulers, yardsticks, measuring tapes, thermometers, balance scales, measuring cups, and centimeter grid paper.
- Use estimation vocabulary. Use words such as *about*, *approximate*, *nearly*, *almost*, and *close to* in the context of real-life situations. Encourage children to check their estimations by measuring.
- Involve children in using recipes and measuring tools to make their own snacks independently.
- Provide opportunities for children to compare how much something will hold. For example, use a snack-size zip bag and see how many snap cubes, bottle tops, or counting bears it will hold when full. Have children count or use a balance scale to compare and record their results.
- Provide a variety of opportunities for children to use ordinal numbers. For example, during cooking experiences, emphasize ordinal words, e.g., *first, second, third,* etc. Use ordinal numbers when inviting children to recall familiar books and stories.

Demonstrates knowledge of patterns

23

A pattern is a regular arrangement of something, e.g., numbers, objects, shapes, colors, sounds, or movements. Guiding children to understand patterns is a foundational skill in mathematics. As they learn to label patterns by having one name stand for something else, they are creating an algebraic representation. Children begin to identify patterns in their environment at an early age. An infant waves her arms in anticipation as you arrive with her bottle. A toddler repeats a repetitive phrase from a storybook while you read aloud. A preschool child describes a simple pattern on a shirt, "Green stripe, red stripe, green stripe, red stripe." A kindergarten child describes how he counts by using even numbers, "Two, four, six, eight. I skip a number every time."

In *repeating patterns*, the core unit repeats a minimum of five times, e.g., red, blue; red, blue; red, blue; red, blue; red, blue. Children often mistakenly believe that something is a pattern because it is repeated once. Young children can recognize the relationship between repeating patterns that share the same core unit but that are perceptually different, e.g., color and movement, as in a color pattern of red, blue; red, blue; red, blue… and a movement pattern of stomp, clap; stomp, clap; stomp, clap… (Sarama & Clements, 2006).

Growing patterns are more complex than repeating patterns. In growing patterns, the pattern increases by at least plus one and continues to increase. A block staircase is an example of a growing pattern (Copley, 2000). The familiar song, "My Aunt Came Back," also is an example of a growing pattern. Children add one phrase and action to each verse, repeating the previous phrases and actions, until they reach the tenth verse with ten actions and phrases (Copley, Jones, & Dighe, 2007).

The study of patterns is exciting for young children. They first learn to copy simple patterns made with objects. They later learn to extend and create their own patterns (Clements, 2004; Klein & Starkey, 2004). Patterns help children know what comes next and to make predictions about things they cannot yet observe. Exploring patterns helps children understand some basic algebraic ideas. Learning experiences that focus on patterns facilitate children's generalizations about number combinations, counting strategies, and problem solving (Copley, 2000).

Students in the primary grades can use their interest in looking for patterns to find and extend numerical patterns and to devise rules and reasoning strategies to solve mathematical problems (Baroody, Lai, & Mix, 2006; Clements, 2004b). They represent their thinking about patterns in various ways, including talking, gesturing, writing, drawing, using arrows or connecting loops, and making organizing charts (Whitin & Whitin, 2012). As students try to make meaning out of the patterns they notice, it is important that teachers guide them to extend their thinking to include generalizations and formalizations that are characteristic of algebraic thinking (Carpenter & Levi, 2000). Some students may benefit from targeted practice to transition from informal pattern awareness to using patterns to assist them in solving mathematical problems (Cross et al., 2009).

Objective 23 Demonstrates knowledge of patterns

Not Yet	1	2	3	4	5	6	7	8	9	10	11	12	13	14	15
		Shows interest in simple patterns in everyday life • Notices that a special song is played whenever it is time to clean up • Points to the tiles in the bathroom and says, "They go this way, that way, this way, that way."		**Copies simple repeating patterns** • Beats a drum as the teacher does, e.g., loud, soft; loud, soft; loud, soft; etc. • Strings beads as her friend does, e.g., red, blue, blue; red, blue, blue; red, blue, blue; etc.		**Extends and creates simple repeating patterns** • Makes a repeating movement pattern, e.g., stomp, stomp, clap, clap; stomp, stomp, clap, clap; stomp, stomp, clap, clap; etc. • When shown pattern of cubes, e.g., red, blue, blue, red; red, blue, blue, red; etc., adds to it correctly		**Recognizes, creates, and explains more complex repeating and simple growing patterns** • Says, "If I add one to three, it's the next number: four. If I add one to four, it's the next number: five." • Extends the growing pattern by adding one cube like a staircase, e.g., one cube, two cubes, three cubes, four cubes, etc.		**Notices more complex patterns in numbers; identifies the core unit of patterns; represents patterns using numerical and letter symbols** • Says, "I see patterns on the '00 to 99 chart.' All the numbers in the ones place in each column are the same. They go from zero to nine." • Circles every second number on the number line in red and then circles every fifth number in blue; uses the visual patterns to assist in skip counting • Looks at a photo of a gate with a distinct pattern and writes *A-B-B* to represent the core unit pattern of one large fleur-de-lis and two small fleurs-de-lis; continues the pattern notation by writing *A-B-B-A-B-B-A-B-B*		**Uses number patterns to count and to solve problems; uses and explains patterns in counting and addition** • Explains that when you have a group with even numbers of objects, each member has "a partner" or can be paired • Accurately fills in the blanks when presented with 26, 22, 18, ___, 10, ___		**Recognizes arithmetic patterns and explains them using properties of operations** • Says, "Hey, if I add 3 + 3 + 3 + 3, that's the same thing as multiplying 3 x 4. Multiplying is faster." • Explains that when you add zero to any number, the sum is still the same because zero is a place holder representing no amount • Remarks that you can add numbers in any order and the sum remains the same • Notices the relationship between a division problem and figuring out a fair share	

Objective 23 Demonstrates knowledge of patterns

Strategies

- Identify patterns in daily routines. For example, you might say, "Every day we follow the same pattern. After choice time, we have cleanup, then snack, then story."
- Call attention to patterns in the environment. For example, you might say, "Magnus, you have a pattern in your shirt: blue stripe, red stripe; blue stripe, red stripe; blue strip, red stripe..." or "Sai, you made a pattern with your blocks: up, down; up, down; up, down... ."
- Support children as they copy and extend patterns. Begin with simple repeating color patterns. Use objects that are identical except for their color. Progress to shape patterns where objects are the same color, same size, but vary in shape. Continue by using same-colored, same-shaped, but differently sized objects. Encourage children to repeat their patterns at least five times.
- Describe patterns with words, sounds, movements, and objects rather than with letters, which can be confusing to children who are learning letters and their sounds.
- Encourage children to talk about and identify patterns. For example, children can become "pattern detectives" as they describe and represent patterns they identify in the environment. Include their discoveries in a class book titled, *Patterns Discovered by Our Class*.
- Read patterning stories and verses. For example, *Mrs. McTats and Her Houseful of Cats* (Alyssa S. Capucilli), *The Napping House* (Audrey Wood), and *The Relatives Came* (Cynthia Rylant) are books that include patterns that children can act out.
- Encourage childen to compare patterns and to find similarities and differences among them. For example, two patterns may use the same colors, but one is a *yellow, green; yellow, green; yellow, green* pattern and the other is a *yellow, green, green; yellow, green, green; yellow, green, green* pattern.
- Have children create growing patterns using materials such as small cube blocks, stacking cubes, or linking chains. They can represent their patterns through drawings.
- Encourage children to listen to familiar songs to identify the patterns they hear, i.e., repeating words, patterns in tones, etc.

Science and Technology

Science content during early childhood typically focuses on living things (life science), the physical properties of materials and objects (physical science), and Earth's environment and how we care for it (earth science). The best way to learn science is to *do* science through integrated, hands-on, child-centered inquiry (Lind, 1997; 2001). Learning to engage in the process of scientific thinking, gaining understanding and making connections are more important than learning scientific facts at an early age.

Young children are natural investigators. They are curious about how things work and what will happen next (Mantzicopoulos, Patrick, & Samarapungavan, 2008). Hands-on science learning begins in infancy with sensory stimulation that sharpens the infant's observation and discrimination skills. With adults' help and encouragement, this leads to more detailed exploration and discovery (Desouza & Czerniak, 2002). During the preschool and kindergarten years, scientific exploration should focus on naturalistic and informal learning that promotes exploration and discovery through everyday experiences. As children become more systematic in their explorations, their understanding deepens and their ideas come closer to current scientific understanding (Chalufour & Worth, 2004). In elementary school, teachers can continue to build on children's curiosity by emphasizing inquiry in science experiences. At this age, children should be encouraged to observe and ask questions about the natural world and to think about what might happen during various scientific processes. Teachers can provide materials and offer experiences and explanations that teach about important scientific concepts and skills (Copple, 2014).

SCIENCE AND TECHNOLOGY OBJECTIVES

24 Uses scientific inquiry skills

25 Demonstrates knowledge of the characteristics of living things

26 Demonstrates knowledge of the physical properties of objects and materials

27 Demonstrates knowledge of Earth's environment

28 Uses tools and other technology to perform tasks

Young children have many scientific understandings, although they may be incomplete or inaccurate (Eshach & Fried, 2005; Hannust & Kikas, 2007; Nobes et al., 2003; Tenenbaum, Rappolt-Schlichtmann, & Zanger 2004). They can think and talk in complex ways about science topics when they have related knowledge and experience (Gelman & Brenneman, 2004; Peterson & French, 2008). Adult-child conversations can support children's evolving theories of science (Tenenbaum & Callanan, 2008). When children have frequent opportunities to hear and use scientific vocabulary in meaningful contexts, they begin to use scientific words accurately (Gelman & Brenneman, 2004).

Science topics should be appropriate for children's developmental levels so that they do not develop scientific misconceptions or become disinterested. Appropriate, integrated scientific-inquiry activities can help children enjoy and feel competent about learning science (Mantzicopoulos, Patrick, & Samarapungavan, 2008). Some language can hinder children's scientific understanding. For example, saying *dead battery* or *lively music* may cloud children's understanding of living and nonliving things. Exploring which items sink or float is more appropriate than discussing the abstract concepts of buoyancy and density, that is, why things sink and float (Eshach & Fried, 2005; Tenenbaum, Rappolt-Schlichtmann, & Zanger, 2004). Some topics, such as astronomy, are difficult for young children to understand because they involve concepts that cannot be explored firsthand and objects that cannot be touched (Hannust & Kikas, 2007).

Young children need many opportunities to explore science concepts firsthand over time so they can connect new understandings to related experiences. Hurried exposure to disconnected science topics does not provide opportunities for rich conceptual growth (Gelman & Brenneman, 2004). In-depth investigations are an appropriate way for children to learn science content, the basic skills needed to use tools and other technology, and such process skills as observing, comparing, classifying, measuring, and communicating. Collaboration with peers and the guidance of a supportive teacher help children acquire basic science concepts and fundamental inquiry skills. Children, whose science learning and inquiry skills are scaffolded by a teacher's guidance and support, express an increased interest in and a stronger motivation for science learning (Samarapungavan, Patrick, & Mantzicopoulos, 2011).

Uses scientific inquiry skills

24

Scientific inquiry is the *doing* of science (Epstein, 2007). Children use a variety of inquiry skills (observing, predicting, using data, and hypothesizing) as they connect what they know to new experiences (Hapgood, Magnuson, & Sullivan Palincsar, 2004). Inquiry skills include making focused observations, posing meaningful questions, determining what is already known by examining books and other resources, making predictions, selecting appropriate techniques and tools, conducting investigations, reflecting on experiences, and communicating their findings (Chalufour & Worth, 2004; National Committee on Science Education Standards and Assessment, National Research Council, 1996). Adults can help children develop scientific inquiry skills through everyday experiences, like observing worms, and helping them represent their observations in various ways, such as recording in science journals (Brenneman & Louro, 2008). The learning experiences provided for students should engage them with fundamental questions about the world and how scientists have investigated and found answers to those questions (National Research Council [NRC], 2012).

As you create exploratory opportunities and plan experiences for children, think about how each child uses the skills of scientific inquiry. Focus your observations on

HOW AND WHEN THE CHILD

- observes and explores things in the environment
- reacts to changes
- manipulates objects to understand their properties
- connects new observations to what she already knows
- identifies problems, makes predictions, thinks of ways to solve problems, and tries possible solutions
- organizes information
- makes comparisons and classifies
- communicates with others about discoveries
- represents his thinking through drawing, dramatizing, graphing, or making models

Objective 24 Uses scientific inquiry skills

Strategies

- Model focused observation by showing curiosity about things in the environment, observing intently, using multiple senses, and calling attention to details. For example, when children wonder in what part of the tank a fish usually stays, encourage them to observe to find out. Involve the children in making a chart to record their observations.
- Support children as they practice scientific inquiry. Use scientific terms like *observe*, *hypothesize*, *predict*, and *estimate*. Guide children as they revisit and extend their investigations. For example, you might document their inquiry with photographs taken with a digital camera. Help children to think about their experiences, talk about the strategies they used, and analyze and synthesize the information they collected.
- Help children connect new discoveries to what they already know. For example, compare children's drawings before and after a site visit. Ask open-ended questions such as, "How is this magnet like/different from the magnet we used last week?"
- Conduct in-depth investigations with children, using living things, objects, and materials from the local environment. Encourage children to communicate their discoveries in multiple ways. For example, they might draw, dictate, write, take photos, dramatize, make models, or graph their findings. Support children's use of explanatory language as they talk about their discoveries.

Demonstrates knowledge of the characteristics of living things

25

Young children are interested in living things. They are especially interested in the plants and animals in their immediate environment. They want to learn about their habitats and how they grow and change. For example, children in Louisiana may want to learn more about the crawfish they see in the bayous, while children in New Mexico may want to explore the different cactus plants they see growing around them (Dodge, Colker, & Heroman, 2002). No matter what topic of the life sciences children study, they can learn the major concepts as they interact with living things. These interactions and experiences help to enhance children's conceptual understanding of living things. Teachers can help students refine and modify their thinking by helping them make connections between things they know as living or nonliving and asking intentional questions that challenge their logic (Legaspi & Straits, 2011). Through regular contact with nature, children expand their curiosity and observation skills, practice nurturing behaviors as they care for living things, and gain knowledge in other academic areas (Rosenow, 2008; Russo, 2008). The life sciences focus on patterns, processes, and relationships of living organisms. Life scientists use observations, experiments, hypotheses, tests, models, theory, and technology to explore how life works. The study of life ranges over scales from single molecules, through organisms and ecosystems, to the entire biosphere, that is all life on Earth (NRC, 2012).

As you create exploratory opportunities and plan experiences for children related to living things, think about how each child is beginning to understand concepts about living things. Focus your observations on

HOW AND WHEN THE CHILD

- shows a growing ability to classify living and nonliving things
- communicates about the characteristics of living things
- demonstrates understanding that living things grow, change, and reproduce
- shows awareness of life in different environments or habitats
- groups or categorizes living things, e.g., appearance, behavior, plant, or animal
- demonstrates awareness that living things go through a growth cycle

Objective 25 Demonstrates knowledge of the characteristics of living things

Strategies

- Include opportunities for children to care for living things. For example, they might care for a pet fish or grow a small garden in the play yard. Discuss what living things need to grow and stay healthy.
- Provide opportunities for children to observe the life cycle of living things. For example, they might observe the life cycle of a frog and record changes that occur by drawing pictures or taking photographs.
- Sing, recite fingerplays, and read stories about how living things grow and change.
- Go on nature walks to look for worms, ladybugs, roly-polies (pill bugs), grasshoppers, or other living things to observe. Use magnifying glasses to get a better look.
- Use correct terminology when discussing living things. Use words like *germinate*, *sprout*, *bud*, or *stalk* when talking about plants. Use words like *habitat*, *camouflage*, *herbivore*, *antennae*, or *predator* when talking about animals.
- Help children understand animal behavior. After observing and talking about specific behaviors, encourage children to act like their favorite animals. For example, they might dramatize how cats stalk, preen themselves, or play.
- Encourage children to categorize living things. They might group according to appearance, behavior, or whether things are plants or animals. Have children explain their classifications.
- Guide children to look up information on the Internet about the habitats or environments of different animals and to record findings in their science journals.
- Support children to measure and document growth of plants and animals. Help them analyze any changes in growth.
- Help children make connections between living and nonliving things, along with the similarities between humans, animals, and plants, and ask intentional questions to further refine their thinking about living things and the life sciences.
- Allow children the time to reflect upon, refine, and shift their original thoughts on living and nonliving things to a more scientific approach thought process.

Demonstrates knowledge of the physical properties of objects and materials

26

By preschool, children have already begun building scientific knowledge about the physical properties of objects and materials (Gelman & Brenneman, 2004). They learn about physical properties by observing and manipulating common objects and materials. As they use their senses to explore things, they learn about shape, color, texture, weight, temperature, and how things move and change. As teachers talk with children about the properties of objects and materials, children develop vocabulary and important background knowledge. This background knowledge helps children observe their environment more closely. For example, the child who has been exposed to ramps at school may notice the ramps they see elsewhere in the community and talk about them at home and school. Without this exposure, the ramps may have gone unnoticed by the child (Eshach & Fried, 2005). Broad questions like "What is everything made of?" and "Why do things happen?" can be applied to explain and predict a wide variety of phenomena that occur in people's everyday lives, such as the evaporation of a puddle of water, the transmission of sound, the digital storage and transmission of information, the tarnishing of metals, and photosynthesis. And because such explanations and predictions rely on a basic understanding of matter and energy, students' abilities to conceive of the interactions of matter and energy are central to their science education (NRC, 2012).

As you create exploratory opportunities and plan experiences for children, think about how each child explores and learns about objects and materials. Focus your observations on

HOW AND WHEN THE CHILD

- examines, describes, and measures the observable features of objects
- demonstrates understanding that objects are made from one or more materials, e.g., metal, wood, plastic, or paper
- communicates that the physical properties of objects and materials can change, e.g., when solid ice becomes a liquid
- displays awareness of natural forces that affect objects and materials, e.g., wind and gravity
- explores and describes ways that objects can be moved in space, e.g., pushing, pulling, rising, or sinking
- explores properties of electricity and magnetism

Objective 26 Demonstrates knowledge of the physical properties of objects and materials

Strategies

- Use everyday activities as opportunities for children to learn about the physical properties of objects and materials and the natural forces that affect them. Talk about what children observe throughout the day. For example, when children paint with water they learn about evaporation. When they cook, they learn about changes that occur in matter. When they push trucks up a ramp or move boats in water, they learn about how objects can be moved in space.
- Use appropriate vocabulary to describe phenomena. Use words like *sink*, *float*, *dissolve*, *melt*, *absorb*, *adhere*, *attract*, *repel*.
- Offer a variety of substances for children to explore and learn their characteristics. Include objects made from metal, wood, plastic, and paper.
- Plan experiences where children can observe changes in the physical properties of objects and materials. For example, leave an ice cube outside in the sun and observe as it becomes a liquid. Mix different materials in water to see if they dissolve.
- Repeat experiences often so children can extend their understandings. For example, use different bubble solution recipes. Offer different materials for children to use as bubble wands. Encourage them to compare their new experiences with what they learned from previous experiences.
- Make charts and/or graphs about the physical properties of objects and materials. For example, children might explore concepts such as absorb/repel, sink/float, hot/cold, or rough/smooth.
- Support children to hypothesize and test predictions during experiments. For example, a child learning about heating and cooling can observe and document changes to matter as a result of a temperature change.

Demonstrates knowledge of Earth's environment

27

When children learn about Earth's environment, they learn about the composition of the Earth: rocks, sand, dirt, mud, and water. They learn about the weather, day and night, shadows, and recycling. Children learn about Earth's environment best by exploring their own natural surroundings. As children explore the properties of the world around them, they notice changes and make predictions. They begin to understand their environment, learn important ideas, and develop respect for their natural surroundings (Dodge, Colker, & Heroman, 2002). Advances in technology have revised conceptions of how Earth was formed and continues to evolve. Vast amounts of new data, especially from satellites, together with modern computational models, are revealing the complexity of the interacting systems that control Earth's ever-changing surface. And many of the conclusions drawn from this science, along with some of the evidence from which they are drawn, are accessible to today's students (NRC, 2012).

As you create exploratory opportunities and plan experiences for children, think about how each child is learning concepts about the Earth and the environment. Focus your observations on

HOW AND WHEN THE CHILD

- demonstrates understanding that there are different kinds of weather and that weather changes
- describes and measures weather
- communicates awareness that the environment changes, e.g., season to season, sometimes slowly and sometimes suddenly
- communicates that the Earth's surface is made of different materials, e.g., rocks, sand, dirt, and water, and each material has properties that can be described
- shows awareness that different objects can be seen in the sky
- demonstrates understanding that people can affect the environment in positive and negative ways

Objective 27 Demonstrates knowledge of Earth's environment

Strategies

- Investigate properties of rocks, soil, and water. For example, children may dig in the dirt, explore puddles, or examine rocks of different hardnesses and talk about their discoveries.
- Point out changes you notice in the environment. For example, you might look out the window during diaper changing and say, "It's snowing outside. Soon the ground will be covered with white snow."
- Use collections of natural objects to help children learn more about the environment. For example, children might collect rocks, shells, leaves, or pinecones and group them by characteristics such as size, color, shape, or texture.
- Observe the Earth's environment during different times of the day and different times of the year. For example, observe the sky at different hours. Talk about what the children see. Go on nature walks at different times of the year. Document and discuss how things are the same and different during each visit.
- Use words such as *evaporation*, *condensation*, *atmosphere*, *windy*, *overcast*, *partly cloudy*, *environment*, *recycling*, *pollution*, and *litter* when talking about the Earth's environment.
- Recite fingerplays, sing, and read seasonal or weather-related books. Compare and contrast the information in books with the current season and weather.
- Go on a litter hunt. Talk about the appropriate place for various kinds of litter (recycling bin or trash can) and how children can help to keep the Earth's environment clean.
- Observe shadows during different times of the day. Measure and compare how they are alike and different.
- Involve older children in making their own recycled paper. Tear scraps of construction paper and put them in a blender with water. Blend and then pour the solution through a rectangular mesh screen. Spread so that the liquid drains and the pulp is left on the screen. During the process, talk about changes that occur. Let the pulp dry for several days, and then use the recycled paper for writing or drawing.

Objective 28

Uses tools and other technology to perform tasks

28

Tools and technology make work easier and help people solve problems (Dodge, Colker, & Heroman, 2002). Technology enables children to respond and represent their learning in individual ways (Northwest Educational Technology Consortium, Northwest Regional Educational Laboratory, 2002). The use of technology-based curriculum in the classroom has a positive impact on children's academic performance, their social and problem-solving skills (Daytner, Johanson, Clark, & Robinson, 2012). Technology can increase participation for English-language learners and children with disabilities (Murphy, DePasquale, & McNamara, 2003). As children use a variety of tools, such as thermometers, funnels, magnifying lenses, balances, hammers, tape measures, measuring cups, cameras, and computers, they learn to select the most appropriate tools for the job. The fields of science and engineering (and the technology used) are mutually supportive. Scientists depend on the work of engineers to produce the instruments and computational tools they need to conduct research. Engineers depend on the work of scientists to understand how different technologies work so they can be improved. As students gain a better understanding of these interactions, their appreciation of the interface of science, engineering, and society should give them deeper insights into local, national, and global issues (NRC Framework, 2012).

As you create exploratory opportunities and plan experiences for children, think about how each child develops important concepts related to tools and technology. Focus your observations on

HOW AND WHEN THE CHILD

- shows understanding that different tools and technology are used in different places for different purposes, e.g., finding information, communicating, and designing
- demonstrates the appropriate use of various tools and other technology

Objective 28 Uses tools and other technology to perform tasks

Strategies

- Offer a variety of tools and other technology for children to use during explorations. For example, you might offer ramps, pulleys, water wheels, egg beaters, and magnets for children to explore their physical world. Include magnifying glasses, tape recorders, and a digital camera as children study living things. Offer sifters, balance scales, plastic thermometers, or rain gauges as they explore the Earth's environment.
- Encourage children to try different tools to accomplish a task. Have them evaluate and compare the results.
- Talk with children about how tools and other technology are used in daily living. For example, you might say, "The hearing aid helps Benny hear what others are saying," or "The mixer helps Mrs. Horton stir the ingredients together to make bread."
- Model technology applications in daily activities. For example, check the weather forecast for the day or look up information about ants on the Internet.
- Demonstrate the appropriate use of tools and other technology, emphasizing safety and proper care. For example, show children how to navigate a software program or operate a digital camera.
- Provide discarded items for children to take apart and find out what is inside or how they work. For example, offer record players, radios, clocks, or telephones. Remove the electrical cord and other unsafe parts before children explore. Offer different sizes and kinds of screwdrivers, pliers, and other tools. As they take these and other things apart, they discover pulleys, magnets, levers, springs, and circuit boards. Remind children not to take things at home apart unless they are given permission.
- Support children as they write and illustrate stories using simple word processing programs, computer art programs, and digital cameras.
- When children find an interesting object outdoors, e.g., rock, fur, pine needles, dandelion helicopters, get them to observe it carefully with their naked eye and then draw what they see. Provide magnifying tools, e.g., magnifying glass, scope on a rope, microscope, jeweler's loupe, for closer study, and discuss how the magnifying devices made their observation better. Have children draw the object again and compare and discuss their drawings.
- Support students as they identify a problem, design a solution, and use the proper tools and technology to solve the problem.

Social Studies

Social studies is the study of people and the ways they relate to others. As a discipline, social studies incorporates concepts and ideas from the fields of history, geography, anthropology, sociology, civics, and economics (Seefeldt, 1995). When young children explore social studies, they learn how to be researchers, critical thinkers, and active members of a classroom community.

Everyday experiences provide the foundation for learning social studies. Teachers can build upon children's interests and use them to introduce children to other places, traditions, and cultures. Many children today are immigrants or come from immigrant-headed households. These children face particular challenges, such as being different or learning a new language (Baghban, 2007a). Issues of human diversity can be addressed through social studies as children learn how people live, work, get along with others, solve problems, and are shaped by their surroundings.

The focus of social studies during infancy and toddlerhood is on self-development within social settings (Mindes, 2005b). Young children begin with an egocentric perspective, showing interest first in themselves and then in their families. Adults enhance this self-development by providing safe, secure environments and materials that foster curiosity and exploration (Epstein, 2007). During the preschool years, children become interested in other people and their community.

As they become more aware of the larger world through their understanding of themselves and their individual experiences, preschool and kindergarten children can engage in long-term studies of meaningful topics. Their interests lead children to ask questions, actively investigate issues, and make connections between what they are learning in their daily lives. In the process of their investigations, children learn how to be researchers, and they become experts on topics related to everyday life.

SOCIAL STUDIES OBJECTIVES

29 Demonstrates knowledge about self

30 Shows basic understanding of people and how they live

31 Explores change related to familiar people or places

32 Demonstrates simple geographic knowledge

Objective 29

Demonstrates knowledge about self

29

Young children describe themselves in terms of age, gender, physical traits, material possessions, behavior, preferences, skills, experiences, role in the family, family routines, and environment. During the preschool years, children begin to develop their racial identities and notice differences in social class (Feeney & Moravcik, 2005; Ramsey, 2003). In elementary school, children's gender identification becomes very strong. Unlike preschool children, children by age 6 clearly understand that their gender is a permanent characteristic that does not vary depending on their clothes or their behavior. During the early school years, children's sense of their own gender becomes connected to culturally accepted roles and expectations, and it more strongly influences their behavior and choice of friends (Copple, 2014). Early elementary students also begin to make social comparisons among multiple individuals, as well as further reflect on personality traits of self and others, both positive and negative (Berk, 2013). The child's culture, family, and social settings (child care, school, and neighborhood) play an important role in determining what features of the self are incorporated into the child's concept of self. Personal storytelling involving family members serves as a rich source of self-knowledge and helps to instill a child's cultural values (Burger & Miller, 1999; Miller, Fung, & Mintz, 1996).

As you create exploratory opportunities and plan experiences for children, think about how each child demonstrates knowledge of herself. Focus your observations on

HOW AND WHEN THE CHILD

- demonstrates understanding that each person has unique characteristics, ways of communicating, and ways of solving problems
- communicates that each person is part of a family that has unique characteristics
- shows awareness that each person has basic needs that must be met to stay healthy, e.g., food, clothing, shelter

Objective 29 Demonstrates knowledge about self

Strategies

- Offer multiple ways for children to express their individuality and preferences. For example, they might communicate their ideas and feelings through painting, drawing, storytelling, song, or dance.
- Encourage children to recognize their unique characteristics as well as characteristics they share with others. For example, use transition times to call attention to similarities and differences by saying, "If you have curly hair, you may go to the rug."
- Use photographs of children involved in classroom activities. Display photos in accessible places so children can refer to them throughout the day. For example, place individual photos in a basket or on rings for children to use during art or writing activities. Create charts or graphs showing children's likenesses and differences (eye color, hair, favorite class activity). Make puzzles using different class pictures.
- Create short stories about children in the class. Take photographs of each child involved in daily activities. Write a short sentence or two about what the child is doing. Make the books accessible during the day. Send them home so children can share them with family members. Encourage kindergarten students to create their own short stories about their daily school activities.
- Encourage families to share traditions, songs, games, or special stories they read at home with their children.
- Include materials that demonstrate awareness of differences among children in the program. For example, include various shades of skin tone paint, crayons, markers, and construction paper. Offer dolls that represent different ethnicities, props, musical instruments, puzzles, books, and other materials that recognize diversity.
- Support the first languages of children in your program. For example, learn a few words in the first languages of the children. Write children's names, *hello* and *good-bye*, or names of familiar objects in English and in the first languages. Involve children and families in the process.
- Help children to learn their full names, addresses, and phone numbers.
- Guide children to illustrate and write books about themselves. Topics might include "My Family," "Things I Like to Do," "Foods I Like to Eat," or "Places in My Neighborhood." Teachers can take dictation for younger children or children who cannot write.

Objective 30

Shows basic understanding of people and how they live

30

Young children are eager to learn about other people and how they live. They are interested in the physical characteristics of people; similarities and differences in habits, homes, and work; family structures and roles; and the exchange of goods and services. It is important for them to learn to respect others and to understand how people rely on each other. Reading appropriate books to children can be an effective way to help them develop positive attitudes about others and to better understand how people live throughout the world (Feeney & Moravcik, 2005). Primary-grade students often have experiences that extend to other parts of the country and even beyond (through travel, immigration, or technology). As our society becomes ever more global, knowledge of the interconnected relationships between groups of people as well as between nations becomes increasingly vital (Copple, 2014).

As you create exploratory opportunities and plan experiences for children, think about how each child demonstrates understandings related to people and how they live. Focus your observations on

HOW AND WHEN THE CHILD

- shows awareness that there are similarities and differences among people and families
- demonstrates understanding of the various jobs of people in the community
- shows understanding that people buy, sell, and trade to get goods and services that they do not raise, make, or find themselves
- communicates about the various means of transportation that people use to move goods and go from place to place
- shows increasing awareness that respect for others, cooperation, and fairness help us get along in communities
- demonstrates increasing understanding that there are rules in our homes, schools, and community and that each rule has a purpose
- communicates understanding that people have various rights and responsibilities

Objective 30 Shows basic understanding of people and how they live

Strategies

- Include puzzles, block people, props, and other materials representing a range of jobs and cultures. As children play, comment on the tools people use in their jobs.
- Take frequent walks in the neighborhood. Help children notice the patterns of life and work as they see people going about their daily activities. For example, they might see street vendors selling their wares, roofers repairing a roof, a delivery person delivering a package, sanitation workers collecting trash, or a bus driver picking up passengers.
- Take trips to visit workplaces in the community. Before the trip read books, introduce new vocabulary words, and discuss what children might see. During the trip, ask workers to demonstrate and talk about what they do. Point out how people work together. Follow up trips by talking about the experience, adding new materials to support play, or documenting through art, writing, or making maps.
- Support children in interviewing people in the school, program, and community to learn more about their jobs. Guide children as they generate questions. For example, they might ask, "Why do you wear a uniform?" or "What tools do you use to do your job?"
- Help children expand their understanding of how children and families in other places are alike and different from themselves. For example, create e-mail partners with children in another part of the country or world. Guide children as they share information about themselves and generate questions to ask.
- Develop a "pen-pal" relationship with a preschool class in another part of the country. Share information through photographs, drawings, and writings about the activities in which the children in the class are involved or community activities that are particularly meaningful to them.
- Include books that show people from other cultures or people in unfamiliar jobs dealing with issues or doing things that are similar to the issues and activities of people with whom the children are familiar.
- Include children when making and discussing classroom rules, solving together the problems that arise in the classroom community, and learning to listen to others' ideas and perspectives.

Objective 31

Explores change related to familiar people or places

31

To gain a sense of history, children must first understand that people and places change over time. Change is difficult for young children to understand because they focus on the here and now (Seefeldt, 1997). Children can learn about time and change in relation to themselves, including their daily schedule, what they did yesterday, and what they will do tomorrow. The calendar, when used appropriately, can help preschool and kindergarten children understand the passage of time. When children use the calendar to count the days until a special event, they are learning about the future. When they count the number of days since they lost their first tooth, they are learning to think about the past. Preschool children love to think about what they can do now that they could not do when they were babies. They can appreciate stories about other times and places that are relevant to their own experiences (Dodge, Colker, & Heroman, 2002). As students explore more in-depth concepts of history in early elementary school, they begin to make sense of events from the past and how those events relate to their own lives (Altun, 2014).

As you create exploratory opportunities and plan experiences for children, think about how each child explores the concept of change. Focus your observations on

HOW AND WHEN THE CHILD

- demonstrates understanding that people and things change over time
- shows that time can be measured
- communicates about time, e.g., uses words such as *yesterday, today, tomorrow, day, week, month, minute, hour*

Objective 31 Explores change related to familiar people or places

Strategies

- Use children in the class to demonstrate change over time. For example, have children place photos of themselves and their friends at different ages in a series from youngest to oldest. Create scrapbooks of each child's life. Include photographs, art, dictations, notes, or other artifacts about important events and accomplishments. Talk about changes over time.
- Take photos of children engaged in the same activity or in the same location during different times of the year. Discuss changes the children notice.
- Provide opportunities for children to recall family memories or events in the community. For example, children might tell a story about something that happened when they were babies or make collages that illustrate a recent visit to grandparents.
- Involve grandparents or other senior citizens in the program. For example, ask them to tell simple stories of what life was like when they were young. Support children to generate interview questions as they talk with elders. They might ask, "What did you like to play when you were little?" or "What was your favorite fruit when you were little?" or "What is your favorite fruit now?"
- Display photographs of buildings in the community. As the year progresses, look for changes that occur. For example, children might notice that a building was painted or another had a "Going out of business" sign in the window. Talk about the changes and about what may have contributed to the changes.
- Avoid spending long periods on "calendar time" activities. Use calendars with children in ways that are meaningful and functional. For example, you might mark special upcoming events at the beginning of the week or month. Indicate special recurring events such as every other Thursday an elder volunteer reads a story. Indicate daily jobs such as who feeds the pet. Show what group project was completed. Involve children in determining what should be marked on the calendar and ways to do it.

Objective 32

Demonstrates simple geographic knowledge

32

Geography is the study of the earth's physical environment and the relationship of this environment to the people who live in it. The study of geography for young children needs to be relevant to their experiences. They can learn about the characteristics of the places where they live and the relationship between that place and other places (Dodge, Colker, & Heroman, 2002).

Preschool and kindergarten children often make simple maps to show their understanding of familiar places, e.g., classroom, play yard, neighborhood. Their first attempts at mapmaking may be with three-dimensional constructions in the Block, Sand, or Art areas. Children's experiences with mapmaking help them to develop the concepts of representation, symbolization, perspective, and scale (Lenhoff & Huber, 2000). The study of geography helps children better understand the world around them with its many patterns and processes and happenings (Heffron & Downs, 2012).

As you create exploratory opportunities and plan experiences for children, think about how they demonstrate simple geographic knowledge. Focus your observations on

HOW AND WHEN THE CHILD

- demonstrates understanding that we are surrounded by geographical features, e.g., mountain, hill, desert, lake, river, creek, bayou, and there is specific information that identifies a location, e.g., address
- communicates that we depend on people who live far away for many necessities and information
- shows increasing understanding that maps are tools with symbols that help us locate objects, find where we are, and where we are going

Objective 32 Demonstrates simple geographic knowledge

Strategies

- Invite children to build, construct, or create various geographic landscapes. Provide materials to support their ideas. For example, you might offer sea shells, large rocks, or grasses for children to use in the sand and water table as they create mountains, the sea shore, or rivers and levees.
- Take walks in the neighborhood. Take photos of landmarks that children can use to create representations of their immediate environment. For example, you might take a picture of a nearby bridge or a hill or large mountain seen from the play yard. Attach photos with laminating paper onto blocks for children to use in block play.
- Support children as they create maps of familiar places. For example, provide chalk and encourage children to make a map of the play yard on the concrete. Offer blocks and landscape toys for children to make a map of the classroom.
- Read books and plan activities that focus on a variety of geographical regions. For example, after reading *Make Way for Ducklings* (Robert McCloskey), support children to work together to create a mural or diorama of the pond and island where the ducklings went to live.
- Use children's personal travels as a springboard for discussion of other places. Talk about possible landmarks such as a lake or tall mountain. Refer to the city and state, and locate children's travels on a map or globe.
- Assist children in creating a "Where does it come from?" web or diagram. For example, kindergarten students might study how the milk they have at school gets to the cafeteria. They might use observation, books, the Internet, and interviews to help them get the needed information.
- Help children examine the relationships between the human world and the physical world by asking engaging, open-ended questions.

The Arts

Children express themselves creatively through the visual arts, music, dance and movement, and drama. In addition to using the arts to create, children can also develop an awareness and appreciation of the art of others. The arts are intrinsically rewarding as an avenue for expressing feelings and ideas that may be difficult to share verbally. Other areas of learning and development are supported when children are involved in the arts (Epstein, 2007). As children draw, paint, construct, mold, weave, dramatize, sing, dance, and move, they make new discoveries and integrate what they are learning.

The early childhood years are very important to children's realizing their creative potential (Kemple & Nissenberg, 2000). Their creative expressions and continued interest in the arts vary greatly according to the quantity and quality of their early experiences (Denac, 2008; Kemple & Nissenberg, 2000; Szechter & Liben, 2007; Zimmerman & Zimmerman, 2000). Children need time, space, supportive adults, opportunities to explore various media, and a variety of world experiences to enhance their creativity. When adults demonstrate techniques, children develop greater skill in expressing their creative ideas, but too much or too little structure can hinder the development of creative expression (Bae, 2004; Epstein, 2007; Jalongo & Isenberg, 2006). Activities such as coloring within the lines, imitating a model, competitions, and highly scripted performances do not further young children's creative expression (Jalongo & Isenberg, 2006). As children progress through the primary years, focusing on individual creativity becomes increasingly necessary to counter the message that accurate representation is most important or that there is only one right way of doing things. Teachers should convey an open, adventurous attitude to the arts that encourages children to explore available media and try new approaches (Copple, 2013).

THE ARTS OBJECTIVES

33 Explores the visual arts

34 Explores musical concepts and expression

35 Explores dance and movement concepts

36 Explores drama through actions and language

For children, the arts involve active exploration and inquiry. Infants respond to musical sounds by babbling and moving (Kenney, 1997). These experimentations satisfy the infants. They gain more control over vocalizations and movements during toddlerhood. During the preschool and kindergarten years, children perform, create, listen to, and describe music (Andress, 1995). Building on their early play behaviors, preschool and kindergarten children enact stories and dramatize a variety of increasingly complex, familiar, and imaginary scenarios.

Children's drawings, paintings, and other visual art creations change dramatically during early childhood (Thompson, 1995). Artwork begins almost by accident as the toddler experiments with materials. Children's creations evolve from what appear to adults to be random, unplanned expressions to more elaborate representations, during preschool and kindergarten, of people, objects, and events. During this time, the arts provide opportunities for collaboration with peers. Children engage in studies and demonstrate what they know through music, drama, dance and movement, and visual arts.

Objective 33

Explores the visual arts

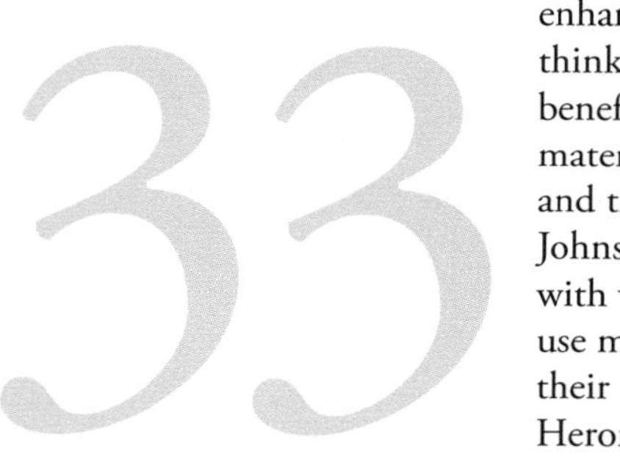

Visual art experiences include painting, drawing, making collages, modeling and sculpting, building, making puppets, weaving and stitching, and printmaking. Children who engage in quality visual arts experiences enhance their self-efficacy skills along with their original thinking skills (Catterall & Peppler, 2007). Children benefit from working with many different kinds of materials and having conversations about their artwork and the work of others (Bae, 2004; Colbert, 1997; Johnson, 2008). The more they are able to experiment with various media and to discuss different ways to use materials, the more children are able to express their ideas through the visual arts (Dodge, Colker, & Heroman, 2002).

In the early primary grades, art often takes a backseat to other curriculum areas, such as math and literacy. However, children benefit from frequent art experiences, both during specialized instruction and from integration of art activities and techniques in the classroom. Children of this age are very aware of physical symbols and how they relate to or represent objects in the world, and the visual arts provide opportunities to explore children's sense of power as symbol makers. Practicing artistic techniques also contributes to greater fine-motor control (e.g., when children experiment with controlling the flow of paint while using watercolors) (Copple, 2014).

As you create exploratory opportunities and plan experiences for children, think about how each child creates and responds to the visual arts. Focus your observations on

HOW AND WHEN THE CHILD

- shows appreciation for various forms of visual art
- shows appreciation for the artwork of peers
- communicates what he sees and how it makes him feel
- uses and cares for art materials
- explores different materials, tools, and processes
- shows increasing awareness of color, line, form, texture, space, and design in her artwork or the work of others
- communicates about his artwork, e.g., what it is made of, what he was thinking, and from where the idea comes

Objective 33 Explores the visual arts

Strategies

- Offer diverse, open-ended materials for children to explore. Include materials with different patterns, textures, and colors.
- Encourage children to explore various art media, tools, and processes. Provide opportunities to draw, paint, print, stitch, sculpt, photograph, and make collages.
- Encourage children to use various media to express their ideas. For example, they may represent the ideas expressed in a drawing by using blocks or collage materials.
- Incorporate technology. For example, offer drawing and painting software. Provide a camera. Invite children to paint while listening to different types of music.
- Encourage close observation as part of creative work. Model the examination of objects from different angles before drawing. Show children how to look from time to time to compare their drawings with the object, and to check when finished to see if anything else needs to be added.
- Demonstrate manipulative skills and how to use and care for art materials. For example, model how to cut and how to wipe a paintbrush on the edge of the cup.
- Display children's art creations attractively and prominently in the room, as much as possible at children's eye level. Show collaborative as well as individual work. Remove displays before the room becomes cluttered or when children lose interest.
- Talk about art techniques used by illustrators. For example, after reading books by Leo Lionni, discuss how he uses torn paper collage in his illustrations. Offer materials for children to experiment with and encourage them to try new techniques.
- Invite family members or local artists to share their work with the children. Get them to talk about the materials, tools, and techniques they use to create their work; how their work has changed over time; and if and where they display or sell their art.
- Ask open-ended questions that invite children to think about their creations and why they made particular choices. Take photos of their work, and record or audiotape their explanations.
- After exploring various art media, provide children with opportunities to classify photographs of art by its medium. For example, they might sort photographs of clay sculptures, wood sculptures, fabric collages, mixed media collages, line drawings, and paintings into piles.
- Give children the opportunity to revisit projects when they have ideas and/or refined skills.

Objective 34

Explores musical concepts and expression

34

Music is combining voice, instrumental, or mechanical sounds to create melody, rhythm, or harmony (Dodge, Colker, & Heroman, 2002). Children learn to appreciate different kinds of music and become comfortable with different forms of musical expression when they listen to recordings, create melodies, learn songs as a group, talk about sounds, and explore musical instruments. When children learn about musical concepts and their connections to other school subjects, children achieve a better understanding of musical concepts (Economidou Stavrou, Chrysostomou, & Socratous, 2011). The teacher's expression of interest and choice of musical activities influence children's interest and musical development (Denac, 2008; Kenney, 1997). Music can affect children's literacy development and academic performance (Shore & Strasser, 2006; Wiggins, 2007). Musical activities that relate to story reading can focus children's attention and enhance their social interactions (de Vries, 2008). Primary-grade students can handle songs with many elements requiring memory and sequencing skills. At this age, teachers can introduce songs with parts, rounds, and harmonies, as primary-grade children now have mature singing voices and a vocal ability to produce 8–10 pitches. Students are also becoming aware of the relationship between printed music and sung notes (Copple, 2014).

As you create exploratory opportunities and plan experiences for children, think about how each child relates to musical concepts and expression. Focus your observations on

HOW AND WHEN THE CHILD

- shows awareness and appreciation of different kinds of music
- expresses thoughts, feelings, and energy through music
- shows increasing awareness of various components of music: melody (tune), pitch (high and low sounds), rhythm (the beat), tempo (speed), dynamics (changes in volume), and timbre (sound quality distinguishing one instrument or voice from another)

Objective 34 Explores musical concepts and expression

Strategies

- Include music and movement experiences and activities throughout the day. Use musical activities as you transition children from one activity to another. Include songs or movement activities as part of most large-group activities. Sing or use musical instruments during outdoor activities.
- Encourage children to make up new lyrics and actions to familiar tunes or to create their own songs. Include software that enables children to create tunes.
- Personalize songs. For example, sing the child's name or the name of a favorite food.
- Create songbooks or song charts with pictures to illustrate songs children frequently sing.
- Play a variety of music. Offer different genres, such as jazz, country, classical, or rock and roll. Include music that inspires children to move quickly (polka) or slowly (lullaby). Discuss differences and how each type of music makes them feel.
- Include songs and lullabies from many cultures. Teach children songs that are familiar to their families so they can sing them together.
- Encourage children to focus on particular musical elements through your comments and questions. Use words such as *pitch* (*high*, *low*, *up*, *down*); *rhythm* or *beat* (*steady*, *fast*, *slow*); *volume* (*loud*, *soft*); and *duration* (*long*, *short*).
- Provide a variety of musical instruments from various cultures for children to explore.
- Involve children in making their own musical instruments. Encourage them to explore sounds by modifying their instruments. For example, compare the sounds of empty coffee can drums to those of drums with water in them.
- Invite musicians to bring instruments. Have them play and talk about their instruments.
- Transform the Dramatic Play area into a musical stage or recording studio. Include musical instruments, a toy microphone, an audio recorder, and other appropriate props.
- Make printed music available to children. Support older preschool and kindergarten children's experimentation with musical symbols and notations. For example, provide staff paper for beginners and encourage children to "write" music. Encourage children to "read" their music and to perform by singing or playing an instrument. Audiotape their creations.
- Integrate music with other curriculum areas.
- Encourage children to listen for specific instruments like the drums or the guitar when listening to music.

Objective 35

Explores dance and movement concepts

One of the first ways that children express themselves is through movement and dance. And it is through these creative activities that children express their emotions, their interests, and their ideas (Purcell Cone, 2009). Children are extremely interested in creative movement and dance (Hun Ping Cheung, 2010). Each new movement gives children more information about the capabilities of their bodies (Lutz & Kuhlman, 2000). Dance involves using one's body to express ideas and feelings and to respond to music. Preschool children demonstrate knowledge of dance and movement in many ways when they imitate animals or use scarves and streamers as they respond to music. Movement, taught with pretend imagery, is beneficial to children's learning and enjoyment of dance (Sacha & Russ, 2006). Teachers can help children learn *how* their bodies can move, *where* their bodies can move, and the *relationships* among parts of their own bodies, relationships with other persons, and relationships among persons in space (Sanders, 2002). As children dance and move, teachers can observe and better understand each individual child's learning and interests (Purcell Cone, 2009).

Music and dance are important to children's overall cognitive development. In the primary years, children are able to follow complex instructions relating to sequences of movement and can learn many dance movements (Copple, 2014). Despite these benefits, the percentage of children who receive movement and dance instruction in the first and third grade has decreased. The percentage of children receiving this instruction decreases the older children get as well (U.S. Department of Education, 2006).

As you create exploratory opportunities and plan experiences for children, think about how each child relates to dance and movement. Focus your observations on

HOW AND WHEN THE CHILD

- communicates feelings and ideas through dance and movement
- demonstrates spatial awareness (*where* the body moves): location (separate or shared space); directions (up or down, forward or backward); levels (low, middle, high); and pathways (straight, curved, zigzag)
- demonstrates effort awareness (*how* the body moves): speed (fast or slow); force (strong or light); and control (bound or free)
- demonstrates relational awareness (*relationships* the body creates): with the physical self (body parts); with body shapes and size (big, small, straight); roles with other people (leading or following, mirroring, alternating); and in space (near or far, over or under, around or through)

Objective 35 Explores dance and movement concepts

Strategies

- Encourage children to participate in various creative movement activities. For example, they might move like an elephant, a swan, falling leaves, a kite, a windstorm, or growing plants.
- Model movements and invite children to join you. Suggest new movements and techniques or ways to combine different actions.
- Use pretend imagery. Have children first imagine the movement and then carry it out. For example, they might close their eyes and imagine reaching for a small bird in a tree, and then they carry out the movements they envisioned.
- Use objects and props to help children focus. For example, use a blue mat as a pond and have children leap over the pond as if they were deer, rabbits, or frogs.
- Provide space and materials for dance and movement activities indoors and outdoors. Use large open spaces to support their exploration of movement and direction. Use small spaces for isolated movement and specific patterns. Offer streamers, ribbons, scarves, balloons, blankets, or parachutes.
- Use vocabulary that supports children's understanding of movement concepts. Describe *how* their bodies move in space (*fast*, *slow*, *heavy*, *light*). Tell *where* their bodies can move (*forward*, *backward*, *low*, *middle*, *high*, *straight*, *curved*, *zigzag*). Describe the *relationship* of their bodies to other people or objects (*near*, *far*, *leading*, *following*, *mirroring*, *together*, *apart*).
- Ask movement experts to visit. For example, invite a member of a dance troupe to demonstrate dance techniques and how to control body movements.
- Watch videos that show examples of a wide variety of dances in other cultures. Take children to see a children's ballet or other dance performance.
- Involve children in designing and making scenery or stage sets for performances.
- Teach children more complex dance movements in a specific sequence.

Objective 36

Explores drama through actions and language

36

Drama is portraying characters and telling stories though action, dialogue, or both (Dodge, Colker, & Heroman, 2002). Drama is an important part of development and learning for young children. It positively affects children's language development and literacy, self-awareness, social–emotional reasoning, and problem solving (Brown, 1990; Pinciotti, 1993; Wright, et al., 2008). As children participate with others in drama-related play, they develop basic skills and knowledge in the use of props, movement, pantomime, sound, speech, character, and story making (Pinciotti, 1993). Drama-related play is also an effective resource to engage children in science learning through play acting and physical interaction, e.g., children can pretend to be planets in the solar system, rotating around the sun (Varelas, Pappas, Tucker-Raymond, Kane, Hankes, Ortiz, & Keblawe-Shamah, 2010).

Children learn to tell stories through repeated exchanges with people who are important to them. Experiences and cultural traditions influence what stories children tell and how they tell stories (Curenton & Ryan, 2006; Wright et al., 2008). Adult guidance is important in helping children develop the skills they need to act out scenarios and stories. This dramatic interpretation (the acting out of scenarios and stories) enhances a child's comprehension of the story and encourages a child's love of reading (Sayers Adomat, 2012).

When teachers read stories for later dramatization or provide children with puppets to act out a story, clothing they can use for dress up, and props that can transform blocks into an imaginary city, they are teaching children drama. As children play with materials such as these, they express their feelings and process their experiences. Children's use of performative actions as a part of read-aloud interactions supports social interactions, builds on individual children's strengths, and helps children better understand stories (Sayers Adomat, 2010).

As you create exploratory opportunities and plan experiences for children, think about how each child explores drama. Focus your observations on

HOW AND WHEN THE CHILD

- shows that real-life roles can be enacted
- communicates a message or story through action and dialogue
- represents ideas through drama, e.g., pretends to be the big bad wolf
- shows appreciation of the dramatizations of others

Note: See Objective 14 for related information about sociodramatic play.

Objective 36 Explores drama through actions and language

Strategies

- Extend the play of children by encouraging additional scenarios. Provide a variety of props for the exploration of different roles.
- Extend children's play by helping them to see a range of actions, solutions, and possibilities. Provide opportunities to act out different characters and feelings. For example, have children make angry, fierce, sad, joyful, kind, and brooding faces.
- Provide an imagination bag with costumes and have children use them in their play.
- Provide verbal prompts to support children's dramatizations. For example, to help children get started you might say, "Act as though...," "Imagine you are...," or "Once there was a... ." To help them continue, say, "Then what happened?" or "What happened next?" To help them close, you might prompt, "How did it end?" or "What happened last?"
- Invite children to dramatize stories you read. Read the story, calling attention to the setting, mood, characters, and plot. Provide puppets or other props for children to use to enact the story. Read the story a second time, pausing so children can act out the various parts.
- Invite children to act out familiar stories such as *Caps for Sale*.
- Encourage children to build scenery and props for dramatization. For example, they might create houses to act out *The Three Little Pigs* or make masks to dramatize *The Three Billy Goats Gruff*.
- Encourage children to dictate stories to act out later. Send copies of stories home for children to enact with their families.
- Attend a children's theater performance or arrange for a mime, actor, or storyteller to visit.
- Provide opportunities for children to try different theater roles. For example, they might be the writer, actor, director, designer, or audience member. Support them as they develop knowledge and skills in the use of props, movement, pantomime, sound, speech, character, and storytelling.

English Language Acquisition

Language learning is a basic feature of the early development of all children. If a child is raised in a family in which English is spoken, she will learn to speak English. If a child is raised in a family in which Spanish is spoken, he will learn to speak Spanish. If a child is raised in a family in which both English and Spanish are spoken, she will become bilingual as she learns both languages. If a child is raised in a family in which Spanish is spoken and the child attends an early childhood classroom in which English is spoken, he will be a second-language learner, adding English to his first language of Spanish. Bilingual children, who are also called *simultaneous* language learners, and second-language-learning children, who are also called *sequential* language learners, are both presented with a challenging cognitive task: They must learn and maintain two languages, rather than just one. Therefore, children in both of these groups are dual-language learners.

The language-learning process for simultaneous language learners closely resembles the process for monolingual children. However, because of simultaneous language learners' need to know twice as many words, their vocabulary development may be less extensive in each language in comparison to monolingual children (Oller & Eilers, 2002).

Young sequential language learners follow a slightly different developmental sequence. At first these children may continue to use their first language in a second-language setting. Later, when they realize that their first language is not being understood, they enter a nonverbal period during which they gain receptive abilities in the new language and may experiment with language sounds. Next, they begin to use memorized words and phrases in their new language, and some of the phrases might be quite long. Finally, they develop productive use of the new language, constructing original sentences with the words and phrases they already know (Tabors, 2008). This sequence is not specific to a particular language, so Objectives 37 and 38 may be adapted to assess progress in acquiring any second language. The language in the examples must be modified to reflect the new language the child is learning.

ENGLISH LANGUAGE ACQUISITION

37 Demonstrates progress in listening to and understanding English

38 Demonstrates progress in speaking English

Learning a second language is cumulative and often uneven. Children may sound very sophisticated in situations where they know the vocabulary and the grammar that they need in order to be understood. In other situations, however, they might be unable to communicate because of emotional or linguistic constraints (Tabors, 2008).

One of the major concerns about young children who are learning a second language in a society where that is the dominant language is that the first language may no longer be developed. The loss of the first language can be detrimental for personal, familial, religious, and cultural reasons (Wong Fillmore, 1991b). Furthermore, research shows that the second-language learners who do best in school are those who have a strong grounding in their first language (Collier, 1987).

There are considerable individual differences in how young children take on the task of learning a second language. Highly motivated children, children with more exposure to the new language, children who are older when they begin the process, and children who have more outgoing personalities may make more rapid progress. Some children may spend an entire year in the nonverbal period, while others may start to use social words right away. Second-language learners may be socially isolated because of their inability to communicate. Effective teachers use strategies to integrate these children into classroom activities, and they develop techniques for helping children begin to understand and use their new language.

Objective 37

Demonstrates progress in listening to and understanding English

37

The first task for second-language learners is to gain receptive understanding of the new language. Once they have learned that they are in an environment where a new language is being used and that they will need to use that language if they want to be understood, they must begin to hear the sounds of the new language and begin the process of connecting those sounds to the objects and activities around them. Children take on this task at different rates (Itoh & Hatch, 1978; Saville-Troike, 1988; Wong Fillmore, 1979). If it is possible to communicate in their first language with adults and children in the classroom, they may choose to do so without making the effort to learn the new language (Meyer, 1989). If they find that nonverbal communication is effective, they may use that for a considerable period of time.

However, once motivated to begin to understand the new language—because they want to play with peers or want to understand the teachers who are using the new language—they begin to observe and listen closely. At this time children use *spectating* behaviors, focusing their attention on how words are formed, and *rehearsing* behaviors, mouthing words or practicing by saying words to themselves (Tabors, 2008). As they acquire the phonology of the new language, children may also play with the sounds of the language by inventing new words (Saville-Troike, 1988).

Classroom routines and the language used in those contexts help children begin to understand the new language. However, assessing children's receptive abilities can be complicated by the fact that young learners are extremely good at guessing meaning from context. In order to check receptive comprehension, teachers must be careful that they are assessing understanding without providing contextual cues like gestures or eye gaze.

Objective 37 Demonstrates progress in listening to and understanding English

1	2 Beginning	3	4 Progressing	5	6 Increasing	7	8 Advancing	9
	Observes others as they converse in English during play or other small-group experiences; may engage in similar activities by imitating behavior; attends to oral use of English • Moves closer to the Dramatic Play area to watch a small group of children • Sits across from two children who are stringing beads and talking, and begins stringing beads, too • Watches another child hold up a cup to request milk and does the same • Participates by doing hand movements while other children and the teacher sing in the new language		**Responds to common words and phrases in English when they are accompanied by gestures or other visual aids** • Joins a group in the Block area when one child motions with a hand to come, and says, "Come play." • Goes to the sink when the teacher says it is time to brush teeth and pantomimes toothbrushing • Nods when classmate says, "Hello." • Sits by the teacher when she holds up a book and asks, "Would you like to read a book?"		**Responds to words and phrases in English when they are not accompanied by gestures or other visual aids** • Goes to table when teacher says, "It's lunchtime. Take your seats at the tables." • Puts the caps on the markers and then puts the markers on the shelf when reminded • Points to ear when asked, "Where's your ear?" • Picks up a car from a group of toys when asked, "Where's the car?" • Picks up the puzzle with the puppy on it when another child says, "Let's do the puppy puzzle together."		**Understands increasingly complex English phrases used by adults and children** • Responds by putting the correct block where directed when another child says, "Hey, put that square block over there by the horse to make the fence." • Points to the correct piece when the teacher asks, "Which circle is the biggest?" • Touches the car at the top of the tallest ramp when the teacher asks, "Which car do you think will roll the fastest?"	

Objective 37 Demonstrates progress in listening to and understanding English

Strategies

- Gather personal information from each family, including what language or languages are spoken at home and which family members speak them. In-depth information includes an estimate of how much time each person in the home spends using a particular language with the child, and what language or languages the child uses when speaking with each family member.
- If the child is using a language other than English at home, ask her family whether or not they feel the child is making appropriate progress in that language.
- If you do not speak the first language of an English-language learner, ask the family members for a few words in the first language that can be used to welcome the child to the classroom. If the family agrees, make a tape recording of these words to use in the classroom to comfort their child or to help other children hear the sounds of the child's first language.
- Set up classroom routines and use consistent language when referring to activities (clean-up time) and objects (cubby, Block area) throughout the day in the classroom.
- Make sure English-language learners are included in situations in the classroom where they can hear English. Assign seating so that English-language learners are near English-speaking children during activities, or snack, group time, and rest time.
- Pair an English-language learner with an outgoing English-speaking child for certain periods during the day, so that the English-speaking child may help to integrate the English-language learner into classroom activities.
- When speaking English with an English-language learner, use these guidelines:
  - Speak slowly. This helps children hear and learn the individual words.
  - Use repetition. When children hear the same word used multiple times for an object, they are more likely to make the connection between the spoken word and the name of the object.
  - Simplify your message.
  - Place important words at the end of a sentence and emphasize those words. For example, "This is your *hand*. Do you want to trace your hand?"
  - Double the message with gestures, actions, visual aids, or directed gaze while you are talking. For example, when asking children to put on their coats, model putting on your own coat. These visual aids help children understand what is being said.
  - Use *running commentary* by telling English-language learners what you are doing as you are doing it. For example say, "Now, I will put the milk in the batter."
  - Use parallel talk, describing the actions of the child, "You are stacking the blue block on top of the red block."
- Be alert to an English-language learner's use of nonverbal communication, such as pointing silently to a paint brush. Supply the words in English for what the child is trying to communicate. For example, "You want the paint brush? Here is the paint brush."
- Talk about what is right in front of the English-language-learning child, so the context will be obvious.
- Provide pictures to accompany the daily schedule, classroom rules, and other print in the classroom. This helps children know the expectations even though they may not yet understand the language.
- Use repetitive songs and games during group times. Children who are English-language learners often say their first words in English when singing familiar songs and fingerplays.
- Read books in children's first languages if possible prior to reading the book in English to them. This helps them become familiar with the words and the story line before hearing it in English. Reading it in the first language should not happen immediately prior to reading it in English, but rather earlier in the day or the week.
- Choose books with repetitive refrains when reading aloud with English-language learners. Read the same books over and over again so that the words become very familiar to them.
- Supply English words for any object that an English-language learner shows interest in (often they will bring objects to you to identify). Then, see if you can elicit what the name for that object is in the child's first language.
- Plan small-group activities so that there are times when an activity is done with only English-language-learning children and all language can be tailored to their needs, and there are times when the group has both English-language-learning children and English-speaking children and the language can be more complex.
- Keep talking. English-language-learning children will need lots and lots of input to hear the sounds of English and to begin to understand what they mean.

Objective 38

Demonstrates progress in speaking English

38

The second task for second-language learners is to begin the process of using their new language. Most children begin by repeating words or phrases, either in one-on-one interactions with adults or in group situations when all of the children are using the same words, for instance, during a group sing-along.

A distinct feature of young children's second-language acquisition is their memorization and use of social interactive terms (Wong Fillmore, 1976, 1979) to help them enter play situations and to have their needs met. Once children have acquired a number of words and socially useful phrases, they can begin to construct original sentences. Eventually second-language learners use the input from speakers of the new language to develop their ability to use questions, negatives, and past and future tenses. Second-language learners make many of the same mistakes made by young children learning their first language. Throughout this process, second-language learners continue to acquire vocabulary so they will have the words they need in order to communicate verbally with other speakers of the new language.

Objective 38 Demonstrates progress in speaking English

1	2 Beginning	3	4 Progressing	5	6 Increasing	7	8 Advancing	9
	Repeats sounds and words in English, sometimes very quietly • Mouths the words of a song during circle time • Echoes a word or phrase, e.g., says, "Monkey," while group chants "Five Little Monkeys Jumping on the Bed" • After teacher says, "Up," child repeats, "Up." • Repeats, "Mil, mil, mil," after the teacher asks, "Would you like more milk?"		**Uses a few socially interactive terms in English appropriately; uses one or two words in English to represent a whole idea** • Says , "Hi"; "Lookit"; "My turn"; and "Stopit." • Hears someone nearby say, "Be careful!" and repeats phrase as a warning in a similar situation later • Points at snack basket and says, "More crackers." • Looks out the window and says, "Go outside." • Says, "No, mine," when another child takes her toy truck		**Develops multiword phrases by using socially interactive terms in English; adds new words to the phrase** • Says, "I do a ice cream"; "I want my mommy"; and "Lookit this, Teacher." • Says, "How you do this flower?" • Says, "Big. I gotta big." • Says, "How do you gonna make dese?"		**Uses increasingly complex grammar in English; makes some mistakes typical of young children** • Develops entire sentences, e.g., "The door is a square," and "The house has a lot of windows." • Uses questions and negatives, e.g., "Your name is what?" and "You no my mommy." • Uses past and future tenses, e.g., "I goed to the park," and "I'll get it." • Interacts in elaborate play schemes, "I be the mommy and you be the baby. Here's your bottle, Baby."	

Objective 38 Demonstrates progress in speaking English

Strategies

- Spend time one-on-one with English-language learners; they may be more likely to start using English if they are not in a group situation.
- Be alert to children beginning to use English very softly, perhaps rehearsing what they want to say.
- Use repetitive songs, games, and fingerplays during group times. Children who are English-language learners often say their first words in English when singing familiar songs and fingerplays. Singing in a group helps give children a secure environment in which to try out their emerging English skills.
- Try to have English-language-learning children repeat words as you demonstrate what objects or illustrations they refer to.
- Validate children's language attempts in either language. If English-language learners use their first language, acknowledge their effort, and if you can guess what they are talking about, respond in English.
- Give English-language learners lots of time to think about what they want to say. If you ask a question ("what would you like to do?") wait longer than you would normally. It may take longer for the children to think of the words they want to say in English.
- For children who are at the beginning stages of learning English, ask close-ended questions and offer some options for response ("Would you like to paint or would you like to build?").
- When reading books with repetitive refrains, pause and let the children fill in the next word. For example, "Brown bear, brown bear, what do you________?" This helps children feel successful and builds confidence when they know what comes next and are able to fill in the missing word.
- Intentionally introduce new vocabulary words. Use those words frequently in different contexts throughout the day. Provide visual aids and gestures to illustrate the meaning of the words.
- Give English-language learners a chance to respond in English in group situations when they can answer in chorus with all of the children.
- Encourage families to bring pictures and objects from home. Children are more likely to talk about things they know and that are familiar to them. Children are also more likely to engage in dramatic play if objects similar to what they see used at home are included in the classroom.
- Engage children in conversations on interesting topics that connect to their daily lives. This provides children opportunities to express ideas and thoughts about things that are relevant and important to them.
- Expand and extend any effort that a child makes to use English. For example, when a child says, "car," you might say, "Yes! That's a racing car."
- Notice which phrases a child uses ("Hey," "OK," "Mine," "Stopit") and help the child build from those phrases ("Hey you," "I'm okay," "That's mine," "Stopit, please")
- Make learning new vocabulary words in English a primary goal of instruction and all communication. Choose words you want all of the children to know and use them repeatedly in the classroom. Introduce the words using objects or illustrations and develop activities during which the children will need to use these words.
- Help children move from nonverbal responses to productive responses by prompting them with questions. For example, when a child points to her untied shoe ask, "What do you need?" If the child does not respond ask, "Do you need me to tie your shoe?" When the child responds, "Tie...shoe," recognize her effort and say, "Okay! I will tie your shoe."
- Encourage interactions between English-language learners and English-speaking children by modeling initiations. For example, you might say to a child, "Ask Sally, 'May I play with you?'"
- Model correct English versions of phrases used by English-language learners. For example, if a child says, "I goed to the store," you respond, "You went to the store? What did you get?"

Glossary

/ /: surrounding a letter, diagonal lines indicate the sound (rather than the name) of that letter, e.g., /k/ for the initial consonant sound in *cat* or /s/ for the initial consonant sound in *cell*

abstract symbol: a sign, figure, mark, image, or numeral that is used to represent an object, person, concept, idea, or number

affix: when functioning as a noun, a letter or group of letters attached to the beginning or end of a word that serves to produce a derivative word or an inflectional form

algorithm: a step-by-step method for solving a problem or accomplishing a goal

alliteration: the repetition of initial consonant sounds in two or more neighboring words, e.g., *big blue balloons*

alphabetic principle: the fact that written words are composed of letters that represent sounds

areas of development and learning: the broadest domains of development and learning, e.g., *Social–Emotional*

array: a group of mathematical elements (numbers, letters) arranged in rows and columns associative: producing the same mathematical value no matter how an expression's elements are grouped so long as the order of those elements is the same. For example, addition is *associative* since $(a + b) + c = a + (b + c)$.

attend: pay attention to an activity or experience

base ten: a number system based on 10, also known as the decimal system. A base-ten system uses the symbols *0–9* and columns for place value.

colored bands: in *Objectives for Development & Learning*, the colored bands or lines (red, orange, yellow, green, blue, purple, pink, silver, and brown) that show the age or the class/grade ranges for widely held developmental and learning expectations

commutative: giving the same mathematical result no matter in which order two numbers are used with an operation. For example, multiplication is *commutative* since $a \times b = b \times a$.

compare and contrast: examine the relationship between two items or groups of items to determine how they are alike and how they are different

count on: a strategy by which a child figures out a quantity by beginning with the sum of a small number of objects and then counting the remaining objects until he counts them all. For example, with a group of five objects, the child might say, "Three," and then point to the remaining objects, saying, "Four, five. I have five." *Counting on* is a more advanced strategy than *counting all*, in which a child would count "One, two, three, four, five. I have five."

decoding: in reading, the ability to make sense of printed words

decontextualized language: language that is not tied to the immediate context, e.g., that refers to past events, future events, or imaginary scenarios

digraph: a group of two successive letters used to write one phoneme (distinctive sound), e.g., /ai/ in *fair*

dimension: a specific aspect or subskill of an objective, e.g., *Manages feelings* or *Follows limits and expectations*

direction: related to where a person or thing is going or from where a person or thing has come

distance: how near or far away a person or object is located

distributive: giving the same mathematical result when an operation is carried out on a whole expression and when it is carried out on each part of an expression with the results then collected together. For example, the *distributive* property of multiplication means $a(b + c) = ab + ac$.

dual-language learners: children who acquire two or more languages simultaneously, as well as those who learn a second language while continuing to develop their first language

engage: interact or become deeply involved with a person or activity

engaged in learning: when children are focused, deeply interested, and involved in experiences through which they learn knowledge and skills. When they are engaged, they exhibit attention, persistence, flexibility, and self-regulation.

examples: in *Objectives for Development & Learning*, different ways that children show what they know and can do, e.g., *Moves to the sand table at the suggestion of an adult when there are too many at the art table*

explanatory talk: talk that consists of explaining and describing, including definitions of words; discussion of cause-and-effect relationships; and discussion of connections between ideas, events, and actions

"fair share" groups: the result of dividing objects, food, etc. into groups so that each person gets an equal or approximately equal amount

fine-motor skills: small movements that involve the small muscles of the fingers and wrists, such as grasping something with one's thumb and index finger

first language: a language spoken in the home that is different from the main language spoken in the community

gallop: a traveling movement that involves leaping (taking a big step forward), keeping the same foot in front of the body at all times, and bringing the rear foot to meet the front foot

genre: a kind or type of art (e.g., folk art and modern art), literature (e.g., picture books and poetry), or music (e.g., classical music and pop music)

gross-motor skills: large movements that involve the large muscles in the arms, legs, torso, and feet, such as running and jumping

growing pattern: a pattern that increases by at least plus one and continues to increase, e.g., a block staircase

indicators: knowledge, skills, or behaviors that children demonstrate at four levels of each developmental progression. In *Objectives for Development & Learning* these statements are in bold print, e.g., *Uses adult support to calm self.*

inflection: a process of word formation in which items are added to the base form of a word to express grammatical meanings, e.g., the plural *–s* and *–ing* forms of verbs

invented spelling: (also called *sound spelling* or *developmental spelling*) a child's attempt to spell words by writing a letter for each sound he or she notices. This is an important step toward conventional spelling.

large ball: a beach ball or playground ball

lowercase letters: the letters of the alphabet that are not uppercase (capital) letters, e.g., *a*, *b*, and *c*. Although children often refer to these as "small" letters, adults should use the term *lowercase* when referring to them because their actual size varies from text to text

levels: in *Objectives for Development & Learning* the rating scale that describes specific points along the progression for each objective

listen (vs. hear): to pay attention to sound, to hear something with thoughtful attention, or to be alert to catch an expected sound

location: relates to positional language that indicates where a person or thing is situated

matrix: a rectangular array of mathematical elements that can be combined to form sums and products with similar arrays having an appropriate number of rows and columns

nonstandard measuring tools: tools that are not formal measuring tools. These may have units of equal length (e.g., same-sized cubes, links, or paper clips) or units of unequal length (e.g., children's strides).

numeral: the symbol that represents a number, e.g., the number *four* is shown as the numeral *4*

objective: a statement of expectations of knowledge, skills, and abilities, e.g., *Regulates own emotions and behaviors*

onset: the first consonant sound(s) before the vowel in a one-syllable word, e.g., /k/ in *cat* and /th/ in *think*

parentese: singsong speech and exaggerated facial expressions. This type of communication encourages young infants to listen and focus on what is said.

persist: remain focused on an activity for an adequate length of time

phoneme: the smallest unit of sound in a word

phonological awareness: the understanding that spoken language can be divided into smaller and smaller units that can be manipulated

pictorial map: a map that uses drawings or pictures to represent objects in the environment

place value: the value of the place, or position, of a digit in a numeral, e.g., 1s, 10s, 100s

position: an indication of where a person or object is located in relation to someone or something else

progress checkpoints: three or four points during the year when teachers determine the progress a child is making toward an objective

progressions of development and learning: paths, or trajectories, that children typically follow when acquiring a skill or behavior

proximity: the closeness or nearness of something, often described as *beside*, *next to*, *touching*, or *alongside*

redirection: guiding children's behavior by restating or providing an attractive alternative

rehearsal strategy: the use of repeated practice of information to learn it, e.g., singing the ABC song to determine whether *R* comes before or after *S*

repeating pattern: a pattern in which the core unit repeats a minimum of five times, e.g., red, blue; red, blue; red, blue; red, blue; red, blue

rhyme: words with the same ending sounds but not necessarily the same ending letters

rime: the vowel sound and all the sounds that follow the vowel in a syllable or one-syllable word, e.g., /at/ in *cat* and /ink/ in *think*

salient: of notable significance

scenario: a series of real or imagined events

secure attachment: the strong emotional bond or trusting relationship between a child and an important person in his or her life

secure base: a familiar, trusted adult to whom a child returns for protection when the child becomes frightened or uneasy while exploring his or her world

self-talk: (sometimes referred to as *private speech*) the language an adult uses with children to describe his or her actions at the time they are being performed, e.g., "Now I am putting milk in the refrigerator."

semantic: relating to meaning in language

sight words: words that young children are taught to recognize instantly, e.g., *and*, *that*, *in*, *you*, *was*. Many sight words cannot be sounded out, have unusual spelling patterns, and/or cannot be learned through the use of pictures.

skip: a traveling movement involving a step and a hop, using alternating feet

skip counting: counting forward or backward in multiples or intervals of a given number, e.g., by 2s, 5, or 10s

sociodramatic play: dramatic play, e.g., role-playing or fantasy play, with the additional component of social interaction with either a peer or an adult

standard measuring tools: formal tools that mark units of measurement with numerals, e.g., rulers, measuring tapes, and meter sticks

story-related problems: in sophisticated picture books, the difficulties characters face that the reader must infer from the information provided. These problems require the reader to analyze information and make predictions.

subitize: to quickly glance at a small group of objects and identify the quantity without counting the objects one at a time

tally: use marks to keep a record of whatever has been counted

tally marks: one-to-one representations of counted items, usually vertical and diagonal lines arranged in groups of five with four vertical lines in a row "crossed" by one diagonal line

teaching strategies: what teachers can do to support and scaffold children's learning as it relates to a particular objective

three-dimensional shape: a figure that has width, height, and depth (thickness), e.g., a sphere, cube, triangular prism, cone, cylinder, or pyramid

two-dimensional shape: a figure that has width and height only, e.g., a circle, square, rectangle, triangle, or pentagon

uppercase letters: the capital letters of the alphabet, e.g., *A*, *B*, and *C*. Although children often refer to these as "big" letters, adults should use the term *uppercase* when referring to them because their actual size varies from text to text

References

Ackerman, B. P. (1978). Children's understanding of speech acts in unconventional directive frames. *Child Development*, 49, 311–318.

Adams, M. J. (1990). *Beginning to read: Thinking and learning about print.* Urbana, IL: University of Illinois Center for the Study of Reading.

Adams, M. J. (2001). Alphabetic anxiety and explicit systematic phonics instruction: A cognitive science perspective. In S. B. Neuman & D. K. Dickinson (Eds.), *Handbook of early literacy research* (pp. 66–80). New York: Guilford Press.

Afflerbach, P., Pearson, P. D., & Paris, S. G. (2008). Clarifying differences between reading skills and reading strategies. *The Reading Teacher, 61*, 364–373.

Allen, K. E. (2003). *Developmental profiles pre-birth through twelve.* (4th ed.). Clifton Park, NY: Delmar Learning.

Allen, K. E., & Marotz, L. R. (2007). *Developmental profiles: Prebirth through twelve*. Clifton Park, NY: Thomson/Delmar Learning.

Altun, Adnan. (2014). The trajectory of elementary and middle school students' perceptions of the concepts of history. *Educational Sciences: Theory and Practice, 14*(6), 2320–2326.

American Academy of Pediatrics (2003). *Baby & child health.* J. Shu (Ed.). New York: DK Publishing.

Andress, B. (1991). From research to practice: Preschool children and their movement responses to music. *Young Children, 47*(1), 22–27.

Andress, B. (1995). Transforming curriculum in music. In S. Bredekamp & T. Rosegrant (Eds.), *Reaching potentials: Transforming early childhood curriculum and assessment,* Vol. 2 (pp. 99–108). Washington, DC: National Association for the Education of Young Children.

Anthony, J. L., Lonigan, C., Driscoll, K., Phillips, B. M., & Burgess, S. R. (2003). Preschool phonological sensitivity: A quasi-parallel progression of word structure units and cognitive operations. *Reading Research Quarterly, 38*, 470–487.

Apel, K., Wilson-Fowler, E. B., Brimo, D., & Perrin, N. A. (2012). Metalinguistic contributions to reading and spelling in second and third grade students. *Reading and Writing*, 25, 1283–1305.

Araujo, N., & Aghayan, C. (2006). *Easy songs for smooth transitions in the classroom.* St. Paul, MN: Redleaf Press.

Arnold, H. D., Kupersmidt, J. B., Voegler-Lee, M. E. & Marshall, N. A. (2012). The association between preschool children's social functioning and their emergent academic skills. *Early Childhood Research Quarterly*, 27(3), 376–386.

Arnone, M. P. (2003). *Using instructional design strategies to foster curiosity.* Retrieved July 9, 2007, from http://www.marilynarone.com/ERIC Digeston Curiosity and 1D.pdf

Arste, J. C., Woodward, V. A., & Burcke, C. I. (1984). *Language stories and literacy lessons.* Portsmouth: Heinemann.

Aubrey, C. (2001). Early mathematics. In T. David (Ed.), *Promoting evidenced-based practice in early childhood education: Research and its implications, Vol. 1*, (pp. 185–210). Amsterdam: Elsevier Science.

August, D., & Hakuta, K. (1998). *Educating language minority children.* New York: National Academy Press.

August, D., & Shanahan, T. (2010). Response to a review and update on *Developing literacy in second-language learners: Report of the National Literacy Panel on Language Minority Children and Youth. Journal of Literacy Research, 42*, 341–348.

Ayoub, C. C., & Fischer, K. W. (2006). Developmental pathways and intersections among domains of development. In K. McCartney & D. Phillips (Eds.), *Blackwell handbook of early childhood development* (pp. 62–81).

Bae, J. (2004). Learning to teach visual arts in an early childhood classroom: The teacher's role as a guide. *Early Childhood Education Journal, 31*(1), 247–254.

Baghban, M. (2007a). Immigration in childhood: Using picture books to cope. *The Social Studies, 98*(2), 71–76.

Baghban, M. (2007b). Scribbles, labels, and stories: The role of drawing in the development of writing. *Young Children, 62*(1), 20–26.

Bailey, A. (2008). Assessing the language of young learners. In N. H. Hornberger, P. Clapham, & C. Corson (Eds.), *Encyclopedia of language and education,* Vol. 7., *Language testing and assessment* (2nd ed.), (pp. 379–400). New York: Springer Science Business Media.

Baker, B. L., & Brightman, A. J. (2004). *Steps to independence: Teaching everyday skills to children with special needs* (4th ed.). Baltimore, MD: Paul H. Brookes.

Barbour, A. C. (1999). The impact of playground design on the play behaviors of children with differing levels of physical competence. *Early Childhood Research Quarterly, 14,* 75–98.

Barkley, R. A. (1997). *ADHD and the nature of self-control.* New York: Guilford Press.

Baron-Cohen, S. (1995). *Mindblindness: An essay on autism and theory of mind.* London: MIT Press.

Baroody, A. J. (1987a). The development of counting strategies for single-digit addition. *Journal for Research in Mathematics Education, 18*(2), 141–157.

Baroody, A. J. (1987b). *Children's mathematical thinking: A developmental framework for preschool, primary, and special education teachers.* New York: Teachers College, Columbia University.

Baroody, A. J. (2000). Research in review: Does mathematics instruction for three-to five-year-olds really make sense? *Young Children, 55*(4), 61–67.

Baroody, A. J. (2004). The developmental bases for early childhood number and operations standards. In D. H. Clements, J. Sarama, & A. -M. DiBiase (Eds.), *Engaging young children in mathematics: Standards for early childhood mathematics education* (pp. 173–219). Mahwah, NJ: Lawrence Erlbaum Associates.

Baroody, A. J., Lai, M -L., & Mix, K. S. (2006). The development of young children's early number and operation sense and its implications for early childhood education. In B. Spodek & O. N. Saracho (Eds.), *Handbook of research on the education of young children* (2nd ed., pp. 187–221). Mahwah, NJ: Lawrence Erlbaum Associates.

Baroody, A. J., & Wilkins, J. L. M. (1999). The development of informal counting, number, and arithmetic skills and concepts. In J. V. Copley (Ed.), *Mathematics in the early years* (pp. 48–65). Reston, VA: National Council of Teachers of Mathematics.

Barry, E. S. (2006). Children's memory: A primer for understanding behavior. *Early Childhood Education Journal, 33,* 405–411.

Baumann, J. & Kame'enui, E. (2012). *Vocabulary instruction: Research to practice* (2nd ed.). New York: Guilford Press.

Beals, D. E. (2001). Eating and reading: Links between family conversations with preschoolers and later language and literacy. In D. K. Dickenson & P. O. Tabors (Eds.), *Beginning literacy with language: Young children learning at home and school* (pp. 75–92). Baltimore: Paul H. Brookes.

Beckman, M., & Edwards, J. (2000). The ontogeny of phonological categories and the primacy of lexical learning in linguistic development. *Child Development, 71,* 240–249.

Beland, K. R. (1996). A school wide approach to violence prevention. In R. L. Hampton, P. Jenkins, & T. P. Gulatta (Eds.), *Preventing violence in America* (pp. 209–231). Thousand Oaks, CA: Sage Publications.

Benigno, J. P., & Ellis, S. (2004). Two is greater than three: Effects of older siblings on parental support of preschoolers' counting in middle-income families. *Early Childhood Research Quarterly, 19,* 4–20.

Benoit, L., Lehalle, H., & Jouen, F. (2004). Do young children acquire number words through subitizing or counting? *Cognitive development, 19*(3), 291–307.

Bergen, D. (2002). The role of pretend play in children's cognitive development. *Early Childhood Research and Practice, 4*(1). Retrieved May 27, 2007, from http://www.ecrp.uiuc.edu/v4n1/bergen.html

Berger, K. S. (2008). *The developing person through the life span* (7th ed.). New York: Worth Publishers.

Berger, S. E., Adolph, K. E., & Lobo, S. A. (2005). Out of the toolbox: Toddlers differentiate wobbly and wooden handrails. *Child Development, 76*, 1294–1307.

Bergin, C., & Bergin, D. (2009). Attachment in the classroom. *Educational Psychology Review, 21*(2), 141–170.

Berk, L. E. (2002). *Infants, children, & adolescents* (4th ed.). Boston: Allyn & Bacon.

Berk, L. E. (2003). *Child development* (6th ed.). Boston: Allyn & Bacon.

Berk, L. E. (2006). Looking at kindergarten children. In D. F. Gullo (Ed.), *K today: Teaching and learning in the kindergarten year* (pp. 11–25). Washington, DC: National Association for the Education of Young Children.

Berk, L. E. (2009). *Child Development*. (8th ed.). Boston: Pearson.

Berk, L. E. (2012). *Infants, children, & adolescents* (7th ed.). Boston: Pearson/Allyn & Bacon.

Berk, L. E., & Winsler, A. (1995). *Scaffolding children's learning: Vygotsky and early childhood education.* Washington, DC: National Association for the Education of Young Children.

Bernstein, B. (1971). *Class codes and control* (Vol. 1). London: Routledge and Kegan Paul.

Bialystok, E., & Martin, M. M. (2004). Attention and inhibition in bilingual children: Evidence from the dimensional change card sort task. *Developmental Science, 7*, 325–339.

Bialystok, E., McBride-Chang, C., & Luk, G. (2005). Bilingualism, language proficiency, and learning to read in two writing systems. *Journal of Educational Psychology, 97*, 580–590.

Bialystok, E., & Senman, L. (2004). Executive processes in appearance-reality tasks: The role of inhibition of attention and symbolic representation. *Child Development, 75*, 562–579.

Biemiller, A. (2001). Teaching vocabulary: Early, direct, and sequential. *American Educator, 25*(1), 24–28, 47.

Biemiller, A. (2005). Vocabulary development and instruction: A prerequisite for school learning. In D. K. Dickinson & S. B. Neuman (Eds.), *Handbook of early literacy research* (Vol. 2, pp. 41–51). New York: The Guilford Press.

Biemiller, A., & Boote, C. (2006). An effective method for building meaning vocabulary in primary grades. *Journal of Educational Psychology, 98*(1), 44–62.

Bilmes, J. (2004). *Beyond behavior management: The six life skills children need to thrive in today's society*. St. Paul, MN: Redleaf Press.

Bilmes, J. (2006). *Common psychological disorders in young children: A handbook for childcare professionals.* St. Paul, MN: Redleaf Press.

Birbili, M. (2006). Mapping knowledge: Concept maps in early childhood education. *Early Childhood Research and Practice. 8*(2). Retrieved June 20, 2007, from http://www.ecrp.uiuc.edu/v8n2/birbili.html

Birch, S., & Ladd, G. (1997). The teacher-child relationship and children's early school adjustment. *Journal of School Psychology, 35*, 61–69.

Bisgaier, C. S., Samaras, T., & Russo, M. J. (2004). Young children try, try again: Using wood, glue, and words to enhance learning. *Young Children, 59*(4), 22–29.

Bjorklund, D. F. (2005). *Children's thinking: Cognitive development and individual differences.* Belmont, CA: Thomson/Wadsworth.

Black, B., & Hazen, N. L. (1990). Social status and patterns of communication in acquainted and unacquainted preschool children. *Developmental Psychology, 26*, 379–387.

Blades, M., & Spencer, C. (2001). Young children's ability to use coordinate references. *The Journal of Genetic Psychology, 150*(1), 5–18.

Blair, C. (2002). School readiness: Integrating cognition and emotion in a neurobiological conceptualization of children's functioning at school entry. *American Psychologist, 57*(2), 111–127.

Blair, C. (2003). *Self-regulation and school readiness.* Retrieved May 24, 2007, from http://www.ericdigests.org/2004-1/self.htm

Blair, C., & Razza, R. P. (2007). Relating effortful control, executive function, and false belief understanding to emerging math and literacy ability in kindergarten. *Child Development, 78*, 647–663.

Blaut, J. M., & Stea, D. (1974). Mapping at the age of three. *Journal of Geography, 73*(7), 5–9.

Bloodgood, J. W. (1999). What's in a name? Children's name writing and literacy acquisition. *Reading Research Quarterly, 34*, 342–367.

Blume, L. B., & Zembar, M. J. (2007). *Middle childhood to middle adolescence: Development from ages 8 to 18.* Boston: Pearson.

Bodrova, E., & Leong, D. J. (2001). *The tools of the mind project: A case study of implementing the Vygotskyian approach in American early childhood and primary classrooms.* Geneva, Switzerland: International Bureau of Education, UNESCO.

Bodrova, E., & Leong, D. J. (2004). Chopsticks and counting chips: Do play and foundational skills need to compete for the teacher's attention in an early childhood classroom? In D. Koralek (Ed.), *Spotlight on young children and play* (pp. 4–11). Washington, DC: National Association for the Education of Young Children.

Bodrova E., & Leong, D. J. (2005). Self-regulation as a key to school readiness: How can early childhood teachers promote this critical competency? In M. Zaslow & I. Martinez-Beck (Eds.), *Critical issues in early childhood professional development* (pp. 223–270). Baltimore: Paul H. Brookes.

Bodrova, E., & Leong, D. J. (2008). Developing self-regulation in kindergarten: Can we keep all the crickets in the basket? *Young Children, 63*(2), 56–58.

Borra, S. T., Kelly, L., Shirreffs, M. B., Neville, K., & Geiger, C. J. (2003). Developing health messages: Qualitative studies with children, parents, and teachers help identify communications opportunities for healthful lifestyles and the prevention of obesity. *Journal of the American Dietetic Association, 103*(6), 721–728.

Borzekowski, D. L. G. (2009). Considering children and health literacy: A theoretical approach. *Pediatrics, 124*(3), 5282–5288.

Bosma, A. Domka, A., & Peterson, J. (2000). *Improving motor skills in kindergartners.* St. Xavier University (ERIC Document Reproduction Service No. ED453913). Retrieved August 10, 2008 from http://www.eric.ed.gov/contentdelivery/servlet/ERICServlet?accno=ED453913

Bowey, J. A., & Francis, J. (1991). Phonological analysis as a function of age and exposure to reading instruction. *Applied Psycholinguistics, 12*(1), 91–121.

Bowman, B., Donovan, M. S., & Burns, M. S. (Eds.). (2001). *Eager to learn: Educating our preschoolers.* Washington, DC: National Academy Press.

Bowman, B., & Moore, E. K. (2006). *School readiness and social-emotional development: Perspectives on cultural diversity.* Washington, DC: National Black Child Development Institute.

Bowman, B., & Stott, F. (1994). Understanding development in a cultural context: The challenge for teachers. In B. L. Mallory & R. S. New (Eds.), *Diversity and developmentally appropriate practices: Challenges for early childhood education* (pp. 119–133). New York: Teachers College Press.

Bredekamp, S., & Copple, C. (1997). *Developmentally appropriate practice in early childhood programs.* Washington, DC: National Association for the Education of Young Children.

Bredekamp, S., & Rosegrant, T. (1992). *Reaching potentials: Appropriate curriculum and assessment for young children* (Vol. 1). Washington, DC: National Association for the Education of Young Children.

Brenneman, K., & Louro, I. F. (2008). Science journals in the preschool classroom. *Early Childhood Education Journal, 36*(2), 113–119.

Breslin, C. M., Morton, J. R., & Rudisill, M. E. (2008). Implementing a physical activity curriculum into the school day: Helping early childhood teachers meet the challenge. *Early Childhood Education Journal, 35,* 429–437.

Briody, J., & McGarry, K. (2005). Using social studies to ease children's transitions. *Young Children, 60*(5), 38–42.

Bronson, M. B. (1995). *The right stuff for children birth to 8: Selecting play materials to support development.* Washington, DC: National Association for the Education of Young Children.

Bronson, M. B. (2000). *Self-regulation in early childhood.* New York: Guilford Press.

Bronson, M. B. (2006). Developing social and emotional competence. In D. F. Gullo, (Ed.), *K today: Teaching and learning in the kindergarten year* (pp. 47–56). Washington, DC: National Association for the Education of Young Children.

Brophy, J. E. (2004). *Motivating students to learn* (2nd ed.). Mahwah, NJ: Erlbaum.

Brown, B. B. (2004). Adolescents' relationships with peers. In R. M. Lerner & L. Steinberg (Eds.), *Handbook of Adolescent Psychology* (2nd ed., pp. 363–394). New York: Wiley.

Brown, V. (1990). Drama as an integral part of the early childhood curriculum. *Design for Arts in Education, 91*(6), 26–33.

Burger, L. K., & Miller, P. J. (1999). Early talk about the past revisited: Affect in working-class and middle-class children's co-narrations. *Journal of Child Language, 26*(1), 133–162.

Burgess, S. R., & Lonigan, C. J. (1998). Bidirectional relations of phonological sensitivity and prereading abilities: Evidence from a preschool sample. *Journal of Experimental Child Psychology, 70*(2), 117–141.

Burhans, K. K., & Dweck, C. S. (1995). Helplessness in early childhood: The role of contingent worth. *Child Development, 66,* 1719–1738.

Burton, M. (2012). Five strategies for creating meaningful mathematics experiences in the primary grades. In A. Shillady (Ed.), *Spotlight on young children: Exploring math* (pp. 10–14). Washington, DC: National Association for the Education of Young Children.

Burton, R. A., & Denham, S. A. (1998). Are you my friend?: How two young children learned to get along with others. *Journal of Research in Childhood Education, 12,* 210–224.

Bus, A. G., & van IJzendoorn, M. H. (1988). Mother-child interactions, attachment, and emergent literacy: A cross-sectional study. *Child Development, 50,* 1262–1273.

Buysse, V. (1993). Friendships of preschoolers with disabilities in community-based child care settings. *Journal of Early Intervention, 17,* 380–395.

Buysse, V., Goldman, B. D., & Skinner, M. L. (2003). Friendship formation in inclusive early childhood classrooms: What is the teacher's role? *Early Childhood Research Quarterly, 18,* 485–501.

Calkins, L. M., (2001). *The art of teaching reading.* Upper Saddle River, NJ: Pearson Education.

Campbell, F. A., Ramey, C. T., Pungello, E., Sparling, J., & Miller-Johnson, S. (2002). Early childhood education: Young adult outcomes from the Abecedarian project. *Applied Developmental Science, 6,* 42–57.

Campbell, N. E., & Foster, J. E. (1993). Play centers that encourage literacy development. *Early Childhood Education Journal, 21*(2), 22–26.

Campbell, S. B. (1995). Behavior problems in preschool children: A review of recent research. *Journal of Child Psychology and Psychiatry and Allied Disciplines, 36,* 113–149.

Campbell, S. B., Pierce, E. W., March, C. L., Ewing, I. J., & Szumowski, E. K. (1994). Hard-to-manage preschool boys: Symptomatic behavior across contexts and time. *Child Development, 65,* 836–851.

Canobi, K. H. (2004). Individual differences in children's addition and subtraction knowledge. *Cognitive Development, 19,* 81–93.

Carpendale, J., & Lewis, C. (2006). *How children develop social understanding.* Malden, MA: Blackwell Publishing.

Carpenter, T. P., & Levi, L. (2000). *Research report: Developing conceptions of algebraic reasoning in the primary grades.* Madison: National Center for Improving Student Learning and Achievement in Mathematics and Science. Retrieved April 16, 2013 from http://mathematics.ocde.us/Assets/Math/Developing Conceptions of Algebraic Reasoning in the Primary Grades.pdf

Carpenter, T. P., & Levi, L. (2000). *Developing conceptions of algebraic reasoning in the primary grades* (Research Rep. No. 00-2). University of Wisconsin, National Center for Improving Student Learning and Achievement in Mathematics and Science.

Carpenter, T. P., Franke, M. L., Jacobs, V. R., Fennema, E., & Empson, S. B. (1998). A longitudinal study of invention and understanding in children's multidigit addition and subtraction. *Journal for Research in Mathematics Education, 29*(1), 3–20.

Carroll, J. M., Snowling, J. J., Hulme, C., & Stevenson, J. (2003). The development of phonological awareness in preschool children. *Developmental Psychology, 39*(5), 913–923.

Carruthers, P. (1996). *Autism as mind-blindness: An elaboration and partial defense.* Retrieved July 18, 2007, from http://cogprints.org/1193/00/autism.htm

Cartwright, K. B. (2002). Cognitive development and reading: The relation of reading-specific multiple classification skills to reading comprehension in elementary school children. *Journal of Educational Psychology, 94*(1), 56–63.

Casby, M. W. (1997). Symbolic play of children with language impairment: A critical review. *Journal of Speech, Language, and Hearing Research, 40*(3), 468–479.

Cats, H. W., Fey, M. E., Zhang, X., & Tomblin, J. B. (2001). Estimating the risk of future reading difficulties in kindergarten children: A research-based model and clinical implications. *Language, Speech and Hearing Services in School, 32,* 38–50.

Catterall, J., & Peppler, K.A. (2007). Learning in the visual arts and the worldviews of young children. *Cambridge Journal of Education, 37*(4), 542–560.

Chalufour, I., & Worth, K. (2004). *Building structures with young children: The Young Scientist Series.* St. Paul, MN: Redleaf Press.

Chalufour, I., & Worth, K. (2006). Science in Kindergarten. In D. F. Gullo (Ed.), *K today: Teaching and learning in the kindergarten year* (pp. 95–106). Washington, DC: National Association for the Education of Young Children.

Chaney, C. (1992). Language development, metalinguistic skills, and print awareness in 3-year-old children. *Applied Psycholinguistics, 13,* 485–514.

Chapin, J. R. (2006). The achievement gap in social studies and science starts early: Evidence from the Early Childhood Longitudinal Study (Survey). *The Social Studies, 97*(6), 231–238.

Charlesworth, R. (2005a). *Experiences in math for young children* (5th ed., pp. 258–355). Clifton Park, NY: Thomson Delmar Learning.

Charlesworth, R. (2005b). Prekindergarten mathematics: Connecting with national standards. *Early Childhood Education Journal, 32,* 229–236.

Charlesworth, R. (2007). *Understanding child development* (7th ed.). New York: Thomson Delmar Learning.

Charlesworth, R. (2011). *Understanding child development.* (8th ed.). New York: Thomson Delmar Learning.

Charlesworth, R., & Lind, K. K. (2009). *Math and science for young children* (6th ed.). Albany, NY: Delmar.

Chen, S. (1996). Are Japanese young children among the gods? In D. W. Shwalb & B. J. Shwalb (Eds.), *Japanese child rearing: Two generations of scholarship* (pp. 31–43). New York: Guilford Press.

Chen, A., & Zhu, W. (2005). Young children's intuitive interest in physical activity: Personal, school, and home factors. *Journal of Physical Activity and Health, 2,* 1–15.

Chen, J -Q., Masur, A., & McNamee, G. (2011). Young children's approaches to learning: A sociocultural perspective. *Early Child Development and Care, 181*(8), 1137–1152.

Chen, Z., Sanchez, R. P., & Cambell, T. (1997). From beyond to within their grasp: The rudiments of analogical problem solving in 10- and 13-month-olds. *Developmental Psychology, 33,* 790–801.

Christie, J. F. (1983). The effects of play tutoring on young children's cognitive performance. *Journal of Educational Research, 76,* 326–330.

Cillessen, A. H. N., & Bellmore, A. D. (2002). Social skills and interpersonal perception. In P. K. Smith & C. H. Hart (Eds.), *Blackwell handbook of childhood social development* (pp. 355–374). Oxford: Blackwell.

Clay, M. M. (1979a). *The early detection of reading difficulties* (2nd ed.). Auckland, New Zealand: Heinemann.

Clay, M. M. (1979b). *Reading recovery: A guidebook for teachers in training.* Auckland, New Zealand: Heinemann.

Clements, D. H. (1999). Geometry and spatial thinking in young children. In J. V. Copley (Ed.), *Mathematics in the early years* (pp. 66–79). Reston, VA: National Council of Teachers of Mathematics.

Clements, D. H. (2001). Mathematics in the preschool. *Teaching Children Mathematics, 7*(5), 270–275.

Clements, D. H. (2003, September). *Good beginnings in mathematics: Linking a national vision to state action.* New York: Carnegie Corporation.

Clements, D. H. (2004a). Geometric and spatial thinking in early childhood education. In D. H. Clements, J. Sarama, & A. -M. DiBiase, (Eds.), *Engaging young children in mathematics* (pp. 267–297). Mahwah, NJ: Lawrence Erlbaum Associates.

Clements, D. H. (2004b). Major themes and recommendations. In D. H. Clements, J. Sarama, & A. -M. DiBiase (Eds.), *Engaging young children in mathematics: Standards for early childhood mathematics education* (pp. 7–72). Mahwah, NJ: Lawrence Erlbaum Associates.

Clements, D. H., Battista, M. T., & Sarama, J. (2001). Logo and geometry. *Journal for Research in Mathematics Education Monograph Series, 10.*

Clements, D. H., Battista, M. T., Sarama, J., & Swaminathan, S. (1997). Development of students' spatial thinking in a unit on geometric motions and area. *Elementary School Journal, 98*(2), 171–186.

Clements, D. H., Battista, M. T., Sarama, J., & Swaminathan, S., & McMillen, S. (1997). Students' development of length concepts in a Logo-based unit on geometric paths. *Journal of Research in Mathematics Education, 28*(1), 70–95.

Clements, D. H., & Sarama, J. (2000). Young children's ideas about geometric shapes. *Teaching Children Mathematics, 6*(8), 482–488.

Clements, D. H., & Sarama, J. (2003). Young children and technology: What does the research say? *Young Children, 58*(6), 34–40.

Clements, D. H., & Sarama, J. (2009). *Learning and teaching early math: The learning trajectories approach.* New York: Routledge.

Clements, D. H., Sarama, J., & DiBiase, A. -M. (Eds.). (2004). *Engaging young children in mathematics: Standards for early childhood mathematics education.* Mahwah, NJ: Lawrence Erlbaum Associates.

Clements, D. H., & Stephan, M. (2004). Measurement in pre-K to grade 2 mathematics. In D. H. Clements, J. Sarama, & A. -M. DiBiase (Eds.). *Engaging young children in mathematics: Standards for early childhood mathematics education* (pp. 299-317). Mahwah, NJ: Lawrence Erlbaum Associates.

Clements, D. H., Wilson, D. C., & Sarama, J. (2004). Young children's composition of geometric figures: A learning trajectory. *Mathematical Thinking and Learning, 6*(2), 163–184.

Cohen, L., & Uhry, J. (2007). Young children's discourse strategies during block play: A Bakhtinian approach. *Journal of Research in Childhood Education, 21*, 302–315.

Colbert, C. (1997). Visual arts in the developmentally appropriate integrated curriculum. In C. H. Hart, D. C. Burts, & R. Charlesworth (Eds.), *Integrated curriculum and developmentally appropriate practice: Birth to age eight* (pp. 201–223). Albany, NY: SUNY Press.

Collier, V. (1987). Age and rate of acquisition of second language for academic purposes. *TESOL Quarterly, 21*(4), 617–641.

Collier, V. (1989, September). How long? A synthesis of research on academic achievement in second language. *TESOL Quarterly, 23*(3), 509–531.

Coloroso, B. (2008). *The bully, the bullied, and the bystander.* New York: HarperCollins Publishers.

Committee for Children. (2002). *Second Step: A violence-prevention curriculum.* Seattle: Author.

Conezio, K., & French, L. (2002). Science in the preschool classroom: Capitalizing on children's fascination with the everyday world to foster language and literacy development. *Young Children, 57*(5), 12–18.

Cook, R. E., Klein, M. D., & Tessier, A. (2004). *Adapting early childhood curricula for children in inclusive settings* (6th ed.). Upper Saddle River, NJ: Pearson Merrill Prentice Hall.

Coplan, R. J., Findlay, L. C., & Nelson, L. J. (2004). Characteristics of preschoolers with lower perceived competence. *Journal of Abnormal Child Psychology, 32*, 399–408.

Coplan, R. J., & Prakash, K. (2003). Spending time with teacher: Characteristics of preschoolers who frequently elicit versus initiate interactions with teachers. *Early Childhood Research Quarterly, 18*, 143–158.

Copley, J. V. (Ed.). (1999). *Mathematics in the early years* (pp. 11–20; 39–99). Washington, DC: National Association for the Education of Young Children.

Copley, J. V. (2000). *The young child and mathematics.* Washington, DC: National Association for the Education of Young Children.

Copley, J. V. (2005). *Measuring with young children.* Paper presented at the International Conference for the Education of the Young Child, Madrid, Spain.

Copley, J. V. (2010). *The young child and mathematics* (2nd ed.). Washington, DC: National Association for the Education of Young Children.

Copley. J. V., & Hawkins, J. (2005). *Interim report of C3 coaching grant: Mathematics professional development.*

Copley, J. V., Jones, C., & Dighe, J. (2007). *Mathematics: The Creative Curriculum® approach.* Washington, DC: Teaching Strategies, Inc.

Copple, C. (2012). *Growing minds: Building strong cognitive foundations in early childhood.* Washington, DC: National Association for the Education of Young Children.

Copple, C., & Bredekamp, S. (2006). *Basics of developmentally appropriate practice: An introduction for teachers of children 3 to 6.* Washington, DC: National Association for the Education of Young Children.

Copple, C., & Bredekamp, S. (Eds.). (2009). *Developmentally appropriate practice in early childhood programs serving children from birth to age 8* (3rd ed.). Washington, DC: National Association for the Education of Young Children.

Copple, C. (2014). *Developmentally appropriate practice: Focus on children in first, second, and third grades.* Washington, DC: National Association for the Education of Young Children.

Cornelius-White, J. (2007). Learner-centered teacher-student relationships are effective: A meta-analysis. *Review of Educational Research, 77*(1), 113–143.

Cross, C. T., Woods, T. A., & Schweingruber, H. (Eds.) (2009). *Mathematics learning in early childhood: Paths toward excellence and equity.* Washington, DC: National Research Council, National Academies Press.

Cummins, J. (1984). *Bilingualism and special education: Issues in assessment and pedagogy.* San Diego: College-Hill Press.

Cunningham, J. W., Spadorcia, S. A., Erickson, K. A., & Koppenhaver, D. A. (2004). Investigating the instructional supportiveness of leveled texts. *Reading Research Quarterly, 40*(4), 410–427.

Curenton, S. M., & Ryan, S. K. (2006). Oral storytelling: A cultural art that promotes school readiness. *Young Children, 61*(5), 78–89.

Curry, N. E., & Johnson, C. N. (1991). *Beyond self-esteem: Developing a genuine sense of human value.* Washington, DC: National Association for the Education of Young Children.

Curtis, D., & Carter, M. (2003). *Designs for living and learning: Transforming early childhood environments.* St. Paul, MN: Redleaf Press.

Cutler, K. M., Gilderson, D., Parrott, S., & Browne, M. T. (2003). Developing math games based on children's literature. In D. Koralek (Ed.), *Spotlight on young children and math* (pp. 14–18). Washington, DC: National Association for the Education of Young Children.

D'Addesio, J., Grob, B., Furman, L., Hayes, K., & David, J. (2005). Social studies: Learning about the world around us. *Young Children, 60*(5), 50–57.

Daniels, D. H., & Perry, K. E. (2003). "Learner-centered" according to children. *Theory into Practice, 42*(2), 102–108.

Danoff-Burg, J. A. (2002). Be a bee and other approaches to introducing young children to entomology. *Young Children, 57*(5), 42–47.

Day, C. B. (2006). Leveraging diversity to benefit children's social-emotional development and school readiness. In B. Bowman & E. K. Moore (Eds.), *School readiness and social-emotional development: Perspectives on cultural diversity* (pp. 23–32). Washington, DC: National Black Child Development Institute, Inc.

Daytner, K., Johanson, J., Clark, L., & Robinson, L. (2012). Accessing curriculum through technology tools (ACTTT): A model development project. *Early Childhood Research and Practice, 14*(1).

Deak, G. O. (2003). *The development of cognitive flexibility and language abilities.* Retrieved May 25, 2007, from http://cogsci.ucsd.edu/~deak/publications/Deak_Advances03pdf

Deater-Deckard, K., Petrill, S. A., Thompson, L. A., & DeThorne, L. S. (2005). A cross-sectional behavioral genetic analysis of task persistence in the transition to middle childhood. *Developmental Science, 8*(3), F21–F26.

DeBord, K. (n.d.) *Childhood years: Ages six through twelve.* NC: North Carolina Cooperative Extension Service. Retrieved April 2, 2013, from http://www.ces.ncsu.edu/depts/fcs/pdfs/fcs465.pdf

Deci, E. L., Koestner, R., & Ryan, R. M. (2001). Extrinsic rewards and intrinsic motivation in education: Reconsidered once again. *Review of Educational Research, 71*(1), 1–27.

Deli, E., Bakle, I., & Zachopoulou, E. (2006). Implementing intervention movement programs for kindergarten children. *Journal of Early Childhood Research, 4*(1), 5–18.

DeLoache, J. S. (1987). Rapid change in the symbolic functioning of very young children. *Science, 238*(4833), 1556–1557.

DeLoache, J. S. (1991). Symbolic functioning in very young children. Understanding of pictures and models. *Child Development, 62*, 736–752.

DeLoache, J. S. (2000). Dual representation and young children's use of scale models. *Child Development, 71*, 329–338.

DeLoache, J. S. (2004). Becoming symbol-minded. *Trends in Cognitive Sciences, 8*(2), 66–70.

Denac, O. (2008). A case study of preschool children's musical interests at home and at school. *Early Childhood Education Journal, 35*(5), 439–444.

Denham, S. A. (2007). Dealing with feelings: How children negotiate the worlds of emotions and social relationships. *Cognitie, Creier, Comportament, 11*(1), 1–48.

Denham, S. A., Blair, K., Schmidt, M., & DeMulder, E. (2002). Compromised emotional competence: Seeds of violence sown early? *American Journal of Orthopsychiatry. 72*(1), 70–82.

Denham, S. A., & Burton, R. (1996). A social-emotional intervention for at-risk 4-year-olds. *Journal of School Psychology, 34*(3), 225–245.

Denham, S. A., & Burton, R. (2003). *Social and emotional prevention and intervention programming for preschoolers*. New York: Springer.

Denham, S. A., Caverly, S., Schmidt, M., Blair, K., DeMulder, E., Caal, S., et al. (2002). Preschool understanding of emotions: contributions to classroom anger and aggression. *Journal of Child Psychology and Psychiatry, 43*(7), 901–916.

Denham, S. A., & Kochanoff, A. T. (2002). Parental contributions to preschoolers' understanding of emotion. *Marriage and Family Review, 34*, 311–343.

Denham, S. A., McKinley, M., Couchoud, E. A., & Holt, R. (1990). Emotional and behavioral predictors of preschool peer ratings. *Child Development, 61*, 1145–1152.

Denham, S., von Salisch, M., Olthof, T., Kochanoff, A., & Caverly, S. (2002). Emotional and social development in childhood. In P. K. Smith & C. H. Hart (Eds.), *Blackwell handbook of childhood social development* (pp. 307–328). Oxford: Blackwell.

Desouza, J. M. S., & Czerniak, C. M. (2002). Social behaviors and gender differences among preschoolers: Implications for science activities. *Journal of Research in Childhood Education, 16*(2), 175–188.

de Vries, P. A. (2008). Parental perceptions of music in storytelling sessions in a public library. *Early Childhood Education Journal, 35*(5), 473–478.

DeVries, R. (2006). Games with rules. In D. P. Fromberg & D. Bergen (Eds.), *Play from birth to twelve: Contexts, perspectives, and meanings.* (2nd ed., pp. 119–125). New York: Routledge/Taylor & Francis Group.

DeVries, R., Haney, J., & Zan, B. (1991). Sociomoral atmosphere in direct-instruction, eclectic, and constructivist kindergartens: A study of teachers' enacted interpersonal understanding. *Early Childhood Research Quarterly, 6*(4), 449–471.

de Wied, M., Branje, S. J. T., & Meeus, W H. J. (2007). Empathy and conflict resolution in friendship relations among adolescents. *Aggressive Behavior, 33*, 48-55.

Diamond, K. E. (2002). Social competence in children with disabilities. In P. K. Smith & C. H. Hart (Eds.), *Blackwell handbook of childhood social development* (pp. 571–587). Oxford: Blackwell.

Diamond, K. E., & Hestenes, L. L. (1996). Preschool children's conceptions of disabilities: The salience of disabilities in children's ideas about others. *Topics in Early Childhood Special Education, 16*(4), 458–475.

Dickinson, D., & Neuman, S., Eds. (2002). *Handbook of Early Literacy Research.* New York: Guilford Press.

Dickinson, D., & Neuman, S., Eds. (2006). *Handbook of Early Literacy Research,* Volume 2. New York: Guilford Press.

Dickinson, D. K., & Tabors, P. O. (1991). Early literacy: Linkages between home, school, and literacy achievement at age five. *Journal of Research in Childhood Education, 6,* 30–46.

Dickinson, D. K., & Tabors, P. O. (Eds.). (2001). *Building literacy with language: Young children learning at home and school.* Baltimore: Paul H. Brookes.

Dickinson, D. K., Golinkoff, R. M., & Hirsh-Pasek, K. (2010). Speaking out for language: Why language is central to reading development. *Educational Researcher, 39*(4), 305–310.

Diesendruck, G., Hammer, R., & Catz, O. (2003). Mapping the similarity space of children and adults' artifacts categories. *Cognitive Development, 18,* 217–231.

Dinwiddle, S. A. (1994). The saga of Sally, Sammy, and the red pen: Facilitating children's social problem solving. *Young Children, 49,* 13–19.

Dodd, J. (1992). *Preventing American Indian children from overidentification with learning disabilities: Cultural considerations during the pre-referral process.* Paper presented at the Council for Exceptional Children, Division for Early Childhood, Topical Conference on Culturally and Linguistically Diverse Exceptional Children (Minneapolis, MN, November 12–14, 1992).

Dodge, D. T., Colker, L. J., & Heroman, C. (2002). *The Creative Curriculum® for preschool* (4th ed.). Washington, DC: Teaching Strategies.

Dodge, D. T, Rudick, S., & Berke, K. (2006). *The Creative Curriculum® for infants, toddlers & twos* (2nd ed.). Washington, DC: Teaching Strategies.

Dodge, K. A., Schlundt, D. C., Schocken, I., & Delugach, J. D. (1983). Social competence in children's sociometric status: The role of peer group strategies. *Merrill-Palmer Quarterly, 29,* 309–336.

Dougherty Stahl, K. A. (2004). Proof, practice, and promise: Comprehension strategy instruction in the primary grades. *The Reading Teacher, 57*(7), 598–609.

Downey, G. & Walker, E. (1989). Social cognition and adjustment in children at risk for psychopathology. *Developmental Psychology, 25,* 835–845.

Drew, W. F., & Rankin, B. (2004). Promoting creativity for life using open-ended materials. *Young Children, 59*(4), 38–45.

Duncan, G. J., Dowsett, C. J., Claessens, A., Magnuson, K., Huston, A. C., Klebanov, P., et al. (2007). School readiness and later achievement. *Developmental Psychology, 43*(6), 1428–1446.

Dunn, J., & Brown, J. (1991). Relationships, talk about feelings, and the development of affect regulation in early childhood. In J. Garber & K. A. Dodge (Eds.), *The development of emotional regulation and dysregulation* (pp. 89–108). New York: Cambridge University Press.

Dymock, S. & Nicholson, T. (2007). *Teaching text structures: A key to nonfiction reading success.* New York: Scholastic.

Dymock, S., & Nicholson, T. (2010). "High 5!" Strategies to enhance comprehension of expository text. *Reading Teacher, 64*(3), 166–178.

Eccles, J. A., Wigfield, R. D., Harold, & Blumfeld, P. (1993). Age and gender differences in children's self- and task perceptions during elementary school. *Child Development 64*(3), 8330-8347.

Economidou Stavrou, N., Chrysostomou, S., & Socratous, H. (2011). Music learning in the early years: Interdisciplinary approaches based on multiple intelligences. *Journal for Learning through the Arts, 7*(1), 1–16.

Education Northwest. (n.d.). *6 + 1 Trait® definitions.* Retrieved April 18, 2013, from http://educationnorthwest.org/resource/503

Ehrenworth, M. & Vinton, V. (2005). *The power of grammar: Unconventional approaches to the conventions of language.* Portsmouth, NH: Heinemann.

Ehri, L. C. (2005). Learning to read words: Theory, findings, and issues. *Scientific Studies of Reading, 9*(2), 167–188.

Ehri, L. C., Nunes, S. R., Willows, D. M., Schuster, B. V., Yaghoub-Zadeh, Z., & Shanahan, T. (2001). Phonemic awareness instruction helps children learn to read: Evidence from the national reading panel's meta-analysis. *Reading Research Quarterly, 36,* 250–297.

Eisenberg, A. R. (1985). Learning to describe past experiences in conversation. *Discourse Processes, 8,* 177–204.

Eisenberg, A. R. (1999). Emotion talk among Mexican-American and Anglo-American mothers and children from two social classes. *Merrill-Palmer Quarterly, 45*(2), 267–284.

Eisenberg, N., Fabes, R. A., Shepard, S. A., Murphy, B. C., Guthrie, I. K., Jones, S., et. al. (1997). Contemporaneous and longitudinal prediction of child's social functioning from regulation and emotionality. *Child Development, 68,* 642–664.

Elbro, C. I., Borstrom, D. K., & Peterson, P. (1998). Predicting dyslexia from kindergarten: The importance of directness of phonological representations of lexical items. *Reading Research Quarterly, 3,* 36–60.

Elias, C. L., & Berk, L. E. (2002). Self-regulation in young children: Is there a role for sociodramatic play? *Early Childhood Research Quarterly, 17,* 216–238.

Elliot, A. J., & Dweck, C. S. (Eds.). (2005). *Handbook of competence and motivation.* New York: Guilford Press.

Ellis, R. (2000). *Second language acquisition.* New York: Oxford University Press.

Emma, L., & Jarrett, M. (2010). *How we play: Cultural determinants of physical activity in young children.* Reston, VA: Head Start Body Start National Center for Physical Development and Outdoor Play. Retrieved April 24, 2013, from http://www.aahperd.org/headstartbodystart/activityresources/upload/HowWePlay_LitReview.pdf

Empson, S. B. (1999). Equal sharing and shared meaning: The development of fraction concepts in a first-grade classroom. *Cognition and Instruction, 17*(3), 283–342.

Engel, B. S. (1995). *Considering children's art: Why and how to value their works.* Washington, DC: National Association for the Education of Young Children.

Epstein, A. S. (2007). *The intentional teacher: Choosing the best strategies for young children's learning.* Washington, DC: National Association for the Education of Young Children.

Epstein, A. S. (2009). *Me, you, us: Social-emotional learning in preschool.* Ypsilanti, MI: HighScope Press.

Eshach, H., & Fried, N. N. (2005). Should science be taught in early childhood? *Journal of Science Education and Technology, 14*(3), 315–336.

Erdley, C. A., & Asher, S. R. (1999). A social goals perspective on children's social competence. *Journal of Emotional and Behavioral Disorders, 7,* 156–167.

Espinosa, L. M. (2005). Curriculum and assessment considerations for young children from culturally, linguistically, and economically diverse backgrounds. *Psychology in the Schools, 42*(8), 837–853.

Espinosa, L. M. (2015). Challenges and benefits of early bilingualism in the United States context. *Global Education Review 2*(1),14–31.

Fabes, R. A., Eisenberg, N., Karbon, M., Bernzweig, J., Speer, A. L., & Carlo, G. (1994). Socialization of children's vicarious emotional responding and prosocial behavior: Relations with mothers' perceptions of children's emotional reactivity. *Developmental Psychology, 30*, 44–55.

Fahey, T. D., Insel, P. M., & Roth, W. T. (2003). *Fit and well.* New York: McGraw-Hill.

Fantini, A. (1985). *Language acquisition of a bilingual child.* San Diego: College-Hill Press.

Fantuzzo, J., & McWayne, C. (2002). The relationship between peer-play interactions in the family context and dimensions of school readiness for low-income preschool children. *Journal of Educational Psychology, 94*(1), 79–87.

Fantuzzo, J., Perry, M. A., & McDermott, P. (2004). Preschool approaches to learning and their relationship to other relevant classroom competencies for low-income children. *School Psychology Quarterly, 19*(3), 212–230.

Farver, J. A. M. (1992). Communicating shared meaning in social pretend play. *Early Childhood Research Quarterly, 7*, 501–516.

Feder, K.P., & Majnemer, A. (2007). Handwriting development, competency, and intervention. *Developmental Medicine & Child Neurology, 49*, 312–317.

Feeney, S., & Moravcik, E. (2005). Children's literature: A window to understanding self and others. *Young Children 60*(5), 20–28.

Feldman, R. S., McGee, G., Mann, L. & Strain, P. S. (1993). Nonverbal affective decoding ability in children with autism and in typical preschoolers. *Journal of Early Intervention, 17*(4), 341–350.

Fenson, L., Dale, P. S., Reznick, J. S., Bates, E., Thal, D. J., & Pethick, S. J. (1994). Variability in early communicative development. *Monographs of the Society for Research in Child Development, 59* (5, Serial No. 242).

Ferreiro, E., & Teberosky, A. (1982). Children's metalinguistic knowledge of syntactical constituents: Effects of age and schooling. *Developmental Psychology, 30*, 663–674.

Fisher, E. P. (1992). The impact of play on development: A meta-analysis. *Play and Culture, 5*(2), 159–181.

Fletcher, K. L., & Sabo, J. (2006). Picture book reading experience and toddlers' behaviors with photographs and books. *Early Childhood Research and Practice, 8*(1). Retrieved June 20, 2007, from http://ecrp.uiuc.edu/v8n1/fletcher.html

Florida Center for Reading Research (n.d.). Retrieved April 24, 2013, from http://www.fcrr.org

Flynn, L. L., & Kieff, J. (2002). Including everyone in outdoor play. *Young Children, 57*(3), 20–26.

Forbes, S. & Briggs, C. (2003). *Research in reading recovery* (Vol. 2). Portsmouth, NH: Heinemann.

Fountas, I. C. & Pinnell, G. S. (1996). *Guided reading: Good first teaching for all children.* Portsmouth, NH: Heinemann.

Fountas, I. C. & Pinnell, G. S. (2011). *Literacy beginnings: A prekindergarten handbook.* Portsmouth, NH: Heinemann.

Fox, B. (2003). *Word identification strategies: Phonics from a new perspective.* Upper Saddle River, NJ: Prentice Hall.

Frank, R. E. (1987). *The emergence of route map reading skills in young children.* Abstract retrieved February 12, 2013, from http://www.eric.ed.gov/ERICWebPortal/search/detailmini.jsp?_nfpb=true&... (ERIC Reproduction Service Number ED288785)

Fredricks , J. A., Blumenfeld , P. C., & Paris, A. H. (2004). School engagement: Potential of the concept, state of the evidence. *Review of Educational Research, 74*(1), 59–109.

Friedman, S. (2005). Social studies in action. *Young Children, 60*(5), 44–47.

Friedman, W. J. (2005). Developmental and cognitive perspectives on humans' sense of times of past and future events. *Learning and Motivation, 26*, 145–158.

Friel, S. N., Curcio, F. R., & Bright, G. W. (2001). Making sense of graphs: Critical factors influencing comprehension and instructional implications. *Journal for Research in Mathematics Education, 32*(2), 124–158.

Fromberg, D. P., & Bergen, D. (Eds.) (2006). *Play from birth to twelve: Contexts, perspectives, and meanings* (2nd ed.). New York: Routledge/Taylor & Francis Group.

Fromkin, V., Rodman, R., & Hyams, N. (2007). *An introduction to language*. Boston: Thomson Wadsworth.

Fuchs, D., Compton, D. L., Fuchs, L. S., Bryant, V. J., Hamlett, C. L., & Lambert, W. (2012). First-grade cognitive abilities as long-term predictors of reading comprehension and disability status. *Journal of Learning Disabilities, 45*(3), 217–231.

Fuson, K. C. (2004). Pre-K to grade 2 goals and standards: Achieving 21st century mastery for all. In D. H. Clements, J. Sarama, & A -M. DiBiase (Eds.), *Engaging young children in mathematics: Standards for early childhood mathematics education* (pp. 105–148). Mahwah, NJ: Lawrence Erlbaum Associates.

Gabbard, C. (1998). Windows of opportunity for early brain and motor development. *Journal of Physical Education, Recreation & Dance, 69*(8), 54–56.

Gajria, M., Jitendra, A. K., Sacks, S., & Sood, S. (2007). Improving content area instruction for students with learning disabilities: A meta-analysis. *Journal of Learning Disabilities, 40*(3), 210–225.

Gallahue, D. A. (1995). Transforming physical education curriculum. In S. Bredekamp & T. Rosegrant (Eds.), *Reaching potentials: Transforming early childhood curriculum and assessment* (Vol. 2, pp. 125–144). Washington, DC: National Association for the Education of Young Children.

Gallahue, D. A. (2008). Developmental physical education for all. Champaign, IL: Human Kinetics Publishers.

Gambrell, L. B., & Jawitz , P. B. (1993). Mental imagery, text illustrations, and children's story comprehension and recall. *Reading Research Quarterly, 28*(3), 264–276.

Gargiulo, R., & Kilgo, J. (2007). *Young children with special needs* (2nd ed). Albany, NY: Thomson Delmar Learning.

Gartrell, D., & Gartrell, J. J. (2008). Guidance matters: Understand bullying. *Young Children, 63*(3), 54–57.

Gauvain, M., & Rogoff, B. (1989). Ways of speaking about space: The development of children's skills in communicating spatial knowledge. *Cognitive Development, 4*(3), 295–307.

Geary, D. C., Bailey, D. H., Littlefield, A., Wood, P., Hoard, M. K., & Nugent, L. (2009). First-grade predictors of mathematical learning disability: A latent class trajectory analysis. *Cognitive Development, 24,* 411–429.

Geist, E. (2001). Children are born mathematicians: Promoting the construction of early mathematical concepts in children under five. *Young Children, 56*(4), 12–19.

Geist, E. (2003). Infants and toddlers exploring mathematics. In D. Koralek (Ed.), *Spotlight on young children and math* (pp. 4–6). Washington, DC: National Association for the Education of Young Children.

Geist, E. (2009). *Children are born mathematicians: Supporting mathematical development, birth to age 8.* Upper Saddle River, NJ: Pearson.

Gelman, R., & Brenneman, K. (2004). Science learning pathways for young children. *Early Childhood Research Quarterly, 19*(1), 150–158.

Gelman, R., & Gallistel, C. R. (1978). *The Child's Understanding of Number.* Cambridge, MA: Harvard University Press.

Gelman, S. A. (1998). Categories in young children's thinking. *Young Children, 53*(1), 20–26.

Gelman, S. A., Chesnick, R., & Waxman, S. (2005). Mother-child conversations about pictures and objects: Referring to categories and individuals. *Child Development, 76,* 1129–1143.

Gelman, S. A., & Coley, J. D. (1990). The importance of knowing a dodo is a bird: Categories and inferences in 2-year-old children. *Developmental Psychology, 26,* 796–804.

Gelman, S. A., Coley, J. D., Rosengren, K. S., Hartman, E., & Pappas, A. (1998). Beyond labeling: The role of maternal input in the acquisition of richly structured categories. *Monographs of the Society for Research in Child Development, 63* (1, Serial No. 253).

Genishi, C., & Brainard, M. (1995). Assessment of bilingual children: A dilemma seeking solutions. In E. E. García & B. McLaughlin (Eds.), *Meeting the challenge of linguistic and cultural diversity in early childhood education* (pp. 49–63). New York: Teachers College Press.

Gentry, J. R. (2008). *Step-by-step assessment guide to code breaking*. New York: Scholastic.

George, J., & Greenfield, D. B. (2005). Examination of a structured problem-solving flexibility task for assessing approaches to learning in young children: Relation to teacher ratings and children's achievement. *Applied Developmental Psychology, 26*, 69–84.

Gifford-Smith, M. E., & Brownell, C. A. (2003). Childhood peer relationships: Social acceptance, friendships, and peer networks. *Journal of School Psychology, 41*, 235–284.

Ginsburg, H. P., & Baroody, A. J. (2003). *Test of early mathematics ability: Examiner's manual* (3rd ed.). Austin, TX: Pro-Ed.

Ginsburg, H. P. & Golbeck, S. L. (2004). Thoughts on the future of research on mathematics and science learning and education. *Early Childhood Research Quarterly 19*, 190–200.

Ginsburg, A., & Leinwand, S. (2009). *Informing grades 1–6 mathematics standards development: What can be learned from high-performing Hong Kong, Korea and Singapore?* Washington, DC: American Institutes for Research.

Ginsburg, H. P., Inoue, N., & Seo, K. (1999). Young children doing mathematics. In J. V. Copley (Ed.), *Mathematics in the early years* (pp. 88–91). Washington, DC and Reston, VA: National Association for the Education of Young Children and National Council of Teachers of Mathematics.

Gober, S. Y. (2002). *Six simple ways to assess young children*. Albany, NY: Delmar Thomson Learning.

Golbeck, S. L. (2005). Research in review: Building foundations for spatial literacy in early childhood. *Young Children, 60*(6), 72–83.

Goldstein, P. (2004). Helping young children with special needs develop vocabulary. *Early Childhood Education Journal, 32*, 1–43.

Gonzalez, V. (1998). *Language and cognitive development in second language learners*. Boston: Allyn & Bacon.

Gonzalez, V., Bauerle, P., & Felix-Holt, M. (1996). Theoretical and practical implications of assessing cognitive and language development in bilingual children with qualitative methods. *Bilingual Research Journal, 20*(1), 93–131.

Gonzalez-Mena, J. (2002). *The child in the family and the community* (3rd ed.). Upper Saddle River, NJ: Merrill Prentice Hall.

Gopnik, A., & Choi, S. (1995). *Beyond names for things: Children's acquisition of verbs*. Hillsdale, NJ: Erlbaum.

Gordon, A. M., & Williams-Brown, K. (1996). *Beginnings and beyond* (4th ed.). Albany, NY: Delmar.

Gould, P., & Sullivan, J. (1999). *The inclusive early childhood classroom: Easy ways to adapt learning centers for all children*. Beltsville, MD: Gryphon House.

Gowen, J. W. (1995). Research in review: The early development of symbolic play. *Young Children, 50*(3), 75–84.

Graham, G., Holt/Hale, S., & Parker, M. (2010). *Children moving: A reflective approach to teaching physical education*. Boston, MA; McGraw Hill.

Graham, S., Gillespie, A., & McKeown, D. (2013). Writing: Importance, development, and instruction. *Reading and Writing, 26*(1), 1–15.

Graham, S., & Harris, K. R. (2015). Common Core State Standards and writing: Introduction to the special issue. *The Elementary School Journal, 115*(4), 457–463.

Green, L. (2009). Morphology and literacy: Getting our heads in the game. *Language, Speech, and Hearing Services in Schools, 40*, 283–285.

Grissmer, D., Grimm, K.J., Aiyer, S.M., Murrah, W.M., & Steele, J.S. (2010). Fine motor skills and early comprehension of the world: Two new school readiness indicators. *Developmental Psychology, 46*(5), 1008–1017.

Gullo, D. F. (Ed.). (2006). *K today: Teaching and learning in the kindergarten year.* Washington, DC: National Association for the Education of Young Children.

Gundlach, R., McLane, J., Scott, F. M., & McNamee, G. D. (1985). The social foundations of early writing development. In M. Farr (Ed.), *Advances in writing research: Vol. 1: Studies in children's early writing development.* Norwood, NJ: Ablex.

Hair, E., Halle, T., Terry-Humen, E., Lavelle, B., & Calkins, J. (2006). Children's school readiness in the ECLS-K: Predictions to academic, health, and social outcomes in first grade. *Early Childhood Research Quarterly, 21*(4), 431–454.

Hakuta, K. (1978). A report on the development of grammatical morphemes in a Japanese girl learning English as a second language. In E. M. Hatch (Ed.), *Second language acquisition: A book of readings* (pp. 132–147). Rowley, MA: Newbury House Publishers.

Hakuta, K. (1986). *Mirror of language: The debate on bilingualism.* New York: Basic Books.

Halliday, M. A. K. (2002). Relevant models of language. In B. M. Power & R. S. Hubbard (Eds.), *Language development: A reader for teachers* (2nd ed., pp. 49–53). Upper Saddle River, NJ: Merrill.

Hammond, W. D., & Nessel, D. D. (2011). *The comprehension experience: Engaging readers through effective inquiry and discussion.* Portsmouth, NH: Heinemann.

Hamre, B., & Pianta, R. C. (2001). Early teacher–child relationships and the trajectory of children's school outcomes through eighth grade. *Child Development, 72*(2), 625–638.

Hannust, T., & Kikas, E. (2007). Children's knowledge of astronomy and its change in the course of learning. *Early Childhood Research Quarterly, 22*(1), 89–104.

Hapgood, S., Magnuson, S. J., & Sullivan Palincsar, A. (2004). Teacher, text, and experience: A case of young children's scientific inquiry. *The Journal of the Learning Sciences, 13*(4), 455–505.

Harper, L. V., & McCluskey, K. S. (2002). Caregiver and peer responses to children with language and motor disabilities in inclusive preschool programs. *Early Childhood Research Quarterly, 17*, 148–166.

Hart, B., & Risley, T. R. (1995). *Meaningful differences in the everyday experience of young American children.* Baltimore: Paul H. Brookes.

Hart, B., & Risley, T. R., (2003). The early catastrophe. *Education Review, 17*(1), 110–118.

Hart, C. H., McGee, L. M., & Hernandez, S. (1993). Themes in the peer relations literature: Correspondence to outdoor peer interactions portrayed in children's storybooks. In C. H. Hart (Ed.), *Children on playgrounds: Research perspectives and applications* (pp. 371–416). Albany, NY: SUNY Press.

Harter, S. (1998). The development of self-representations. In W. Damon & N. Eisenberg (Eds.), *Handbook of child psychology: Vol. 3. Social, emotional, and personality development* (pp. 553–617). New York: John Wiley & Sons.

Harter, S. (1999). *The construction of the self: A developmental perspective.* New York: Guilford Press.

Hartup, W. W., & Abecassis, M. (2002). Friends and enemies. In P. K. Smith & C. H. Hart (Eds.), *Blackwell handbook of childhood social development* (pp. 285–306). Oxford: Blackwell.

Hartup, W. W., & Laursen, B. (1999). Relationships as developmental contexts: Retrospective themes and contemporary issues. In W. A. Collins (Ed.), *Relationships as developmental contexts: Vol. 30. The Minnesota symposia on child psychology* (pp.13–35). Mahwah, NJ: Erlbaum.

Harwood, R. L., Miller, J. G., & Irizarry, N. L. (1995). *Culture and attachment: Perceptions of the child in context.* New York: Guilford.

Haugland, S. W. (2000). What role should technology play in young children's learning? Part 2: Early childhood classrooms in the 21st century: Using computers to maximize learning. *Young Children, 55*(1), 12–18.

Head Start Bureau. (2002). *Identifying strategies to support English language learners in Head Start and Early Head Start programs.* (English Language Learners Focus Group Report.) Washington, DC: Author.

Heath, S. M., & Hogben, J. H. (2004). Cost-effective prediction of reading difficulties. *Journal of Speech, Language, and Hearing Research, 47*(4), 751–765.

Heffron, S., & Downs, R. (2012). *Geography for life: National geography standards,* (2nd ed.). Washington, DC: National Council for Geographic Education.

Heise-Baigorria, C. & Tabors, P. O. (2004). *Bilingual early language and literacy assessment (BELA).* Cambridge, MA: Cambridge 0–8 Council/Cambridge Public Schools. Retrieved July 2, 2007, from http://www.cpsd.us/bela

Heisner, J. (2005). Telling stories with blocks: Encouraging language in the block center. *Early Childhood Research and Practice, 7*(2). Retrieved September 23, 2008, from http://ecrp.uiuc.edu/v7n2/heisner.html

Henniger, M. L. (1991). Play revisited: A critical element of the kindergarten curriculum. *Early Child Development and Care, 70,* 63–71.

Henrich, C. C., Wheeler, C. M., & Zigler, E. F. (2005). Motivation as a facet of school readiness in a Head Start sample. *NHSA Dialog, 8*(1), 72–87. Retrieved July 17, 2007, from https://webftp.gsu.edu/~wwwcch/Henrich,Wheeler,&Zigler(2005).pdf

Hensen, R. (2005). Real super-hero play. *Young Children, 60*(5), 37.

Herbert, J., Gross, J., & Hayne, H. (2007). Crawling is associated with more flexible memory retrieval by 9-month old infants. *Developmental Science, 10*(2), 183–189.

Heroman, C., & Jones, C. (2004). *Literacy: The Creative Curriculum® Approach.* Washington, DC: Teaching Strategies, Inc.

Hess, K. (2006). *Teaching and assessing understanding of text structures across grades.* Dover, NH: Center for the Improvement of Educational Assessments.

Hess, K. (2011). *Learning progressions frameworks designed for use with the Common Core State Standards in English Language Arts and Literacy K-12.* Retrieved April 30, 2013, from http://www.naacpartners.org/publications/ELA_LPF_12.2011_final.pdf

Hesse, P., & Lane, F. (2003). Media literacy starts young: An integrated curriculum approach. *Young Children, 58*(6), 20–26.

Hildreth, G. (1936). Developmental sequences in name writing. *Child Development, 7,* 291–302.

Hirsch, P. L., & Sandberg, E. H. (2012). Development of map construction skills in childhood. *Journal of Cognition and Development.* Retrieved abstract February 12, 2013, DOI:10.1080/15248372.2012.669219

Hirschler, J. A. (1994, Winter). Preschool children's help to second language learners. *Journal of Educational Issues of Language Minority Students, 14,* 227–240.

Hirsch-Pasek, K., Golinkoff, R. M., & Naigles, L. (1996). *The origins of grammar: Evidence from early language comprehension.* Cambridge, MA: MIT Press.

Hoisington, C. (2002). Using photographs to support children's science inquiry. *Young Children, 57*(5), 26–32.

Holowka, S., & Petitto, L. A. (2002, August). Left hemisphere cerebral specialization for babies while babbling. *Science, 297,* 1515.

Honig, A. S. (2005). The language of lullabies. *Young Children, 60*(5), 36, 30–36.

Hooper, S. R., Roberts, J. E., Zeisel, S. A., & Poe, M. (2003). Core language predictors of behavioral functioning in early elementary school children: Concurrent and longitudinal findings. *Behavioral Disorders, 29,* 10–24.

Howes, C. (2000). Social-emotional classroom climate in child care: Child-teacher relationships and children's second grade peer relations. *Social Development, 9*(2), 191–204.

Howes, C., Burchinal, M., Pianta, R., Bryant, D., Early, D., Clifford, R., et al. (2008). Ready to learn? Children's pre-academic achievements in pre-kindergarten programs. *Early Childhood Research Quarterly, 23,* 27–50.

Howes, C., Hamilton, C. E., & Matheson, C. C., (1994). Children's relationships with peers: Differential associations with aspects of the teacher-child relationship. *Child Development, 65,* 253–263.

Howes, C., & James, J. (2002). Children's social development within the socialization context of childcare and early childhood education. . In P. K. Smith & C. H. Hart (Eds.), *Blackwell handbook of childhood social development* (pp. 137–155). Oxford: Blackwell.

Howes, C. & Matheson, C. C. (1992). Sequences in the development of competent play with peers: Social and social pretend play. *Developmental Psychology, 94*(1), 79–87.

Howes, C., & Ritchie, S. (1998). Changes in child-teacher relationships in a therapeutic preschool. *Early Education and Development, 4,* 411–422.

Howse, R. B., Lange, G., Farran, D. C., & Boyles, C. D. (2003). Motivation and self-regulation as predictors of achievement in economically disadvantaged young children. *The Journal of Experimental Education, 71*(2), 151–174.

Huang, J., & Hatch, E. M. (1978). A Chinese child's acquisition of English. In E. M. Hatch (Ed.), *Second language acquisition: A book of readings* (pp. 118–131). Rowley, MA: Newbury House Publishers.

Hubbard, J. A., & Coie, J. D. (1994). Emotional correlates of social competence in children's peer relationships. *Merrill-Palmer Quarterly, 20,* 1–20.

Hughes, J. (2007). *Oral and visual literacy: The four cueing systems.* Retrieved May 4, 2013, from University of Ontario, Institute of Technology Web site: http://faculty.uoit.ca/hughes/Oral_Visual_Literacy/CueingSystems.html

Hulit, L. M., & Howard, M. R. (2002). *Born to talk: An introduction to speech and language development* (3rd ed., pp. 215–275). Boston: Allyn & Bacon.

Hull, G., & Moje, E. B. (2013). *What is the development of literacy the development of?* Stanford, CA: Stanford University. Retrieved May 15, 2013, from http://ell.stanford.edu/sites/default/files/pdf/academic-papers/05-Hull %26 Moje CC Paper FINAL.pdf

Humphryes, J. (2000). Exploring nature with children. *Young Children, 55*(2), 16–20.

Hun Ping Cheung, R. (2010). Designing movement activities to develop children's creativity in early childhood education. *Early Childhood Development and Care, 180*(3), 377–385.

Hurley, D. S. (2000). *Developing fine and gross motor skills: Birth to three.* Austin, TX: PRO-ED.

Husby, I., Heitmann, B. L., & Jensen, K. O. (2009). Meals and snacks from the child's perspective: The contribution of qualitative methods to the development of dietary interventions. *Public Health Nutrition, 12,* 739–747.

Hyson, M. (2005). Enthusiastic and engaged: Strengthening young children's positive approaches to learning. *Young Children, 60*(6), 68–70.

Hyson, M. (2008). *Enthusiastic and engaged learners: Approaches to learning in the early childhood classroom.* New York: Teachers College Press.

Hyson, M. C. (2003). *The emotional development of young children: Building an emotion-centered curriculum* (2nd ed.). New York: Teachers College Press.

Hyson, M., Buch, L., Fantuzzo, J., & Scott-Little, C. (2006). *Enthusiastic and engaged: Why are positive approaches to learning so important, and how can we support their development in young children?* Paper presented at the Annual Conference of the National Association for the Education of Young Children, Atlanta, GA.

Iaquinta, A. (2006). Guided reading: A research-based response to the challenges of early reading instruction. *Early Childhood Education Journal, 33*(6), 413–418.

Itoh, H., & Hatch, E. M. (1978). Second language acquisition: A case study. In E. M. Hatch (Ed.), *Second language acquisition: A book of readings* (pp. 76–88). Rowley, MA: Newbury House Publishers.

Izard, C., Fine, S., Schultz, D., Mostow, A., Ackerman, B., & Youngstrom, E. (2001). Emotion knowledge as a predictor of social behavior and academic competence in children at risk. *Psychological Science, 12*(1), 18–23.

Jablon, J. R., Dombro, A. L., & Dichtelmiller, M. L. (2007). *The power of observation.* (2nd ed.). Washington, DC: Teaching Strategies, Inc. and National Association for the Education of Young Children.

Jablon, J. R., & Wilkinson, M. (2006). Using engagement strategies to facilitate children's learning and success. *Young Children, 61*(2), 12–16.

Jacobs, V. R., Franke, M. L., Carpenter, T. P., Levi, L., & Battey, D. (2007). Professional development focused on children's algebraic reasoning in elementary school. *Journal for Research in Mathematics Education, 38*(3), 258–288.

Jalongo, M. R. (2008). *Learning to listen, listening to learn: Building essential skills in young children.* Washington, DC: National Association for the Education of Young Children.

Jalongo, M. R., & Isenberg, J. P. (2006). Creative expression and thought in kindergarten. In D. F. Gullo (Ed.), *K today: Teaching and learning in the kindergarten year* (pp. 116–126). Washington, DC: National Association for the Education of Young Children.

Jambunathan, S., Burts, D. C., & Pierce, S. H. (1999). Developmentally appropriate practice as predictors of self-competence among preschoolers. *Journal of Research in Childhood Education, 13*, 167–174.

Jipson, J. L., & Gelman, S. A. (2007). Robots and rodents: Children's inferences about living and nonliving kinds. *Child Development, 78*(6), 1675–1688.

Johnson, J. E. (2006). Play development from ages four to eight. In D. P. Fromberg & D. Bergen (Eds.). *Play from birth to twelve: Contexts, perspectives, and meanings.* (2nd ed., pp. 13–20). New York: Routledge/Taylor & Francis Group.

Johnson, M. H. (2008). Developing verbal and visual literacy through experiences in the visual arts. *Young Children, 63*(1), 74–79.

Jones, N. P. (2005). Big jobs: Planning for competence. *Young Children, 60*(2), 86–93.

Jordan, N. C. (2007). The need for number sense. *Educational Leadership, 65*(2), 63–65.

Jordan, N. C., Glutting, J., & Ramineni, C. (2010). The importance of number sense to mathematics achievement in first and third grades. *Learning and Individual Differences, 20*, 82–88.

Jordan, N. C., Kaplan, D., Olah, L. N., & Locuniak, M. N. (2006). Number sense growth in kindergarten: A longitudinal investigation of children at risk for mathematics difficulties. *Child Development, 77*, 153–175.

Juel, C. (2006). The impact of early schooling experiences on initial reading. In D. K. Dickinson & S. B. Neuman (Eds.), *Handbook of early literacy research* (Vol. 2), pp. 410–426. New York: Guilford Press.

Jung, M., Kloosterman, P., & McMullen, M. B. (2007). Research in review. Young children's intuition for solving problems in mathematics. *Young Children, 62*(5), 50–57.

Kagan, S. L., Britto, P. R., Kauerz, K., & Tarrant, K. (2005). *Washington state early learning and development benchmarks: A guide to young children's learning and development: From birth to kindergarten entry*. Retrieved March 23, 2009, from http://www.k12.WA.US/Earlylearning/pubdocs/earlylearningbenchmarks.pdf

Kaiser, B., & Rasminsky, S. (2003). *Challenging behavior in young children: Understanding, preventing, and responding effectively*. Boston: Allyn & Bacon.

Kalmar, K. (2008). Let's give children something to talk about! Oral language and preschool literacy. *Young Children, 63*(1), 88–92.

Kantor, R., Elgas, P. M., & Fernie D. (1993). Cultural knowledge and social competence within a preschool peer-culture group. *Early Childhood Research Quarterly, 8*, 125–148.

Karlsdottir, R., & Steffanson, T. (2002). Problems in developing functional handwriting. *Perceptual & Motor Skills, 94*(2), 623–62.

Katz, L. F., Kramer, L., & Gottman, J. M. (1992). Conflict and emotions in marital, sibling, and peer relationships. In. C. U. Shantz & W. W. Hartup (Eds.), *Conflict in child and adolescent development* (pp. 122–149). New York: Cambridge University Press.

Katz, L. G. (1999). *Another look at what young children should be learning*. Retrieved June 16, 2007, from http://ecap.crc.uiuc.edu/eecearchive/digests/1999/katzle99.pdf

Katz, L. G., & Chard, S. C. (1995). *Engaging children's minds: The project approach*. Norwood, NJ: Ablex.

Kelley, S. A., Brownell, C. A., & Campbell, S. B. (2000). Mastery motivation and self-evaluative affect in toddlers: Longitudinal relations with maternal behavior. *Child Development, 71*, 1061–1071.

Kemple, K. M. (1991). Research in review: Preschool children's peer acceptance and social interaction. *Young Children, 46*(5), 47–54.

Kemple, K. M., Batey, J. J., & Hartle, L. C. (2004). Music play: Creating centers for musical play and exploration. *Young Children, 59*(4), 30–37.

Kemple, K. M., & Nissenberg, S. A. (2000). Nurturing creativity in early childhood education: Families are part of it. *Early Childhood Education Journal, 28*(1), 67–71.

Kenney, S. H. (1997). Music in the developmentally appropriate integrated curriculum. In C. H. Hart, D. C. Burts, & R. Charlesworth (Eds.), *Integrated curriculum and developmentally appropriate practice: Birth to age eight* (pp. 103–144). Albany, NY: SUNY Press.

Kerem, E. A., Kamaraj, I., & Yelland, N. (2001). An analysis of Turkish pre-school teachers' ideas about the concept of creativity and the activities that can foster creativity in young children. *Contemporary Issues in Early Childhood, 2*(2), 248–252.

Kilmer, S. J., & Hofman, H. (1995). Transforming science curriculum. In S. Bredekamp & T. Rosegrant (Eds.), *Reaching potentials: Transforming early childhood curriculum and assessment,* Vol. 2 (pp. 43–64). Washington, DC: National Association for the Education of Young Children.

Kilpatrick, J., Swafford, J., & Findell, B. (2001). *Adding it up: Helping children learn mathematics*. Washington, DC: National Academy Press.

Kim, H., Park, E., & Lee, J. (2001). "All done! Take it home." Then into a trashcan?: Displaying and using children's art projects. *Early Childhood Education Journal, 29*(1), 41–50.

Kim, Y -S., Otaiba, S. A., Sidler, J. F., & Gruelich, L. (2013). Language, literacy, attentional behaviors, and instructional quality predictors of written composition for first graders. *Early Childhood Research Quarterly, 28*, 461–469.

Kim, Y.- S.; Puranik, C., & Al-Otaiba, S. (2015). Developmental trajectories of writing skills in first grade: Examining the effects of SES and language and/or speech impairments. *The Elementary School Journal, 115*(4), 593–613.

Kim, S. D. G. (2005). Kevin: "I gotta get to the market": The development of peer relationships in inclusive early childhood settings. *Early Childhood Education Journal, 33*(3), 163–169.

Klein, A., & Starkey, P. (2004). Fostering preschool children's mathematical knowledge: Findings from the Berkeley math readiness project. In D. H. Clements, J. Sarama, & A. -M. DiBiase (Eds.), *Engaging young children in mathematics: Standards for early childhood mathematics education* (pp. 343–360). Mahwah, NJ: Lawrence Erlbaum Associates.

Klein, M. D., & Chen, D. (2001). *Working with children from diverse backgrounds.* Albany, NY: Delmar.

Klein, T. P., Wirth, D., & Linas, K. (2004). Play: Children's context for development. In D. Koralek (Ed.), *Spotlight on young children and play* (pp. 28–34). Washington, DC: National Association for the Education of Young Children.

Kohn, A. (1993). Choices for children: Why and how to let students decide. *Phi Delta Kappan, 75*, 8–20.

Kopp, C. B. (1982). Antecedent of self-regulation: A developmental perspective. *Developmental Psychology, 18*, 199–214.

Koralek, D. (Ed.). (2003). *Spotlight on young children and math.* Washington, DC: National Association for the Education of Young Children.

Koralek, D. (Ed.). (2004). *Spotlight on young children and play.* Washington, DC: National Association for the Education of Young Children.

Krafft, K. C., & Berk, L. E. (1998). Private speech in two preschools: Significance of open-ended activities and make-believe play for verbal self-regulation. *Early Childhood Research Quarterly, 13*, 637–658.

Kreidler, W. J., & Whittall, S. T. (2003). Resolving conflict. In C. Copple (Ed.), *A world of difference: Readings on teaching young children in a diverse society* (pp. 52–56). Washington, DC: National Association for the Education of Young Children.

Kruk, R. S., & Bergman, K. (2013). The reciprocal relations between morphological processes and reading. *Journal of Experimental Child Psychology, 114*, 10–34.

Ladd, G. W. (1990). Having friends, keeping friends, making friends, and being liked by peers in the classroom: Predictors of children's early school adjustment? *Child Development, 61*, 1081–1100.

Ladd, G. W. (1999). Peer relationships and social competence during early and middle childhood. *Annual Review of Psychology 50*, 333–359.

Ladd, G. W., Birch, S. H., & Buhs, E. S. (1999). Children's social and scholastic lives in kindergarten: Related spheres of influence? *Child Development, 70*, 1373–1400.

Ladd, G. W., Buhs, E. S., & Seid, M. (2000). Children's initial sentiments about kindergarten: Is school liking an antecedent of early classroom participation and achievement? *Merrill-Palmer Quarterly, 46*, 255–279.

Lamb, M. E., Bornstein, M. H., & Teti, D. M. (2002). *Development in infancy: An introduction.* Mahwah, NJ: Lawrence Erlbaum Associates.

Landy, S. (2009). *Pathways to competence.* Baltimore: Brookes Publishing.

Lane, K. L., Givner, C. C., & Pierson, M. R. (2004). Teacher expectations of student behavior: Social skills necessary for success in elementary school classrooms. *The Journal of Special Education, 38*(2), 104–110.

Lanvers, U. (1999). Lexical growth patterns in a bilingual infant: The occurrence of significance of equivalents in the bilingual lexicon. *International Journal of Bilingual Education and Bilingualism, 2.* 30–32.

Larkina, M., Guler, O. E., Kleinknect, E., & Bauer, P. J. (2008). Maternal provision of structure in a deliberate memory task in relation to their preschool children's recall. *Journal of Experimental Child Psychology, 100,* 235–251.

Lee, S. M., Nihiser, A., Strouse, D., Das, B., Michael, S., & Huhman, M. (2010). Correlates of children and parents being physically active together. *Journal of Physical Activity and Health, 7,* 776–783.

Legaspi, B., & Straits, W. (2011). Living or nonliving? First-grade lessons on life science and classification address misconceptions. *Science and Children, 48*(8), 27–31.

Lemaire, P. & Lecacheur, M. (2011). Age-related changes in children's executive functions and strategy selection: A study in computational estimation. *Cognitive Development, 26,* 282– 294.

Lenhoff, R., & Huber, L. (2000). Young children make maps. *Young Children, 55*(3), 6–11.

Lenski, S., & Nierstheimer, S. (2002). Strategy instruction from a sociocognitive perspective. *Reading Psychology, 23,* 127–143.

Levin, D. E. (2003). *Teaching young children in violent times: Building a peaceable classroom* (2nd ed.). Washington, DC: National Association for the Education of Young Children.

Levy, A. K., Wolfgang, C. H., & Koorland, M. A. (1992). Sociodramatic play as a method for enhancing the language performance of kindergarten age students. *Early Childhood Research Quarterly, 7,* 245–262.

Lewis, M., & Michalson, L. (1993). *Children's emotions and moods: developmental theory and measurement.* New York: Plenum Press.

Lewis, V. (2003). *Development and disability.* (2nd ed.). Malden, MA: Blackwell.

Liben, L. S., & Downs, R. M. (1993). Understanding person-space map relations: Cartographic and developmental perspectives. *Developmental Psychology, 29*(4), 739–752.

Li-Grining, C. P., Votruba-Drzal, E., Maldonado-Carreño, C., & Haas, K. (2010). Children's early approaches to learning and academic trajectories through fifth grade. *Developmental Psychology, 46,* 1062–1077.

Lin, P., Schwanenflugel, P. J., & Wisenbaker, J. M. (1990). Category typicality, cultural familiarity, and the development of category knowledge. *Developmental Psychology, 26,* 805–813.

Lind, K. K. (1997). Science in the developmentally appropriate integrated curriculum. In C. H. Hart, D. C. Burts, & R. Charlesworth (Eds.), *Integrated curriculum and developmentally appropriate practice: Birth to age eight* (pp. 75–101). Albany, NY: SUNY Press.

Lind, K. K. (2001). *Science in early childhood: Developing and acquiring fundamental concepts and skills.* Presentation handout retrieved October 21, 2008 from www.hsnrc.org/CDI/pdfs/klind1.pdf

Linder, S. M. (2012). Interactive whiteboards in early childhood mathematics: Strategies for effective implementation in pre-K–grade 3. *Young Children, 67*(3), 26–32; 34–35.

Lomax, R. G., & McGee, L. M. (1987). Young children's concepts of print and reading: Toward a model of word reading acquisition. *Reading Research Quarterly, 22,* 237–256.

Lonigan, C. J., Burgess, S. R., & Anthony, J. L. (2000). Development of emergent literacy and early reading skills in preschool children: Evidence from a latent-variable longitudinal study. *Developmental Psychology, 36*, 596–613.

Lonigan, C. J., Burgess, S. R., Anthony, J. L., & Barker, T. A. (1998). Development of phonological sensitivity in 2- to 5-year-old children. *Journal of Educational Psychology, 90*(2), 294–311.

Lorenzo-Lasa, R., Ideishi, R. I., & Ideishi, S. K. (2007). Facilitating preschool learning and movement through dance. *Early Childhood Education Journal, 35*(1), 25–31.

Lu, M. (2000). *Language development in the early years.* Bloomington, IN: ERIC Clearinghouse on Reading, English, and Communication.

Lutz, T. & Kuhlman, W. D. (2000). Learning about culture through dance in kindergarten classrooms. *Early Childhood Education Journal, 28*(1), 35–40.

Macrina, M., Hoover, D., & Becker, C. (2009). The challenge of working with dual language learners: Three perspectives: Supervisor, mentor, and teacher. *Young Children 64*(2), 27–34.

Mallory, B. L., & New, R. S. (Eds.). (1994). *Diversity and developmentally appropriate practices: Challenges for early childhood education.* New York: Teachers College Press.

Manning, M. L. (2006). Play development from ages eight to twelve. In D. P. Fromberg & D. Bergen (Eds.), *Play from birth to twelve: Contexts, perspectives, and meanings.* (2nd ed., pp. 21–29). New York: Routledge/Taylor & Francis Group.

Manross, M. A. (2000). Learning to throw in physical education class: Part 3. *Teaching Elementary Physical Education, 11*(3), 26–29.

Mantzicopoulos, P., Patrick, H., & Samarapungavan, A. (2008). Young children's motivational beliefs about learning science. *Early Childhood Research Quarterly, 23*(3), 378–394.

Marcus, G. F. (1995). Children's overregularization of English plurals: A quantitative analysis. *Journal of Child Language, 22,* 447–460.

Marcus, G. F., Pinker, S., Ullman, M., Hollander, M., Rosen, T. J., & Xu, F. (1992). Overregularization in language acquisition. *Monographs of the Society for Research in Child Development, 57* (Serial No. 228).

Markman, E. M. (1979). Realizing that you don't understand: Elementary school children's awareness of inconsistencies. *Child Development, 50,* 643–655.

Marotz, L. R. (2012). *Health, safety, and nutrition for the young child* (8th ed.). Belmont, CA: Wadsworth Cengage Learning.

Marotz, L. R. & Allen, K. E. (2013). *Developmental profiles: Pre-birth through adolescence.* (7th ed.). Stamford, CT: Cengage Learning.

Mason, J. (1980). When do children begin to read? An exploration of four-year-old children's letter and word reading competencies. *Reading Research Quarterly, 15,* 203–227.

Matlock, R., & Hornstein, J. (2004). Sometimes a smudge is just a smudge, and sometimes it's a saber-toothed tiger: Learning and the arts through the ages. *Young Children, 59*(4), 12–17.

Mayeux, L., & Cillessen, A. H. N. (2003). Development of social problem solving in early childhood: Stability, change, and associations with social competence. *Journal of Genetic Psychology, 164*(2), 153–173.

McAfee, O., & Leong, D. (1994). *Assessing and guiding young children's development and learning.* Boston: Allyn & Bacon.

McAfee, O., & Leong, D. (2007). *Assessing and guiding young children's development and learning* (4th ed.). Boston: Pearson/Allyn & Bacon.

McAfee, O., Leong, D. J., & Bodrova, E. (2004). *Basics of assessment: A primer for early childhood educators.* Washington, DC: National Association for the Education of Young Children.

McCabe, A. (1997). Developmental and cross-cultural aspects of children's narration. In M. Bamberg (Ed.), *Narrative development: Six approaches* (pp. 137–174). Mahwah, NJ: Erlbaum.

McClelland, M. M., Morrison, F. J., & Holmes, D. L. (2000). Children at risk for early academic problems: The role of learning-related social skills. *Early Childhood Research Quarterly, 15*(3), 307–329.

McCormick, C. E., & Mason, J. M. (1986). Intervention procedures for increasing preschool children's interest in and knowledge about reading. In W. H. Teale & E. Sulzby (Eds.), *Emergent literacy: Writing and reading* (pp. 90–115). Norwood, NJ: Ablex.

McDonald, N., & Messinger, D. (2011). The development of empathy: How, when, and why. In A. Acerbi, J. A. Lombo, & J. J. Sanguineti (Eds), *Free will, emotions, and moral actions: Philosophy and neuroscience in dialogue.* Rome: Pontifica Università della Santa Croce.

McGee, L., Lomax, R., & Head, M. (1988). Young children's written language knowledge: What environmental and functional print reading reveals. *Journal of Reading Behavior, 20,* 99–118.

McGee, L., & Richgels, D. J. (1996). *Literacy's beginnings: Supporting young readers and writers.* Boston: Allyn & Bacon.

McGee, L., & Richgels, D. J. (2003). *Designing early literacy programs: Strategies for at-risk preschool and kindergarten children.* New York: Guilford Press.

McHale, S. M., Crouter, A. C., & Tucker, C. J. (2001). Free-time activities in middle childhood: Links with adjustment in early adolescence. *Child Development, 72*(6), 1764–1778.

McHenry, J. D., & Buerk, K. J. (2008). Infants and toddlers meet the natural world. *Young Children, 63*(1), 40–41.

McKay, P. (2006). *Assessing young language learners.* New York: Cambridge University Press.

McKenzie, T. L., Sallis, J. F., Elder, J. P., Berry, C. C., Hoy, P. L., Nader, P. R., et al. (1997). Physical activity levels and prompts in young children at recess: A two-year study of a bi-ethnic sample. *Research Quarterly for Exercise and Sport, 68*(3), 195–202.

McLaughlin, B., Blanchard, A., & Osanai, Y. (1995, June). *Assessing language development in bilingual preschool children* [National Clearinghouse for Bilingual Education Rep. No. 22]. Washington, DC: George Washington University. Retrieved August 16, 2007, from http://www.ncela.gwu.edu/pubs/pigs/pig22.htm

McLaughlin, M. (2012). Reading comprehension: What every teacher needs to know. *The Reading Teacher, 65,* 432-440.

McLaughlin, M., & DeVoogd, G. L. (2004). *Critical literacy: Enhancing students' comprehension of text.* New York: Scholastic.

McLaughlin, M., & Overturf, B. J. (2012). The Common Core: Insights into the K–5 standards. *The Reading Teacher, 66*(2), 153–164.

McNeil, N. M., Fyfe, E. R., Petersen, L. A., Dunwiddie, A. E., & Brletic-Shipley, H. (2011). Benefits of practicing 4 = 2 + 2: Nontraditional problem formats facilitate children's understanding of mathematical equivalence. *Child Development, 82,* 1620–1633.

McWayne, C. M., Fantuzzo, J. W., & McDermott, P. A. (2004). Preschool competency in context: An investigation of the unique contribution of child competencies to early academic success. *Developmental Psychology*, 40(4), 633–645.

McWilliams, R. A., Scarborough, A. A., & Kim, H. (2003). Adult interactions and child engagement. *Early Education and Development, 14*(1), 7–28.

Meisel, J. (1989). Early differentiation of languages in bilingual children. In K. Hylterstam & L. Obler (Eds.), *Bilingualism across the lifespan: Aspects of acquisition, maturity, and loss* (pp. 13–54). Cambridge, England: Cambridge University Press.

Meisels, S. (1994). Designing meaningful measurements for early childhood. In B. L. Mallory & R. S. New (Eds.), *Diversity and developmentally appropriate practices: Challenges for early childhood education* (pp. 202–222). New York: Teachers College Press.

Menn, L., & Stoel-Gammon, C. (2001). Phonological development: Learning sounds and sound patterns. In J. B. Gleason (Ed.), *The development of language* (pp. 39–100). Boston: Allyn & Bacon.

Metsala, J. L., & Walley, A. C. (1998). Spoken vocabulary growth and the segmental restructuring of lexical representations: Precursors to phonemic awareness and early reading ability. In J. L. Metsala & L. C. Ehri (Eds.), *Recognition in beginning literacy* (pp. 89–120). Mahwah, NJ: Lawrence Erlbaum Associates.

Meyer, C. (1989). *The role of peer relationships in the socialization of children to preschool: A Korean example.* Unpublished doctoral dissertation, Ohio State University, Columbus.

Miller, P. J., Fung, H., & Mintz, J. (1996). Self-construction through narrative practices: A Chinese and American comparison of early socialization. *Ethos, 24*(2), 237–280.

Miller, S. E. (1999). Balloons, blankets, and balls: Gross-motor activities to use indoors. *Young Children, 54*(5), 58–63.

Mindes, G. (2005a). Resources for teaching and learning about social studies. *Young Children 60*(5), 58–60.

Mindes, G. (2005b). Social studies in today's early childhood curricula. *Young Children, 60*(5), 12–18.

Mindes, G. (2006). Social studies in kindergarten. In D. F. Gullo (Ed.), *K today: Teaching and learning in the kindergarten year* (pp. 107–115). Washington, DC: National Association for the Education of Young Children.

Mitchell, L. C. (2004). Making the most of creativity in activities for young children with disabilities. *Young Children 59*(4), 46–49.

Mix, K. S., Huttenlocher, J., & Levine, S. C. (2002). *Quantitative development in infancy and early childhood.* New York: Oxford University Press.

Miyakawa, Y., Kamii, C., & Nagahiro, M. (2005). The development of logico-mathematical thinking at ages 1–3 in play with blocks and an incline. *Journal of Research in Childhood Education, 19*, 292–301.

Monhardt, L., & Monhardt, R. (2006). Creating a context for the learning of science process skills through picture books. *Early Childhood Education Journal, 34*(1), 67–71.

Montelongo, J. A. & Hernandez, A. C. (2007). Reinforcing expository reading and writing skills: A more versatile sentence completion task. *The Reading Teacher, 60*(6), 538-546.

Mooney, C. (2005). *Use your words: How teacher talk helps children learn.* St. Paul, MN: Redleaf Press.

Moore, S. G. (1985). Social effects of peers on curiosity. *Early Report, 12*(3), 1–2.

Morrison, F. J., Connor, C. M., & Bachman, H. J. (2006). The transition to school. In D. K. Dickinson, & S. B. Neuman (Eds.), *Handbook of early literacy research,* Vol. 2, (pp. 375–394). New York: The Guilford Press.

Morrow, L. (2005). *Literacy development in the early years: Helping children read and write* (5th ed.). Boston: Allyn & Bacon.

Morrow, L. M. (1985). Retelling stories: A strategy for improving children's comprehension, concept of story structure, and oral language complexity. *The Elementary School Journal, 85*, 647–661.

Morrow, L. M. (1990). Preparing the classroom environment to promote literacy during play. *Early Childhood Research Quarterly, 5*, 537–554.

Mostow, A. J., Izard, C. E., Fine, S., & Trentacosta, C. J. (2002). Modeling emotional, cognitive, and behavioral predictors of peer acceptance. *Child Development, 73(6)*, 1775–1788.

Murnan, J., Price, J. H., Telljohann, S. K., Dake, J. A., & Boardley, D. (2006). Parents' perceptions of curricular issues affecting children's weight in elementary schools. *Journal of School Health, 76*(10), 502–511.

Murphey, D. A., & Burns, C. E. (2002). Development of a comprehensive community assessment of school readiness. *Early Childhood Research and Practice, 2.* Retrieved June 16, 2007, from http://ecrp.uiuc.edu/v4n2/murphey.html

Murphy, K. L., DePasquale, R., & McNamara, E. (2003). Meaningful connections: Using technology in primary classrooms. *Young Children, 58*(6), 12–18.

Mussen, P. H., Conger, J. J., Kagan, J., & Huston, A. C. (1990). *Child development and personality* (7th ed.). New York: Harper and Row.

National Association for the Education of Young Children. (1996). NAEYC position statement: Responding to linguistic and cultural diversity—Recommendations for effective early childhood education. *Young Children, 52*(2), 4–12.

National Association for the Education of Young Children. (2005a). *Screening and assessment of young English-language learners: Supplement to the NAEYC position statement on early childhood curriculum, assessment, and program evaluation.* Washington, DC: Author.

National Association for the Education of Young Children. (2005b). *Where we stand on the screening and assessment of young English-language learners.* Washington, DC: Author.

National Association for Sport and Physical Education. (2004). *Moving into the future: National standards for physical education.* (2nd ed.). Reston, VA: Author.

National Center for Education Statistics (NCES). (1993). *Public school kindergarten teachers' views on children's readiness for school.* Washington, DC: Author. Retrieved July 6, 2007, from http://nces.ed.gov/surveys/frss/publications/93410/index.asp?sectionID=3

National Center for Education Statistics (NCES). (2000). *Special analysis 2000. Entering kindergarten: A portrait of American children when they begin school.* Retrieved September 12, 2007, from http://nces.ed.gov/programs/coe/2000/essay/e03g.asp

National Center for Education Statistics (NCES). (2002). *Children's reading and mathematics achievement in kindergarten and first grade.* Washington, DC: Author. Retrieved July 6, 2007, from http://nces.ed.gov/pubs2002/kindergarten/24.asp?nav=4

National Committee on Science Education Standards and Assessment, National Research Council (1996). *National Science Education Standards.* Retrieved October 20, 2008, from http://books.nap.edu/openbook.phprecord_id=4962&page=105

National Council of Teachers of Mathematics (NCTM). (2000). *Principles and standards for school mathematics.* Reston, VA: Author.

National Council of Teachers of Mathematics (NCTM). (2006). *Curriculum focal points for prekindergarten through grade 8 mathematics: A quest for coherence.* Reston, VA: Author.

National Early Literacy Panel. (2004). *A synthesis of research on language and literacy.* Retrieved June 2004, from http://www.famlit.org/ProgramsandInitiatives/FamilyPartnershipinReading/index.cfm

National Early Literacy Panel. (2008). *Developing early literacy: Report of the National Early Literacy Panel.* Retrieved January 2009, from http://www.nifl.gov/nifl/publications/pdf/NELPReport09.pdf

National Early Literacy Panel, (2008). *Developing Early Literacy: Report of the National Early Literacy Panel—Executive Summary.* Washington, DC: National Institute for Literacy.

National Governors Association Center for Best Practices & Council of Chief State School Officers. (2010). *Common Core State Standards.* Washington, D.C.: National Governors Association Center for Best Practices & Council of Chief State School Officers.

National Institute of Child Health and Human Development. (2000). *Report of the national reading panel. Teaching children to read: An evidence-based assessment of the scientific research literature on reading and its implications for reading instruction* (NIH Publication No. 00-4769). Washington, DC: U.S. Government Printing Office.

National Institute on Deafness and Other Communication Disorders (NIDCD). (2000, April.) *Speech and language developmental milestones.* Retrieved July 21, 2007, from http://www.nidcd.nih.gov/health/voice/speechandlanguage.asp/

National Reading Panel. (2000). *Teaching children to read: An evidence-based assessment of the scientific research literature on reading and its implications for reading instruction.* NIH Publication No. 00-4769. Washington, DC: National Institute of Child Health and Human Development.

National Research Council. (1998a). *Preventing reading difficulties.* Washington, DC: National Academy Press.

National Research Council. (1998b). *Starting out right.* Washington, DC: National Academy Press.

National Research Council. (2009). *Mathematics learning in early childhood: Paths toward excellence and equity.* Committee on Early Childhood Mathematics, C. T. Cross, T. A. Woods, & H. Schweingruber, Eds. Center for Education, Division of Behavioral and Social Sciences and Education. Washington, DC: The National Academies Press.

National Research Council: Committee on Conceptual Framework for the New K–12 Science Education Standards. (2012). *A framework for k–12 science education: Practices, crosscutting concepts, and core ideas.* The National Academies Press.

National Scientific Council on the Developing Child. (2004). *Children's emotional development is built into the architecture of their brain: Working paper no. 2.* Retrieved August 31, 2007, from www.developingchild.net/pubs/wp/emotional_development_is_built.pdf

Neuman, S., Copple, C., & Bredekamp, S. (1999). *Learning to read and write: Developmentally appropriate practices for young children.* Washington, DC: National Association for the Education of Young Children.

Neuman, S., & Roskos, K. (1990). Play, print and purpose: Enriching play environments for literacy development. *Reading Teacher, 44*(3), 214–221.

Neuman, S., & Roskos, K. (1993). Access to print for children of poverty: Differential effects of adult mediation and literacy-enriched play settings on environmental and functional print tasks. *American Educational Research Journal, 30,* 95–122.

Neuman, S. B. (2003). From rhetoric to reality: The case for high-quality compensatory prekindergarten programs. *Phi Delta Kappan, 85*(4), 286–291.

Neuman, S. B., Copple, C., & Bredekamp, S. (2000). *Learning to read and write: Developmentally appropriate practice for children.* Washington, DC: National Association for the Education of Young Children.

Neuman, S. B., & Gambrell, L. B. (Eds.) (2013). *Quality reading instruction in the age of Common Core standards.* Newark, DE: International Reading Association.

Neuman, S. B., & Roskos, K. (2012). More than teachable moments: Enhancing oral vocabulary instruction in your classroom. *The Reading Teacher, 66*(1), 63–67.

Newman, L. S. (1990). Intentional and unintentional memory in young children: Remembering vs. playing. *Journal of Experimental Child Psychology, 50,* 243–258.

Nicolopoulou, A., & Richner, E. S. (2007). From actors to agents to persons: The development of character representation in young children's narratives. *Child Development, 78,* 412–429.

Nilges, L., & Usnick, V. (2000). The role of spatial ability in physical education and mathematics. *Journal of Physical Education, Recreation & Dance, 71*(6), 29–35.

Nippold, M. A. (1998). *Later language development.* Austin: PRO-ED.

Nobes, G., Moore, D. G., Martin, A. E., Clifford, B. R., Butterworth, G., Panagiotaki, G., et al., (2003). Children's understanding of the earth in a multicultural community: Mental model or fragments of knowledge? *Developmental Science, 6*(1), 72–85.

Normandeau, S., & Guay, F. (1998). Preschool behavior and first-grade school achievement: The mediational role of cognitive self-control. *Journal of Educational Psychology, 90*, 111–121.

Northwest Educational Technology Consortium, Northwest Region Educational Laboratory. (2002). *5 effective ways for young children to use technology.* Portland, OR: Author.

Nourot, P. M., & Van Hoorn, J. L. (1991). Research in review: Symbolic play in preschool and primary settings. *Young Children, 46*(6), 40–50.

O'Reilly, A. W., & Bornstein, M. H. (1993). Caregiver-child interaction in play. *New Directions in Child Development, 59*, 55–66.

Ohman-Rodriquez, J. (2004). Music from inside out: Promoting emergent composition with young children. *Young Children, 59*(4), 50–55.

Oller, D. K., & Eilers, R. E. (Eds.). 2002. *Language and literacy in bilingual children*. Bristol, UK: Multilingual Matters.

Olson, C. B., Scarcella, R., & Matuchniak, T. (2015). English learners, writing, and the Common Core. *The Elementary School Journal, 115*(4), 570–592.

Ontai, L., & Thompson, R. A. (2002). Patterns of attachment and maternal discourse effects on children's emotion understanding from 3 to 5 years of age. *Social Development, 11*(4), 433–450.

O'Shaughnessy, T., Lane, K. L., Gresham, F. M., & Beebe-Frankenberger, M. E. (2002). Students with or at risk for learning and emotional-behavioral difficulties: An integrated system of prevention and intervention. In K. L. Lane, F. M. Gresham, & T. E. O'Shaughnessy (Eds.), *Interventions for children with or at risk for emotional and behavioral disorders* (pp. 3–17). Boston: Allyn & Bacon.

Ostrov, J. M., Woods, K. E., Jansen, E. A., Casas, J. F., & Crick, N. R. (2004). An observational study of delivered and received aggression, gender, and social-psychological adjustment in preschool: "This white crayon doesn't work…" *Early Childhood Research Quarterly, 19*, 355–371.

Overvelde, A., & Hulstijn, W. (2011). Handwriting development in grade 2 and grade 3 primary school children with normal, at risk, or dysgraphic characteristics. *Research in Developmental Disabilities, 32*, 540–548.

Owens, C. V. (1999). Conversational science 101A: Talking it up! *Young Children, 54*(5), 4–9.

Páez, M. M., Tabors, P. O., & López, L. M. (2007). Dual language and literacy development of Spanish-speaking preschool children. *Journal of Applied Developmental Psychology, 28*(2), 85–102.

Palermo, F., Hanish, L. D., Martin, C. L., Fabes, R. A., & Reiser, M. (2007). Preschoolers' academic readiness: What role does the teacher-child relationship play? *Early Childhood Research Quarterly, 22*, 407–422.

Palmer, H. (2001). The music, movement, and learning connection. *Young Children, 56*(5), 13–17.

Parish-Morris, J., Hennon, E. A., Hirsh-Pasek, K., Golinkoff, R. M., & Tager-Flusberg, H. (2007). Children with autism illuminate the role of social intention in word learning. *Child Development, 78*, 1265–1287.

Parker, J. G. & Asher, S. R. (1987). Peer relations and later personal adjustment: Are low-accepted children at risk? *Psychological Bulletin, 102*, 357–389.

Passehl, B., McCarroll, C., Buechner, J., Gearring, C., Smith, A. E., & Trowbridge, F. (2004). Preventing childhood obesity: Establishing healthy lifestyle habits in the preschool years. *Journal of Pediatric Health Care, 18*(6), 315–319.

Pauen, S. (2002). The global-to-basic level shift in infants' categorical thinking: First evidence from a longitudinal study. *International Journal of Behavioral Development, 26*, 492–499.

Payne, J. N., & Huinker, D. M. (1993). Early number and numeration. In R. J. Jensen (Ed.), *Research ideas for the classroom: Early childhood mathematics* (pp. 43–71). New York: Macmillan.

Payne, V. G., & Rink, J. E. (1997). Physical education in the developmentally appropriate integrated curriculum. In C. H. Hart, D. C. Burts, & R. Charlesworth (Eds.), *Integrated curriculum and developmentally appropriate practice: Birth to age eight*, (pp. 145–170). Albany, New York: SUNY Press.

Pearson, B., & Fernández, S. (1994). Patterns of interaction in the lexical growth in two languages of bilingual infants and toddlers. *Language Learning, 44*(4), 617–653.

Pearson, B., Fernández, S., Lewedeg, V., & Oller, D. K. (1997). The relation of input factors to lexical learning by bilingual infants. *Applied Psycholinguistics, 18*, 41–58.

Peisner-Feinberg, E. S., Burchinal, M. R., Clifford, R. M., Culkin, M. L., Howes, C., & Kagan, S. L., et al. (1999). *The children of the cost, quality, and outcomes study go to school: Technical report.* Chapel Hill: University of North Carolina at Chapel Hill, Frank Porter Graham Child Development Center.

Pellegrini, A. D., & Galda, L. (1982). The effects of theme-fantasy play training on the development of children's story comprehension. *American Educational Research Journal, 19*, 443–452.

Peña, E. D., & Mendez-Perez, A. (2006). Individualistic and collectivistic approaches to language learning. *Zero to Three, 27*(1), 34–41.

Perfetti, C. A., Landi, N., & Oakhill, J. (2005). The acquisition of reading comprehension skill. In M. J. Snowling & C. Hulme (eds.), *The science of reading: A handbook* (pp.227-247). Oxford, England: Blackwell.

Perry, M. W. (2006). A splash of color. *Young Children, 61*(2), 83.

Petersen, S., & Wittmer, D. (2008). Relationship-based infant care: Responsive, on demand, and predictable. *Young Children, 63*(3), 40–42.

Peterson, B. (2001). *Literary Pathways: Selecting Books to Support New Readers.* Portsmouth, NH: Heinemann.

Peterson, S. M., & French, L. (2008). Supporting young children's explanations through inquiry science in preschool. *Early Childhood Research Quarterly, 23*(3), 395–408.

Pettit, G. S., & Harrist, A. W. (1993). Children's aggressive and socially unskilled playground behavior with peers: Origins in early family relations. In C. H. Hart (Ed.), *Children on playgrounds: Research perspectives and applications.* Albany, NY: SUNY Press.

Piaget, J., & Inhelder, B. (1967). *The child's conception of space* (F. J. Langdon & J. L Lunzer, Trans.). New York: Norton.

Pianta, R. C. (1999). *Enhancing relationships between children and teachers.* Washington, DC: American Psychological Association.

Pianta, R. C., & Stuhlman, M. W. (2004). Teacher-child relationships and children's success in the first years of school. *School Psychology Review, 33*, 444–458.

Pica, R. (1997). Beyond physical development: Why young children need to move. *Young Children, 52*(6), 4–11.

Pica, R. (2006). Physical fitness and the early childhood curriculum. *Young Children, 61*(3), 12–19.

Pickett, L. (1998). Literacy learning during block play. *Journal of Research in Childhood Education, 12*(2), 225–230.

Pierce, K. L., & Schreibman, L. (1994). Teaching daily living skills to children with autism in unsupervised settings through pictorial self-management. *Journal of Applied Behavioral Analysis 27*(3), 471–481.

Piker, R. A., & Rex, L. A. (2008). Influences of teacher-child interactions on English language development in a Head Start classroom. *Early Childhood Education Journal, 36*, 187–193.

Pinciotti, P. (1993). Creative drama and young children: The dramatic learning connection. *Arts Education Policy Review, 94*(6), 24–28.

Plester, B., Richards, J., Blades, M., & Spencer, C. (2002). Young children's ability to use aerial photographs as maps. *Journal of Environmental Psychology, 22*(1–2), 29–47.

Plumert, J. M., & Hawkins, A. M. (2001). Biases in young children's communication about spatial relations: Containment versus proximity. *Child Development, 72*, 22–36.

Ponitz, C. E. C., McLelland, M. M., Jewkes, A. M., Conner, C. M., Farris, C. L., & Morrison, F. J. (2008). Touch your toes! Developing a direct measure of behavioral regulation in early childhood. *Early Childhood Research Quarterly, 23*(2), 141–158.

Poole, C., & Miller, S. A. (n. d.) *Problem solving in action*. Retrieved February 1, 2009, from http://www2.scholastic.com/browse/article.jsp?id=3746479

Pope, C. E., & Springate, K. W. (1995). Creativity in early childhood classrooms. *ERIC Digest*. ED389474 1995-12-00. Retrieved July 16, 2007, from www.eric.ed.gov

Preissler, M. A., & Carey, S. (2004). Do both pictures and words function as symbols for 18- and 24-month old children? *Cognition and Development, 5*(2), 185–212.

Pressley, M., and Block, C. C. (2002). *Comprehension instruction: Research based best practices.* New York: Guilford.

Public Broadcasting System (PBS). (n.d.). *Child development and early child development advice/PBS parents: Child development tracker*. Retrieved April 24, 2013, from www.pbs.org/parents/childdevelopment/

Purcell Cone, T. (2009). Following their lead: Supporting children's ideas for creating dances. *Journal of Dance Education, 9*(3), 81–89.

Purpura, D. J., Baroody, A. J., & Lonigan, C. J. (2013). The transition from informal mathematical knowledge: Mediation by numeral knowledge. *Journal of Educational Psychology, 105*(2), 453–464.

Putallaz, M., & Gottman, J. M. (1981). Social skills and group acceptance. In S. R. Asher & J. M. Gottman (Eds.), *The development of children's friendships* (pp. 116–149). New York: Cambridge University Press.

Putallaz, M., & Wasserman, A. (1990). Children's entry behavior. In S. R. Asher & J. D. Coie (Eds.), *Peer rejection in childhood* (pp. 60–89). New York: Cambridge University Press.

Raghubar, K. P., Barnes, M. A., & Hecht, S. A. (2010). Working memory and mathematics: A review of developmental, individual difference, and cognitive approaches. *Learning and Individual Differences, 20*, 110–122.

Ramsey, P. G. (2003). Growing up with the contradictions of race and class. In C. Copple (Ed.), *A world of difference: Readings on teaching young children in a diverse society* (pp. 24–28). Washington, DC: National Association for the Education of Young Children.

RANS Reading Study Group. (2002). *Reading for understanding: Toward an R&D program in reading comprehension.* Santa Monica, CA: RAND.

Rasinski, T. V. (2003). *The fluent reader: Oral reading strategies for building word recognition, fluency, and comprehension*. New York: Scholastic.

Rasinski, T. V., Blachowicz, C. & Lems, K., (2012) *Fluency instruction, Second Edition: Research-based best practices*. New York: Guilford Publications.

Ratner, N. B. (2001). Atypical language development. In J. B. Gleason (Ed.), *The development of language* (pp. 369–406). Boston: Allyn & Bacon.

Raver, C. C. (2002). Emotions matter: Making the case for the role of young children's emotional development for early school readiness. *Social Policy Report, 16*, 3–18.

Raver, C. C., & Zigler, E. F. (1997). Social competence: An untapped dimension in evaluating Head Start's success. *Early Childhood Research Quarterly, 12*, 363–385.

Rawson, R. M., & Goetz, E. M. (1983). *Reading-related behavior in preschoolers: Environmental factors and teacher modeling*. Unpublished manuscript.

Ray, A., Bowman, B., & Brownell, J. O. (2006). Teacher-child relationships, social-emotional development, and school achievement. In B. Bowman & E. K. Moore (Eds.), *School readiness and social-emotional development: Perspectives on cultural diversity* (pp. 7–22). Washington, DC: National Black Child Development Institute, Inc.

Reio, T. G., Jr., Petrosko, J. M., Wiswell, A. K., & Thongsukmag, J. (2006). The measurement and conceptualization of curiosity. *The Journal of Genetic Psychology, 16*(2), 117–135.

Resources for exploring the creative arts with young children. (2004). *Young Children, 59*(4), 58–59.

Richard, B. A., & Dodge, K. A. (1982). Social maladjustment and problem-solving in school aged children. *Journal of Consulting and Clinical Psychology, 50*, 226–233.

Richardson, K., & Salkeld, L. (1995). Transforming mathematics curriculum. In S. Bredekamp & T. Rosegrant (Eds.), *Reaching potentials: Transforming early childhood curriculum and assessment* (Vol. 2). Washington, DC: National Association for the Education of Young Children.

Richgels, D. J. (1986). An investigation of preschool and kindergarten children. *Journal of Research and Development in Education, 19*(4), 41–47.

Riley, D., San Juan, R. R., Klinkner, J., & Ramminger, A. (2008). *Social & emotional development: Connecting science and practice in early childhood settings*. St. Paul, MN and Washington, DC: Redleaf Press and National Association for the Education of Young Children.

Riley, J. (1996). *The Teaching of reading*. London: Paul Chapman.

Rimm-Kaufman, S., Pianta, R. C., & Cox, M. (2000). Teachers' judgments of problems in the transition to school. *Early Childhood Research Quarterly, 15*(2), 147–166.

Ritchey, K. D. (2008). The building blocks of writing: Learning to write letters and spell words. *Reading and Writing, 21*(1–2), 27–47.

Robert, D. L. (1999). *The effects of a preschool movement program on motor skill acquisition, movement concept formation, and movement practice behavior.* (Doctoral dissertation, West Virginia University). Retrieved August 10, 2008, from http://eidr.wvu.edu/files/1193/Robert_D_Diss.pdf

Roberts, J. E., Burchinal, M., & Durham, M. (1999). Parents' report of vocabulary and grammatical development of African American preschoolers: Child and environmental associations. *Child Development, 70*, 92–106.

Robinson, C. C., Anderson, G. T., Porter, C. L., Hart, C. H., & Wouden-Miller, M. (2003). Sequential transition patterns of preschoolers' social interactions during child-initiated play: Is parallel-aware play a bidirectional bridge to other play states? *Early Childhood Research Quarterly, 18*, 3–21.

Robinson, L. (2003). Technology as a scaffold for emergent literacy: Interactive storybooks for toddlers. *Young Children, 58*(6), 42–48.

Rodger, L. (1996). Adding movement throughout the day. *Young Children, 51*(3), 4–7.

Rodriguez, R. (1983). *Hunger of memory: The education of Richard Rodriguez.* New York: Bantam Books.

Rogoff, B., Mistry, A., Goncu, A., & Mosier, C. (1993). Guided participation in cultural activity by toddlers and caregivers. *Monographs of the Society for Research in Child Development, 58*, Serial No. 236.

Rosenow, N. (2008). Learning to love the Earth… and each other. *Young Children, 63*(1), 10–13.

Roskos, K., & Neuman, S. B. (2013). Common Core, commonplaces, and community in teaching reading. *The Reading Teacher, 66*(6), 469–473.

Roskos, K., Tabors, P., & Lenhart, L. (2004). *Oral language and early literacy in preschool.* Newark, DE: International Reading Association.

Ross, M. E. (2000). Science their way. *Young Children, 55*(2), 6–13.

Rowe, M. B. (1987). Wait time: Slowing down may be a way of speeding up. *American Educator, 11*, 38–43, 47.

Rubin, K. H., Bukowski, W. M., & Parker, J. G. (1998). Peer interactions, relationships, and groups. In W. Damon & N. Eisenberg (Eds.), *Handbook of child psychology: Vol. 3: Social, emotional, and personality development* (pp. 619–700). New York: John Wiley & Sons.

Rubin, K. H., Bukowski, W. M., & Parker, J. G. (2007). *Peer interactions, relationships, and groups.* Handbook of Child Psychology.

Rule, A. C. (2007). Mystery boxes: Helping children improve their reasoning. *Early Childhood Education Journal, 35*(1), 13–18.

Rule, A. C., & Stewart, R. A. (2002). Effects of practical life materials on kindergartners' fine motor skills. *Early Childhood Education Journal, 30*(1), 9–13.

Russell, S. J. (1991). Counting noses and scary things: Children construct their ideas about data. In D. Vere-Jones (Ed.), *Proceedings of the third international conference on teaching statistics* (pp. 158–164). Voorburg, Netherlands: International Statistical Institute.

Russo, M. (with Colurciello, S. G. & Kelly, R.). (2008). For the birds! Seeing, being, and creating the bird world. *Young Children, 63*(1), 26–30.

Sacha, T. J., & Russ, S. W. (2006). Effects of pretend imagery on learning dance in preschool children. *Early Childhood Education Journal, 33*(5), 341–345.

Salmon, M., & Akaran, S. E. (2005). Cross-cultural e-mail connections. *Young Children, 60*(5), 36.

Saltz, E., Dixon, D., & Johnson, H. (1997). Training disadvantaged preschoolers on various fantasy activities: Effects on cognitive functioning and impulse control. *Child Development, 48*, 367–380.

Saltz, E., Dixon, D., & Johnson, H. (1997). Training disadvantaged preschoolers on various fantasy activities: Effects on cognitive functioning and impulse control. *Child Development, 48*, 367–380.

Samarapungavan, A., Patrick, H., & Mantzicopoulos, P. (2011). *What kindergarten students learn in inquiry-based science classrooms. Cognition and Instruction, 29*(4), 416–470.

Sameroff, A., & McDonough, S. C. (1994). Educational implications of developmental transitions. *Phi Delta Kappan 76*(3),188–93.

Sanders, S. W. (2002). *Active for life: Developmentally appropriate movement programs for young children.* Washington, DC: National Association for the Education of Young Children.

Sanders, S. W. (2006). Physical education in kindergarten. In D. F. Gullo (Ed.), *K today: Teaching and learning in the kindergarten year* (pp. 127–137). Washington, DC: National Association for the Education of Young Children.

Sarama, J., & Clements, D. H. (2003). Early childhood corner: Building blocks of early childhood mathematics. *Teaching Children Mathematics, 9*(8), 480–484.

Sarama, J., & Clements, D. H. (2004). *Building Blocks* for early childhood mathematics. *Early Childhood Research Quarterly, 19*, 181–189

Sarama, J., & Clements, D. H. (2006). Mathematics in kindergarten. In D. F. Gullo (Ed.), *K Today: Teaching and learning in the kindergarten year* (pp. 85–94). Washington, DC: National Association for the Education of Young Children.

Sarama, J., & A. -M. DiBiase (Eds.). *Engaging young children in mathematics: Standards for early childhood mathematics education* (pp. 91–104). Mahwah, NJ: Lawrence Erlbaum Associates.

Satchwell, L. (1994). Preschool physical education class structure. *Journal of Physical Education, Recreation, and Dance, 65*(6), 34–36.

Saunders, G. (1988). *Bilingual children: From birth to teens.* Philadelphia: Multilingual Matters.

Sauter, M., Uttal, D. H., Alman, A. S., Goldin-Meadow, S., & Levine, S. C. (2012). Learning what children know about space from looking at their hands: The added value of gesture in spatial communication. *Journal of Experimental Child Psychology, 111*, 587–606.

Saville-Troike, M. (1987). Dilingual discourse: The negotiation of meaning without a common code. *Linguistics, 25*, 81–106.

Saville-Troike, M. (1988). Private speech: Evidence for second language learning strategies during the "silent" period. *Journal of Child Language, 15*(3), 567–590.

Sayers Adomat, D. (2010). Dramatic interpretations: Performative responses of young children to picturebook read-alouds. *Children's Literature in Education, 41*, 207–221.

Sayers Adomat, D. (2012). Drama's potential for deepening young children's understandings of stories. *Early Childhood Education Journal, 40*, 343–350.

Scarborough, H., & Dobrich, W. (1994). On the efficacy of reading to preschoolers. *Developmental Review, 14*, 245–302.

Scarr, S., & McCartney, K. (1983). How people make their own environments: A theory of genotype environment effects. *Child Development, 54*, 424–435.

Scharmann, M. W. (1998). We are friends when we have memories together. *Young Children, 53*(2), 27–29.

Schickedanz, J. A. (1999). *Much more than the ABCs: The early stages of reading and writing.* Washington, DC: National Association for the Education of Young Children.

Schickedanz, J. A., & Casbergue, R. M. (2009). *Writing in preschool: Learning to orchestrate meaning and marks.* (2nd ed.). Newark, DE: International Reading Association.

Schickedanz, J. A., Schickedanz, D. I., Forsyth, P. D., & Forsyth, G. A. (2001). *Understanding children and adolescents* (4th ed.). Boston: Allyn & Bacon.

Schleepen, T. M. J., & Jonkman, L. M. (2012). Children's use of semantic organizational strategies is mediated by working memory capacity. *Cognitive Development, 27*, 255–269.

Schmidt, D. (1985). Adult influences on curiosity in children. *Early Report, 12*(3), 2–3.

Schmidt, H. M., Burts, D. C., Durham, R. S., Charlesworth, R., & Hart, C. H. (2007). Impact of developmental appropriateness of teacher guidance strategies on kindergarten children's interpersonal relations. *Journal of Research in Childhood Education, 21*, 290–301.

Schmidt, B., Houang, R., & Cogan, L. (2002). A coherent curriculum: The case of mathematics. *American Educator, 26*(2), 1–18.

Schonert-Reichl, K. A. (2011). Promoting empathy in school-aged children: Current approaches and implications for practice. In K. Nader (Ed.), *School rampage shootings and other youth disturbances: Early preventive interventions* (pp.159–203). New York: Routledge. Retrieved April 5, 2013, from http://changingresultsforyoungreaders.bclibraries.ca/downloads/SchonertReichl_PromotingEmpathy_SchoolRampageShootings.pdf

Schultz, D., Izard, C. E., & Ackerman, B. P. (2000). Children's anger attribution bias: Relations to family adjustment and social adjustment. *Social Development, 9*, 284–301.

Seefeldt, C. (1995). Transforming curriculum in social studies. In S. Bredekamp & T. Rosegrant (Eds.), *Reaching potentials: Transforming early childhood curriculum and assessment,* Vol. 2. (pp. 109–124). Washington, DC: National Association for the Education of Young Children.

Seefeldt, C. (1997). Social studies in the developmentally appropriate integrated curriculum. In C. H. Hart, D. C. Burts, & R. Charlesworth (Eds.), *Integrated curriculum and developmentally appropriate practice: Birth to age eight* (pp. 171–199). Albany, NY: SUNY Press.

Segatti, L., Brown-DuPaul, J., & Keyes, T. L. (2003). Using everyday materials to promote problem solving in toddlers. *Young Children, 58*(5), 12–16, 18.

Senechal, M., Ouellette, G., & Rodney, D. (2006). The misunderstood giant: On the predictive role of early vocabulary to future reading. In D. K. Dickinson & S. B. Neuman (Eds.), *Handbook of early literacy,* Vol. 2, (pp. 173–182). New York: The Guilford Press.

Seo, K. (2003). What children's play tells us about teaching mathematics. *Young Children, 58*(1), 28–33.

Seo, K. -H., & Ginsburg, H. P. (2004). What is developmentally appropriate in early childhood mathematics education? Lessons from new research. In D. H. Clements, J. Sarama, & A. -M. DiBiase (Eds.), *Engaging young children in mathematics: Standards for early childhood mathematics education* (pp. 91–104). Hillsdale, NJ: Lawrence Erlbaum Associates.

Sera, M. D., & Millett, K. G. (2011). Developmental differences in shape processing. *Cognitive Development, 26,* 40–56.

Shanahan, T. (2015). What teachers should know about Common Core: A guide for the perplexed. *The Reading Teacher, 68*(8), 583–588.

Share, D. L., & Jaffe-Gur, T. (1999). How reading begins: A study of preschoolers' print identification strategies. *Cognition and Instruction, 17,* 177–213.

Shephard, R. J. (2005). The obesity epidemic: A challenge to pediatric work physiologist? *Pediatric Exercise Science, 17*(1), 3–17.

Shillady, A. (Ed.) (2012). *Spotlight on young children: Exploring math.* National Association for the Education of Young Children: Washington, DC.

Shipman, K. L., & Zeman, J. (2001). Socialization of children's emotion regulation in mother-child dyads: A developmental psychopathology perspective. *Development and Psychopathology, 13,* 317–336.

Shonkoff, J. P., & Phillips, D. A. (Eds). (2000). *From neurons to neighborhoods: The science of early childhood development.* Washington, DC: National Academy Press.

Shore, R. & Strasser, J. (2006). Music for their minds. *Young Children, 61*(2), 62–67.

Shure, M. B. (1997). Interpersonal cognitive problem solving: Primary prevention of early high-risk behaviors in the preschool and primary years. In G. W. Albee & T. P. Gullota (Eds.), *Primary prevention works* (pp. 167–190). Thousand Oaks, CA: Sage Publications.

Siegler, R., Carptenter, T., Fennell, F., Geary, D., Lewis, J., Okamoto, Y. et al. (2010). *Developing effective fraction instruction for kindergarten through 8th grade.* Washington, DC: Institute of Education Sciences, U. S. Department of Education.

Sigman, M., & Ruskin, E. (1999). Continuity and change in the social competence of children with autism, Down syndrome, and developmental delay. *Monographs of the Society for Research in Child Development, 64* (1, Serial No. 256).

Silvern, S., Williamson, P., & Waters, B. (1983). Play as a mediator of comprehension: An alternative to play training. *Educational Research Quarterly, 7,* 16–21.

Slaby, R. G., Roedell, W. C., Arezzo, D., & Hendrix, K. (1995). *Early violence prevention: Tools for teachers of young children.* Washington, DC: National Association for the Education of Young Children.

Smilansky, S., & Shefatya, L. (1990). *Facilitating play: A medium for promoting cognitive, socio-emotional, and academic development in young children.* Gaithersburg, MD: Psychosocial and Educational Publications.

Smetana, J. G. (1984). Toddlers' social interactions regarding moral and conventional transgressions. *Child Development, 55,* 1767–1776.

Smidts, D. P., Jacobs, R., & Anderson, V. (2004). The object classification task for children (OCTC): A measure of concept generation and mental flexibility in early childhood. *Developmental Neuropsychology, 26*(1), 385–401.

Smith, H., & Heckman, P. (1995). The Mexican-American war. In E. García & B. McLaughlin (Eds.), *Meeting the challenge of linguistic and cultural diversity in early childhood education* (pp. 64–84). New York: Teachers College Press.

Smith, P. K., & Hart, C. H. (2002). *Blackwell handbook of childhood social development.* Oxford: Blackwell Publishers.

Smith, S. P. (2006). *Early childhood mathematics* (3rd ed.). Boston: Pearson.

Snow, C. E. (1983a). Age differences in second language acquisition: Research findings and folk psychology. In K. Bailey, M. Long, & S. Peck (Eds.), *Second language acquisition studies* (pp. 141–150). Rowley, MA: Newbury House.

Snow, C. E. (1983b). Literacy and language: Relationships during the preschool years. *Harvard Educational Review, 53*(2), 165–189.

Snow, C. E. (1991). The theoretical basis for relationships between language and literacy development. *Journal of Research in Childhood Education, 6*(1), 5–10.

Snow, C. E., Burns, M. S., & Griffin, P. (Eds.). (1998). *Preventing reading difficulties in young children.* Washington, DC: National Academy Press.

Snow, C. E., & Hoefnagel-Hohle, M. (1977). Age differences in the pronunciation of foreign sounds. *Language and Speech, 20*, 357–365.

Snow, C. E., & Van Hemel, S. B. (Eds.). (2008). *Early childhood assessment: Why, what, and how? Report of the National Research Council of the National Academies.* Washington, DC: National Academies Press. http://www.nap.edu/catalog/12446.html

Son, S. H., & Meisels, S. J. (2006). The relationship of young children's motor skills to later school achievement. *Merrill-Palmer Quarterly, 52*, 755–778.

Spaulding, C., Gottlieb, N. H., & Jensen, J. (2008). Promoting physical activity in low-income preschool children. *Journal of Physical Education, Recreation & Dance, 79*(5), 42–47.

Spivak, G., & Shure, M. B. (1997). *Social adjustment of young children: A cognitive approach to solving real-life problems.* San Francisco: Jossey-Bass.

Stadler, M. A., & Ward, G. C. (2005). Supporting the narrative development of young children. *Early Childhood Education Journal, 33*(2), 73–80.

Staley, L., & Portman, P. A. (2000). Red Rover, Red Rover, it's time to move over. *Young Children, 55*(1), 67–72.

Stark, R. (1978). Features of infant sounds: The emergence of cooing. *Journal of Child Language, 5*, 1–12.

Starkey, P., Klein, A., & Wakely, A. (2004). Enhancing young children's mathematical knowledge through a pre-kindergarten mathematics intervention. *Early Childhood Research Quarterly, 19*, 99–120.

Steglin, D. A. (2005). Making the case for play policy: Research-based reasons to support play-based environments. *Young Children, 60*(2), 76–85.

Stetson, C., Jablon, J., & Dombro, A. L. (2009). *Observation: The key to responsive teaching.* Washington, DC: Teaching Strategies, Inc.

Stevenson, H. W., & Newman, R. S. (1986). Long-term prediction of achievement and attitudes in mathematics and reading. *Child Development 57*, 646–659.

Stevenson, N. C., & Just, C. (2014). In early education, why teach handwriting before keyboarding? *Early Childhood Education Journal, 42*, 49–56.

Stewart, R. A., Rule, A. C., & Giordano, D. A. (2007). The effect of fine motor skill activities on kindergarten student attention. *Early Childhood Education Journal, 35*, 103–109.

Stipek, D. (2002). *Motivation to learn: Integrating theory and practice* (4th ed.). Boston: Allyn & Bacon.

Stipek, D., Recchia, S, & McClintic, S. (1992). Self-evaluations in young children. *Monographs of the Society for Research in Child Development, 57*(1), Serial No. 226.

Stipek, D. J., Feiler, R., Byler, P., Ryan, R., Milburn, S., & Salmon, J. M. (1998). Good beginnings: What difference does the program make in preparing young children for school? *Journal of Applied Psychology, 19*(1), 41–66.

Stoel-Gammon, C., & Menn, L. (2004). Phonological development: Learning sounds and sound patterns. In J. B. Gleason (Ed.), *The development of language* (7th ed.). Boston: Allyn & Bacon.

Strickland, D. S. (2006). Language and literacy in kindergarten. In D. F. Gullo (Ed.), *K today: Teaching and learning in the kindergarten year* (pp. 73–84). Washington, DC: National Association for the Education of Young Children.

Strickland, D. S., & Riley-Ayers, S. (2007). *Literacy leadership in early childhood: The essential guide.* New York: Teacher's College Press.

Strickland, D. S., & Schickedanz, J. A. (2004). *Learning about print in preschool: Working with letters, words, and beginning links with phonemic awareness.* Newark, DE: International Reading Association.

Strickland, D. S., & Shanahan, T. (2004). Laying the groundwork for literacy. *Educational Leadership, 61*(6), 74–77.

Strong, W. B., Malina, R. M., Blimkie, C., Daniels, S. R., Dishman, R. K., Gutin, B., et al. (2005). Evidence- based physical activity for school-age youth. *Journal of Pediatrics, 146*, 732–737.

Stuart, M. (1995). Prediction and qualitative assessment of five- and six-year-old children's reading: A longitudinal study. *British Journal of Educational Psychology, 65*, 287–296.

Sulzby, E. (1985). Children's emergent reading of favorite storybooks: A developmental study. *Reading Research Quarterly, 20*(4), 464.

Sutterby, J. A., & Frost, J. L. (2002). Making playgrounds fit for children and children fit on playgrounds. *Young Children, 57*(3), 36–42.

Swanson, H. L., Rosston, K., Gerber, M., & Solari, E. (2008). Influence of oral language and phonological awareness on children's bilingual reading. *Journal of School Psychology, 46*(4), 413–429.

Szechter, L. E., & Liben, L. S. (2007). Children's aesthetic understanding of photographic art and the quality of art-related parent–child interactions. *Child Development, 78*(3), 879–894.

Tabors, P. O. (1998, November). What early childhood educators need to know: Developing effective programs for linguistically and culturally diverse children and families. *Young Children, 53*(6), 20–26.

Tabors, P. O. (2002). Language and literacy for *all* children. *Head Start Bulletin, 74,* 10–14.

Tabors, P. O. (2008). *One child, two languages: A guide for early childhood educators of children learning English as a second language* (2nd ed.). Baltimore: Paul H. Brookes.

Tabors, P. O., Aceves, C., Bartolomé, L., Páez, M., & Wolf, A. (2000). Language development of linguistically diverse children in Head Start classrooms: Three ethnographic portraits. *NHSA Dialog, 3*(3), 409–440.

Tabors, P. O., Beals, D. E., & Weizman, Z. O. (2001). "You know what oxygen is?" Learning new words at home. In D. K. Dickinson & P. O. Tabors (Eds.), *Beginning literacy with language: Young children learning at home and school* (pp. 93–110). Baltimore: Paul H. Brookes.

Tabors, P. O., & López, L. M. (2005). How can teachers and parents help young children become (and stay) bilingual? *Head Start Bulletin, 78,* 14–17.

Tabors, P. O., Páez, M., & López, L. (2003). Dual language abilities of bilingual four-year olds: Initial findings from the Early Childhood Study of Language and Literacy Development of Spanish-speaking Children. *NABE Journal of Research and Practice, 1*(1), 70–91. Retrieved August 16, 2007, from http://www.uc.edu/njrp/pdfs/Tabors.pdf

Tabors, P. O., & Snow, C. (1994). English as a second language in preschools. In F. Genesee (Ed.), *Educating second language children: The whole child, the whole curriculum, the whole community* (pp. 103–125). New York: Cambridge University Press.

Tabors, P. O., & Snow, C. E. (2001). Young bilingual children and early literacy development. In S. B. Neuman & D. K. Dickinson (Eds.), *Handbook of early literacy research,* Vol. 1 (pp. 159–178). New York: Guilford Press.

Taeschner, T. (1983). *The sun is feminine: A study of language acquisition in bilingual children.* New York: Springer-Verlag.

Taylor, D. (1983). *Family literacy*. Exeter, NH: Heinemann.

Taylor, I. (1981). Writing systems and reading. In G. E. Mackinnon & T. G. Waller (Eds.), *Reading research: Advances in theory and practice* (Vol. 2). New York: Academic Press.

Taylor-Cox, J. (2003). Algebra in the early years? Yes. In D. Koralek (Ed.), *Spotlight on young children and math* (pp. 7–13). Washington, DC: National Association for the Education of Young Children.

Teale, W., & Yokota, J. (2000). Beginning reading and writing: Perspectives on instruction. In D. S. Strickland & L. M. Morrow (Eds.), *Beginning reading and writing: Language and literacy series* (pp. 3–21). Newark, DE: International Reading Association.

Tenenbaum, H. R., & Callanan, M. A. (2008). Parents' science talk to their children in Mexican-descent families residing in the United States. *International Journal of Behavioural Development, 32*(1), 1–12.

Tenenbaum, H. R., Rappolt-Schlichtmann, G., & Zanger, V. V. (2004). Children's learning about water in a museum and in the classroom. *Early Childhood Research Quarterly, 19*(1), 40–58.

Terry, N. P., & Connor, C. M. (2012). Changing nonmainstream American English use and early reading achievement from kindergarten to first grade. *American Journal of Speech-Language Pathology, 21*, 78–86.

Terry, N. P., Connor, C. M., Petscher, Y., & Colin, C. R. (2012). Dialect variation and reading: Is change in nonmainstream American English use related to reading achievement in first and second grades? *Journal of Speech, Language, and Hearing Research, 55*, 55–69.

Thatcher, D. H. (2001). Reading in the math class: Selecting and using picture books for math investigations. *Young Children, 56*(4), 20–26.

Thompson, C. M. (1995). Transforming curriculum in the visual arts. In S. Bredekamp & T. Rosegrant (Eds.), *Reaching potentials: Transforming early childhood curriculum and assessment,* Vol. 2 (pp. 81–98). Washington, DC: National Association for the Education of Young Children.

Thompson, R. A., Winer, A. C., & Goodvin, R. (2011). The individual child: Temperament, emotion, self and personality. In M. H. Bornstein & M. E. Lamb (Eds.), *Developmental Psychology: An Advanced Textbook* (6th ed.). Hillsdale, NJ: Erlbaum.

Thompson, R. A., & Lagattuta, K. H. (2006). Feeling and understanding: Early emotional development. In K. McCartney & D. Phillips (Eds.), *Blackwell handbook of early childhood development* (pp. 317–337). Malden, MA: Blackwell Publishing.

Thompson, S. C. (2005). *Children as illustrators: Making meaning through art and language.* Washington, DC: National Association for the Education of Young Children.

Thornton, S. J., & Vukelich, R. (1988). Effects of children's understanding of time concepts on historical understanding. *Theory and Research in Social Education, 16*(1), 69–82.

Tomlinson, H. B. (2009). Developmentally appropriate practice in the primary grades: ages 6–8. In C. Copple, & S. Bredekamp (Eds.), *Developmentally appropriate practice in early childhood programs serving children from birth through age 8* (3rd ed., pp. 257–288). Washington, DC: National Association for the Education of Young Children.

Tomlinson, H. B. (2012). Cognitive development in the primary grades. In C. Copple (Ed.), *Growing minds: Building strong cognitive foundations in early childhood* (pp. 33–40). Washington, DC: National Association for the Education of Young Children.

Torquati, J., & Barber, J. (2005). Dancing with trees: Infants and toddlers in the garden. *Young Children, 60*(3), 40–47.

Trawick-Smith, J. (1998a). An analysis of metaplay in the preschool years. *Early Childhood Research Quarterly, 13,* 433–452.

Trawick-Smith, J. (1998b). Why play training works: An integrated model for play intervention. *Journal of Research in Childhood Education, 12*, 117–129.

Trawick-Smith, J. (2006). *Early childhood development: A multicultural perspective* (4th ed.). Upper Saddle River, NJ: Pearson/Merrill Prentice Hall.

Trawick-Smith, J. (2010). *Early childhood development: A multicultural perspective* (5th ed.). Upper Saddle River, NJ: Pearson.

Trentacosta, C. J., Izard, C. E., Mostow, A. J., & Fine, S. E. (2006). Children's emotional competence and attentional competence in early elementary school. *School Psychology Quarterly, 21*(2), 148–170.

Tsybina, I., Girolametto, L. E., Weitzman, E., & Greenberg, J. (2006). Recasts used with preschoolers learning English as their second language. *Early Childhood Education Journal, 34*, 177–185.

Tu, T. (2006). Preschool science environment: What is available in a preschool classroom? *Early Childhood Education Journal, 33*(4), 245–251.

U.S. Department of Education. (2006). *The condition of education*. Institute of Education Sciences, National Center for Education Statistics.

Ulrich, B. D., & Ulrich, D. (1985). The role of balancing ability in performance of fundamental motor skills in 3-, 4-, 5-year-old children. In J. E. Clark & J. H. Humphrey (Eds.), *Motor development: Current selected research* (Vol. 1), pp. 87–97. Princeton: Princeton Book Company.

Uttal, D. H. (1996). Angles and distances: Children's and adults' reconstruction and scaling of spatial configurations. *Child Development, 67*, 2763–2779.

Uttal, D. H. (2000). Seeing the big picture: Map use and the development of spatial cognition. *Developmental Science, 3*(3), 247–286.

Uttal, D. H., & Wellman, H. M. (1989). Young children's representation of spatial information acquired through maps. *Developmental Psychology, 25*(1), 128–138.

Van Hiele, P. M. (1986). *Structure and insight: A theory of mathematics education*. Orlando, FL: Academic Press.

Varelas, M., Pappas, C.C., Tucker-Raymond, E., Kane, J., Hankes, J., Ortiz, I., & Keblawe-Shamah, N. (2010). Drama activities as ideational resources for primary-grade children in urban science classrooms. *Journal of Research in Science Teaching, 47*(3), 302–325.

Varol, F., & Farran, D. C. (2006). Early mathematical growth: How to support young children's mathematical development. *Early Childhood Education Journal, 33*, 381–387.

Vaughn, S., Linan-Thompson, S., Pollard-Durodola, S. D., Mathes, P. G., & Hagan, E. C. (2006). In D. K. Dickinson & S. B. Neuman (Eds.), *Handbook of early literacy research*, (Vol. 2, pp. 185–197). New York: Guilford Press.

Verschueren, K., Buyck, P., & Marcoen, A. (2001). Self-representations and socioemotional competence in young children: A 3-year longitudinal. *Developmental Psychology, 37*, 126–134.

Vlach, H. A., & Carver, S. M. (2008). The effects of observation coaching on children's graphic representations. *Early Childhood Research and Practice, 10*(1). Retrieved April 7, 2009, from http://ecrp.uiuc.edu/v10n1/vlach.html

VORT Corporation. (2004a). *HELP for preschoolers—Assessment strands: Ages 3–6 years*. Palo Alto, CA: Author.

VORT Corporation. (2004b). *Revised HELP Checklist: Birth to three years*. Palo Alto, CA: Author.

Vukelich, C. (1990). Where's the paper? Literacy during dramatic play. *Childhood Education, 55*(4), 205–209.

Vygotsky, L. (1997). *The history of the development of higher mental functions*. In R. W. Rieber (Ed.), *The collected works of L. S. Vygotsky* (M. J. Hall, Trans., Vol. 4). New York: Plenum Press.

Wagner, R. K., Torgesen, J. K., Laughon, P., Simmons, K., & Rashotte, C. A. (1993). The development of young readers' phonological processing abilities. *Journal of Educational Psychology, 30*, 73–87.

Wagner, R. K., Torgesen, J. K., Rashotte, C. A., Hecht, S. A., Barker, T. A., Burgess, S. R., et al. (1997). Changing causal relations between phonological processing abilities and word-level reading as children develop from beginning to fluent readers: A 5-year longitudinal study. *Developmental Psychology, 33*, 468–479.

Wang, J. H. T. (2004). A study of gross-motor skills of preschool children. *Journal of Research in Childhood Education, 19*(1), 32–43.

Wang, W. Y., & Ju, Y. H. (2002). Promoting balance and jumping skills in children with Down syndrome. *Perceptual Motor Skills, 94*, 443–438.

Washington state early learning and development benchmarks (2005). Retrieved May 23, 2007, from http://www.k12.wa.us/EarlyLearning/pubdocs/EarlyLearningBenchmarks.pdf

Watts, K., Jones, T. W., Davis. E. A., & Green. D. (2005). Exercise training in obese children and adolescents. *Sports Medicine, 35*(5), 375–392.

Webster-Stratton, C., & Herbert, M. (1994). *Troubled families—Problem children: Working with parents: A collaborative process.* Chichester, England: Wiley.

Weitzman, E., & Greenberg, J. (2002). *Learning language and loving it.* Toronto, Ontario: The Hanen Centre.

Welk, G. J., & Blair, S. N. (2000). Physical activity protects against the health risks of obesity. *Research Digest, 3*(12), 1–8.

Wells, G. (1985). Preschool literacy-related activities and success in school. In D. R. Olance, N. Torrance, & A. Hildyard (Eds.), *Literacy, language, and learning* (pp. 229–255). Cambridge, England: Cambridge University Press.

Wells, G. (1986). *The meaning makers: Children learning language and using language to learn.* Portsmouth, NH: Heinemann.

Wentzel, K., & Asher, S. (1995). The academic lives of neglected, rejected, popular, and controversial children. *Child Development, 66*, 754–763.

West, J., Denton, K., & Germino-Hausken, E. (2000). *America's kindergartners: Findings from the early childhood longitudinal study, kindergarten class of 1998–99, Fall 1998.* Retrieved July 16, 2007, from http://ceep.crc.uiuc.edu/eecearchive/digests/ed-cite/ed438089.html

Wheeler, R., & Swords, R. (2004). Code-switching: Tools of language and culture transform the dialectically diverse classroom. *Language Arts, 81*, 470–480.

Whitehurst, G. J., & Fischel, J. (1994). Practitioner review: Early developmental language delay: What, if anything, should the clinician do about it? *Journal of Child Psychology and Psychiatry, 35*, 613–648.

Whitin, P. (2001). Kindness in a jar. *Young Children, 56*(5), 18–22.

Whitin, D. J., & Piwko, M. (2012). Mathematics and poetry in grades 2 and 3: The right connection. In A. Shillady (Ed.), *Spotlight on young children: Exploring math* (pp. 36-41). Washington, DC: National Association for the Education of Young Children.

Whitin, P., & Whitin, D. J. (2003). Developing mathematical understanding along the yellow brick road. In D. Koralek (Ed.), *Spotlight on young children and math* (pp. 25–28). Washington, DC: National Association for the Education of Young Children.

Whitin, P., & Whitin, D. J. (2012). Second- and third-grade mathematical pattern hunters. In A. Shillady (Ed.), *Spotlight on young children: Exploring math* (pp. 21–27). Washington, DC: National Association for the Education of Young Children.

Whiting, B. B., & Edwards, C. P. (1988). *Children of different worlds.* Cambridge, MA: Harvard University Press.

Whiting, B. B., & Whiting, J. W. M. (1975). *Children of six cultures: A psycho-cultural analysis.* Cambridge, MA: Harvard University Press.

Wien, C. A., Keating, B., Coates, A., & Bigelow, B. (2008). Moving into uncertainty: Sculpture with three- to five-year-olds. *Young Children, 63*(4), 78–86.

Wiggins, D. G. (2007). Pre-K music and the emergent reader: Promoting literacy in a music-enhanced environment. *Early Childhood Education Journal, 35*(1), 55–64.

Williams, A. E. (2008). Exploring the natural world with infants and toddlers in an urban setting. *Young Children, 63*(1), 22–25.

Williams, K. C., & Cooney, M. H. (2006). Young children and social justice. *Young Children, 61*(2), 75–82.

Williams, H., Pfeiffer, K., O'Neill, J., Dowda, M., Mclver, K., Brown, W., & Pate, R. (2008). Motor skill performance and physical activity in preschool children. *Obesity, 16*(6), 1421–1426.

Wishard, A. G., Shivers, E. M., Howes, C., & Ritchie, S. (2003). Child care program and teacher practices: Associations with quality and children's experiences. *Early Childhood Research Quarterly, 18*, 65–103.

Witzel, B. S., Ferguson, C. J., & Mink, D. V. (2012). Number sense: Strategies for helping preschool through grade 3 children develop math skills. *Young Children, 67*(3), 89–94.

Wolter, J. A., Wood, A., & D'zatko, K. W. (2009). The influence of morphological awareness on the literacy development of first-grade children. *Language, Speech, and Hearing Services in Schools, 40*, 286–298.

Wong Fillmore, L. (1976). *The second time around: Cognitive and social strategies in second language acquisition.* Unpublished doctoral dissertation, Stanford University, Palo Alto.

Wong Fillmore, L. (1979). Individual differences in second language acquisition. In C. J. Fillmore, D. Kempler, & W. S. -Y. Wang (Eds.), *Individual differences in language ability and language behavior* (pp. 203–228). New York: Academic Press.

Wong Fillmore, L. (1985). *Second language learning in children: A proposed model.* In *English language development. Proceedings of a conference on issues in English language development for minority language education.* Washington, DC: ERIC Clearinghouse on Languages and Linguistics. (ERIC Document Reproduction Service No. ED273149)

Wong Fillmore, L. (1991a). Language and cultural issues in the early education of language minority children. In S. Kagan (Ed.), *The care and education of America's young children: Obstacles and opportunities. 90th yearbook of the National Society for the Study of Education, Part I* (pp. 30–49). Chicago: University of Chicago Press.

Wong Fillmore, L. (1991b). When learning a second language means losing the first. *Early Childhood Research Quarterly, 6*(3), 323–346.

Wood, C. (2005). *Yardsticks: Children in the classroom ages 4–14.* Turners Falls, MA: Northeast Foundation for Children.

Woodard, C., Haskins, G., Schaefer, G., & Smolen, L. (2004). Let's talk: A different approach to oral language development. *Young Children, 59*(4), 92–95.

Worden, P. E., & Boettcher, W. (1990). Young children's acquisition of alphabet knowledge. *Journal of Reading Behavior, 20*(3), 277–295.

Wright, C., Bacigalupa, C., Black, T., & Burton, M. (2008). Windows into children's thinking: A guide to storytelling and dramatization. *Early Childhood Education Journal, 35*(4), 363–369.

Wrotniak, B., Epstein, L., Dorn, J., Jones, K., & Kondilis, V. (2006). The relationship between motor proficiency and physical activity in children. *Pediatrics, 118*, 1758–1765.

Wu, P., Robinson, C. C., Yang, C, Hart, C. H., Olsen, S. F., Porter, C. L., et al. (2002). Similarities and differences in mothers' parenting of preschoolers in China and the United States. *International Journal of Behavioral Development, 26*, 481–491.

Yamamoto, J., & Kubota, M. (1983). Emotional development of Japanese-American children. In G. J. Powell (Ed.), *The psychosocial development of minority children* (pp. 237–247). New York: Brunner/Mazel.

Yeates, K. O., Schultz, L. H., & Selman, R. L. (1991). The development of interpersonal negotiation strategies in thought and action: A social-cognitive link to behavioral adjustment and social status. *Merrill-Palmer Quarterly, 37*(3), 369–406.

Yeats, K. O., Schultz, L. H., & Selman, R. L. (1991). The development of interpersonal negotiation strategies in thought and action: A social-cognitive link to behavioral adjustment and social status. *Merrill-Palmer Quarterly, 37(3),* 369–406.

Yen, C. J., Konold, T. R., & McDermott, P. A. (2004). Does learning behavior augment cognitive ability as an indicator of academic achievement? *Journal of School Psychology, 42*, 157–169.

Yesil-Dagli, U. (2011). Predicting ELL students' beginning first grade English oral reading fluency from initial kindergarten vocabulary, letter naming, and phonological awareness skills. *Early Childhood Research Quarterly, 26*, 15–29.

Yoon, J., & Onchwari, J. A. (2006). Teaching young children science: Three key points. *Early Childhood Education Journal, 33*(6), 419–423.

Young, D., & Behounek, L. M. (2006). Kindergartners use PowerPoint to lead their own parent–teacher conferences. *Young Children, 61*(2), 24–26.

Youngblade, L. M., & Dunn J. (1995). Individual differences in young children's pretend play with mother and sibling: Links to relationships and understanding of other people's feelings and beliefs. *Child Development, 66*, 1472–1492.

Younger, B. A., & Johnson, K. E. (2004). Infants' comprehension of toy replicas as symbols for real objects. *Cognitive Psychology, 18*, 207–242.

Youngstrom, E., Wolpaw, J. M., Kogos, J. L., Schoff, K., Ackerman, B., & Izard, C. (2000). Interpersonal problem solving in preschool and first grade: Developmental change and ecological validity. *Journal of Clinical Child Psychology, 29*, 589–602.

Yuzawa, M., Bart, W. M., Yuzawa, M., & Junko, I. (2005). Young children's knowledge and strategies for comparing sizes. *Early Childhood Research Quarterly, 20*, 239–253.

Zachopoulou, E., Tsapakidou, A., & Derri, V. (2004). The effects of a developmentally appropriate music and movement program on motor performance. *Early Childhood Research Quarterly, 19*, 631–642.

Zaslow, M., & Martinez-Beck, I. (Eds.). (2005). *Critical issues in early childhood professional development.* Baltimore: Paul H. Brookes.

Zembar, M. J., & Blume, L. B. (2009). *Middle childhood development: A contextual approach.* Upper Saddle River: Merrill/Pearson. Retrieved April 8, 2013, from http://www.education.com/reference/article/peer-relations-middle-childhood/

Zill, N., Collins, M., West, J., & Hausken, E. G. (1995). *Approaching kindergarten: A look at preschoolers in the United States.* Washington, DC: U.S. Department of Education, Office of Education.

Zimmerman, E., & Zimmerman, L. (2000). Art education and early childhood education: The young child as creator and meaning maker within a community context. *Young Children, 55*(6), 87–92.

Zumbrunn, S., & Bruning, R. (2013). Improving the writing knowledge of emergent writers: The effects of self-regulated strategy development. *Reading and Writing, 26*(1), 91–110.

Zur, O., & Gelman, R. (2004). Young children can add and subtract by predicting and checking. *Early Childhood Research Quarterly, 19*, 121–137.